Tears For Grandma

Linda Campbell

PublishAmerica

Baltimore

© 2003 by Linda Campbell.

All rights reserved. No part of this book may be reproduced in any form without written permission from the publishers, except by a reviewer who may quote brief passages in a review to be printed in a newspaper or magazine.

First printing

ISBN: 1-59286-874-6
PUBLISHED BY PUBLISHAMERICA, LLLP
www.publishamerica.com
Baltimore

Printed in the United States of America

For all the special people in my life, especially my mother, Lucy Bishop and father, the late James Bishop for giving me life and doing the best they could.

Acknowledgments

First and foremost, I would like to thank Arlene Uslander for all of her assistance in this endeavor, especially the editing. I am also indebted to her for introducing me to PublishAmerica. In addition, I would like to thank my daughter Jessie Campbell for her immense contribution to the cover design.

Throughout this process there were numerous other family members and special friends that have provided continual encouragement and helped tremendously in this process. Thank all of you for helping me to make my dream become a reality.

"To every thing there is a season, and a time to every purpose under the heaven;
A time to be born, and a time to die; a time to plant, and a time to pluck up that which has been planted;
A time to kill, and a time to heal; a time to break down, and a time to build up;
A time to weep, and a time to laugh; a time to mourn; and a time to dance;
A time to cast away stones, and a time to gather stones together; a time to embrace, and a time to refrain from embracing;
A time to get, and a time to lose; a time to keep, and a time to cast away;
A time to rend, and a time to sew; a time to keep silence, and a time to speak;
A time to love, and a time to hate; a time of war, and a time of peace."

Ecclesiastes 3: 1-8
Holy Bible

Prologue

My son John walked into Mother's living room carrying a large cardboard box filled with decades of family snapshots. He dropped the topless box on the coffee table in the living room and exclaimed, "This thing sure is heavy." As he rummaged through the pictures, searching for snapshots he could use for a family timeline he was working on for his latest school project, he picked up a packet of photos held together with a thick red rubber band. He proceeded to loosen the rubber band and pictures scattered over the tabletop. As they fell from his nine-year-old hands, one lonely photo floated down to the floor.

"Mom, please get the one that fell," John requested as he continued rummaging through the box. I leaned down to retrieve the photo, and there she was staring at me, frozen in time more than thirty years ago: Sallie Irene Merrill, my grandmother. The year was 1964. My sister, Brenda, and I were standing next to her underneath the huge ancient oak tree in our family's front yard. Could it really have been that long ago? I remember my father taking the picture with one of those old Polaroid cameras that took black and white pictures. It would be the last photograph ever taken of my grandma. I was eleven years old, and she was seventy two. At that time there was no way for me to know how her final nine months on earth would drastically alter the remainder of my life.

Sallie Irene Merrill was born in Marion, Alabama, in 1892. Marion was a small community in Perry County; its largest neighbor was Montgomery, Alabama. Marion was the place where the first confederate flag and confederate uniform were designed. The town has a rich history and was named Marion in honor of Francis Marion, the "Swamp Fox," hero of the American Revolution.

Grandma grew up in this fairly quiet town in a beautiful Dixie setting with a rich heritage. When she was in her early twenties, she met a strong, handsome twenty-six year old stave maker named John H. Bishop. Staves are the wooden strips of barrels that are held together with hoops that are generally made of metal. John had relocated to Marion from Pennsylvania to work at the local stave mill due to lack of work in his home state of Pennsylvania.

Within a very short time, Grandma and Pap began courting, fell in love, and eventually became engaged. On June 18, 1918, they were married there in Grandma's hometown of Marion. They initially set up housekeeping near Grandma's parents' home which was located right across from Judson College. Their first child was born the following March on the 28th. Grandma and Pap eventually had five sons: John, Jr., the eldest, March 28, 1919; Clarence, July 23, 1923; Jay, February 6, 1928; James; May 2, 1932, and Harry, who was born and died sometime after the birth of John and before the birth of James.

Harry's death is now somewhat of a family mystery. He died at a very young age while Grandma and Pap were still in Alabama. It is uncertain when he was born and died, but the cause was suffocation according to Grandma. Perhaps he died from SIDS (Sudden Infant Death Syndrome), for doctors were not aware of that diagnosis back then. A search by the Department of Public Health, Center for Health Statistics for the years 1920 – 1935 revealed no certificate of death for Harry Bishop. Maybe he was buried in the family plot, and his death just went unreported.

In the spring of 1930, Grandma and Pap returned to Pennsylvania with their remaining three sons, due to diminished work opportunities in Marion. They set-up housekeeping in central Pennsylvania in the small rural community of McClure, in Snyder County, which was Amish country. Their youngest son, James, was born in McClure in 1932. James was my father.

Pap remained in the central Pennsylvania area for the remainder of his life where he owned and operated sawmills. Grandma always wanted to return to Alabama for she claimed that was where her heart had always been. She never did return to Alabama, however; not even for her parents', Marian's and Rufus', funerals. Pennsylvania would always be Yankee territory to Grandma, no matter how long the war had been over.

Pap had a massive heart attack in 1956, and two days later died in his home with my grandma and their four sons present. I was three-and-a-half years old. My only memories of Pap came from stories I heard from family members through the years and the few photos we had of him.

After his death, Grandma had a hard time making ends meet. They had no savings, and she wasn't eligible for Social Security. The Social Security Act was passed in 1935; however, Pap had never paid into the system, and

Grandma had never worked outside of the home. She was not eligible for Social Security. The Supplemental Security Income (SSI) program that guaranteed the elderly and disabled an annual income was not passed until 1972; that was too late for Grandma.

Grandma was forced to apply for welfare so that she could survive. At that time, the welfare system required elderly individuals to seek support from their children. It was mandatory that she take her remaining four sons to court.

The court ordered John, Clarence, and Jay to pay Grandma parental support. My father, James, was exempted because they stated his income was too low. Due to John's and Clarence's greed, they became very angry about the court order, and refused to talk to Grandma or my father.

Jay was upset about having to pay, also, but he continued to have contact with Grandma. She often spoke about John and Clarence, her two eldest sons. She missed them greatly, and occasionally I would see a tear slip down her cheek when someone mentioned their names. Grandma also missed their children, her grandchildren. John had two sons: John, III, and Albert. Clarence had a son and a daughter: Robert and Barbara.

After Pap's death, Grandma left the big old farm house they had rented in Treaster Valley, a rich valley amidst Amish territory in Mifflin County, Pennsylvania, and eventually moved about ten miles farther north near Milroy, Pennsylvania, approximately two miles from our home. Grandma's home was a small three-room, artificial-red-brick shingled house. The three rooms consisted of a kitchen-dining room combination, a living room, and a bedroom.

There was an old wood cook-stove to the left as you entered her kitchen through the back door. She never had an electric or gas stove. Grandma kept that old stove burning even during the hot summer months whenever she was cooking.

Brenda, my younger sister, and I spent many weekends with Grandma. We loved to stay overnight. On Saturdays, my parents and Uncle Jay and his family all gathered at Grandma's house for supper. She sure could cook on her old cook-stove. Her specialties were country ham, biscuits, peach cobbler, divinity candy, and sweet potato pie.

Uncle Jay and Aunt Betty had one child, a daughter named Carol. She was two years older than me. Carol, Brenda, and I would watch *American Band Stand* on Grandma's old secondhand, thirteen-inch, octagon-shaped-screen black and white TV. We loved dancing along with all the teenagers on the show. Dick Clark hosted the show, and I remember seeing different rising stars like Stevie Wonder.

Our private little world was simple, but I was extremely content, and my soul was satisfied. That period was probably the most carefree era I would ever experience. It was my generation's age of innocence. Times were a-changing, though.

In November of the previous year, 1963, John F. Kennedy was assassinated. I still remember the day well. My sixth grade teacher, Mrs. Headings, was called to the office, and when she returned, she was crying and announced to the class that President Kennedy had been shot.

We were in the "freedom movement" decade between 1954 and 1966. During that period, Dr. Martin Luther King, Jr. was leading "Freedom Rides" and massive demonstrations in the Southern states. He delivered his infamous "I have a dream…" speech in front of the Lincoln Memorial during the March on Washington on August 28, 1963. That movement eventually led to the passing of the Civil Rights Act of 1964, followed by the Voting Rights Act of 1965. Ironically, many of the demonstrations were held in Grandma's home state of Alabama, very near Marion, her hometown.

The Viet Nam war was another cause of social protest in the sixties. More than 58,000 Americans would lose their lives in that war. I recall that on April 14, 1966, Dennis G. Harmon became the first graduate from our high school to get killed in the Viet Nam war. It was sad, and sadder still, when viewing the war with hindsight. What a terrible waste!

Beatlemania was another sign of the times in 1964. My friends and I all watched the Beatles go from practically unknown musicians to mega stars on the *Ed Sullivan Variety Show*. My friends and I, like most teenagers during that period, were caught up in the frenzy of the music. Other popular musicians I liked were Bob Dylan, the Rolling Stones, Simon and Garfunkle, the Byrds, and the Mamas and Papas.

The music my generation listened to reflected the changes that were occurring throughout our nation and the world. It was a turbulent time in history, and the beginning of a turbulent time in my life.

PART I
JULY 1964 – JUNE 1965
Time Line

July 2, 1964 – Lyden Baines Johnson signed the Civil Rights Act.
July – August 1964 – Black uprisings in Harlem, Brooklyn, Rochester, New Jersey, and Chicago.
August 20, 1964 – Lyden Baines Johnson signs War on Poverty Bill.
August 1964 - Beatles "Hard Day's Night" released in the United States.
August – September, 1964 – Beatles first United States tour.
September 1964 – Selective Service calls up 27,500 individuals.
September 1964 – Linda begins 7th grade.
October 26, 1964 – Rolling Stones on Ed Sullivan.
December 10, 1964 - Martin Luther King awarded Nobel Peace Prize.
December 12, 1964 – Linda's 12th birthday.
February 8, 1965 – United States starts bombing North Viet Nam.
February 1965 – Martin Luther King and 770 others arrested in Selma, Alabama for picketing county courthouse to end discrimination of voting rights.
February 21, 1965 – Malcolm X shot and killed in the Harlem auditorium.
March 6, 1965 – First American soldier officially sets foot on Viet Nam battlefields.
March 1965 – Police violence in Selma, Alabama against march; police break-up demonstration of 600 in Montgomery, Alabama; Martin Luther King leads thousands in march from Selma to Montgomery; Martin Luther King calls for boycott of Alabama.
April 17, 1965 – First Anti-Viet Nam war march in Washington.
April 1965 – 25,000 troops in Viet Nam.

Popular Songs

"Rag Doll," The 4 Seasons; "Where Did Our Love Go," The Supremes; "The House of the Rising Sun," The Animals; "Oh, Pretty Woman," Roy Orbison & The Candy Man; "Baby Love" The Supremes; "I Feel Fine/She's A Woman," The Beatles; "Come See About Me," The Supremes; "Downtown," Petula Clark; "Stop In The Name Of Love," The Supremes; "I'm Telling You Now," Freddie & The Dreamers; "Mrs. Brown You've Got A Lovely Daughter," Herman's Hermits; "Wooly Bully," Sam The Sham & The Pharaohs

Chapter 1

It was Wednesday, July 29, 1964 in Mount Pleasant, Pennsylvania. I was in my eleventh year. Sounds of crickets and katydids echoed all around me as my best friend, Cathy, and I played badminton in my yard at the side of our one and a half story green and white wood-framed house. It was our third game. It was now dusk in Lingle Valley, a part of Mount Pleasant, a small village nestled at the base of the Seven Mountains between Milroy and State College. During the last several years, those badminton games had become a ritual between Cathy and me. We would play and count down the days until summer vacation would end and we would be going back to school.

"The score is ten to two," Cathy said as I missed the birdie and leaned over to scoop it up.

"Are you sure?" I countered. "I thought I had three."

"No way!" she insisted. "Ten, Two."

"All right, here we go," I said as I swiftly batted the birdie back across the net in her direction.

"What are you wearing to school the first day?" Cathy asked as she swung her racket and hit the birdie back over the net directly to me.

"I don't know yet," I replied, swinging as hard as I could and making contact with the birdie. "I need to do some shopping yet. What are you going to wear?"

Cathy swung and missed. "Oh, probably my new plaid skirt and white blouse and one of my new mohair sweaters. I think I'm getting a pair of those big-tongued penny loafers, too," she continued as she walked over to where the birdie had landed and scooped it up.

"That will look great," I stated.

"Yeah, I think so, too," Cathy said as she leaned over to pick the scab on her knee before she hit the birdie back toward me.

"I can't believe there are only four more weeks to go!" I exclaimed again hitting the birdie back over the net to Cathy. "It's really going to be strange starting high school. I won't be able to find anything."

"I wish I could go, too. Another whole year until it's my turn," Cathy said. There was a seven month age difference between Cathy and me, but because my birthday was in December and hers was in July, I was a year ahead of her in school.

There were four of us who ran around together most of the time: Cathy, Betsy, Brenda, and me. My sister Brenda is a year younger than I and was in the same class as Cathy. Betsy was my age and in my class. She buddied around more with Brenda, but we all hung out together a lot, too.

We were quite a foursome! Brenda was shorter than the rest of us. She had very curly short brown hair, and she had bowed legs that were very noticeable when she wore shorts. She was a tomboy just like Betsy. That's probably why they got along so well. They both often wore boys' clothing, and they showed no interest in female accessories as Cathy and I did. Betsy had a big frame and very wide hips. She had long straight blond hair that she usually wore in a ponytail. Cathy was the petite one of the group. She had the smallest feet and a little nose that turned slightly upward, and she had long slightly wavy black hair. I was tall like Betsy, but I was very thin. My arms seemed too long for the rest of my body. I had short light brown wavy hair. When Brenda and I were younger, people thought we looked alike, but as we got older, we no longer resembled each other.

"Betsy thinks we're probably going to get lost the first day," I stated. "You know last week at orientation, I really got mixed up. There's an upstairs and a downstairs. The cafeteria is in the basement. They have a gym, too, and you have to take showers all together."

"Yuck," Cathy squealed. "That's disgusting. Everybody will see you nude."

"I know," I persisted. "But you have to. There's a special shower for girls who have their periods."

"Totally yucko," Cathy replied.

That year I was going into seventh grade at Kishacoquillas High School. Elementary school consisted of grades one through six. We had no kindergarten. The high school consisted of grades seven through twelve. It was one of life's major milestones to switch from elementary school to the high school.

The high school had many more students than the elementary school. They combined the elementary schools from Brown, Armaugh, and Meno townships to make up the student population at the high school of approximately

1,200. In addition, the age difference would range from eleven year olds to eighteen year olds. That meant a tremendous difference in maturity.

Cathy finished me off with one more speeding birdie that landed behind me on the left.

"I win!" she declared exuberantly as I picked up the birdie and went back with her around the side of our house to the front porch and sat on the swing beside her.

"Yeah, I know. This just wasn't my night," I stated.

"Admit it," Cathy said. "I'm the best and you know it."

"No way!" I exclaimed, and we both continued swinging and debating who was the best player for several more minutes.

"Well, I better get home. It's dark and I'm tired," Cathy eventually said as she stood up to leave.

"I'm tired too." I replied.

Cathy started out our front walk, turned right, and headed toward her house. Her parents had divorced a few years before. She had lived at the top of the hill in a cute light blue, Cape Cod style house. It stood right along Route 322, a major route between Lewistown and State College, and the exit to Lingle Valley Road. My home was the second house on the left at the bottom of the hill along Lingle Valley Road. Back then I kind of envied Cathy's house.

Cathy's first house had a knotty-pine kitchen and dining room. Knotty pine was really "in" during the sixties. There also was a fireplace in the den. Not too many homes in our neighborhood had fireplaces. I really liked her bedroom because it had a large window seat that looked out over the highway, and she had white lace Priscilla curtains that had ruffles along the edge and on the valance. Best of all, though, I liked her canopy bed with the butterfly comforter.

After Cathy's parents divorced, Cathy, her mother Faye, and her brother Steve moved down to the bottom of the hill and back a side alley into a blue and white mobile home. Her alley was right across from ours; you turned right instead of left off Lingle Valley Road. Cathy's grandfather Bud owned the house in front of the trailer, which sat along Route 322. Faye was Bud's daughter, and he allowed her to park her trailer on his property. Bud had built a cinder-block swimming pool in his backyard which turned out to be Cathy's front yard. We spent many summer afternoons and evenings in that pool discussing life's most important events like who our current boyfriends were and what we would wear to the next school dance.

Cathy's brother Steve was six years older than me. Shortly after his parents divorced, he graduated and joined the Air Force. When Steve was home, we would hang around him and his friends while they played the latest hits on their guitars. "I Get Around" by the Beach Boys was one of their favorites.

It seemed to me that Cathy got anything she wanted, and Faye was much more lenient with her than my parents were with me. Her grandparents spoiled her, too. They always bought her the latest fashions and newest records. Her grandmother worked at Dank's department store, and at that time, it was the most fashionable store in Lewistown, our closest shopping area. She bought Cathy's clothes at that store because she received a discount.

The next few weeks passed quickly, and before I knew it, school was going to start the following day. I was extremely excited as well as nervous, and I could hardly contain myself. It was going to be so different to be in the high school. I called Cathy and Betsy several times during the day to discuss the next day. We talked for hours, and later in the evening, we got together for a few hours. When I finally got into bed that night, I was still wound so tight anticipating the next day's events that I had a very difficult time getting to sleep.

The following morning, Mom was standing at the bottom of the stairs calling, "Time to get up; there's school today!" That's all I needed to get myself up and going. I really wanted to get there. Brenda was the opposite; she would lay in bed until the last minute, then jump up when I was going out the door to the bus stop. I was a compulsive early bird. I would get to the bus stop thirty minutes early. The bus stop was located at the top of the hill along Route 322, right beside Cathy's old house. On days when it rained, we would wait on Irene and Percy Walter's front porch. Their house was next to the highway and the Lingle Valley Road exit, right in front of the bus stop.

It seemed as though I had been waiting for hours, but the bus finally arrived and stopped in front of Walter's porch. I, along with the other high school students, boarded and made my way back the aisle until I came to the seat occupied by Betsy. "Hi, I saved you a seat," she stated.

"Great, I hoped you would," I said as I slipped into the seat beside her. We continued chatting as our bus traveled east on Route 322. It made several stops along the way picking up students. The bus ride lasted approximately twenty minutes, and then we arrived at the high school.

The high school was a two-story, red brick building that had a new one-story wing extension on the left. There was a circular drive and sidewalk directly in front of the school that began at the doors leading into the old section of the building and on around to the doors that led into the new addition where the auditorium and main offices were located. The new section was added when the "baby boomers" began reaching seventh grade. That wing was used mainly for the junior high classes. Both junior high and senior high classes were held in the same building.

Our bus driver stopped directly in front of the six doors leading into the old section of the building. We exited the bus and moved inside. On the right was the gymnasium. To the extreme left was the stairwell that led upstairs to the ninth and tenth grade homerooms or down to the basement where the cafeteria was located.

I was lost. Betsy and I both pulled out our maps that we had gotten at orientation to see where we were. It was very complicated, but we eventually found our way to the new addition where my homeroom was located. My homeroom was in Room 171, and Mrs. Baker was my homeroom teacher. Betsy was in my homeroom. We double checked the number and went inside. I immediately saw Kenny Cooper. He had been in my class in elementary school. I slid into a seat near him, and Betsy sat behind me. I didn't recognize any of the other kids.

The seventh grade class was made up of students from four different townships. The homerooms were then broken down alphabetically. As I sat there adjusting to my new environment, several more students I recognized came into my room. They were all boys. I later learned that the girls I ran around with in elementary school were scattered throughout different homerooms; that is, all except Betsy.

After all the students arrived, Mrs. Baker entered the room and closed the door behind her. She proceeded to introduce herself and explain the rules we must abide by while in homeroom. After that all was accomplished, she seated us in alphabetical order. Then she passed out the schedules. Some of us had already gotten schedules when we had gone to orientation several weeks before. Not everyone had gone, though. Shortly after the schedules were reviewed, the bell rang, and we were all off to experience our first day of high school.

I felt completely overwhelmed. The schedules and class switching was difficult getting used to. My sense of direction wasn't the best, and I found myself wandering around the halls, trying to find the right rooms. Of course, all the old veterans in eighth grade and up thought it was fun to laugh and tease us. That was intimidating. The level of maturity between a twelfth grader and a seventh grader was very different. High school was still a lot of fun, though, and I felt that I had arrived. I thought I was really grown up.

When the first day of school was over, we all stampeded back onto our buses and headed home. Betsy and I discussed everything that happened that day on our bus ride home. She got off the bus first because we had to wait until the bus turned around at Wagner's, the last house along Route 322, before starting over the Seven Mountains, and coming back down Route 322 in the opposite direction so we wouldn't have to cross the highway. I exited the bus near the Walters' front porch.

Thoughts of the school day were going through my mind, as I walked down the hill to our house. I took the shortcut down over the bank between our two dog boxes. Spot and Brownie were our dogs' names. Brenda and I always picked such original names! Spot was a Dalmatian and Brownie was some sort of mixed terrier breed, and, of course, he was brown.

When I walked into the house, I heard Mom telling someone on the phone that she had made a doctor's appointment for Grandma that evening for 6:30 with Dr. McNabb. I had previously heard Mom and Dad discussing Grandma because she was losing several pounds a week and had a lump on her left side about six inches below her rib cage. Mom said Grandma had told her she thought she better get a checkup.

Mom never got her driver's license, and Grandma didn't drive, either. It was up to Dad to provide all the family's transportation. His prize vehicle was a 1953 two-tone blue Desoto. He had a 1956 light green Ford Thunderbird, too, that he had bought and fixed up. It's engine had blown up, and he had put in a new one. I recall him having a chain hoist attached to the big branch of the old oak tree that hung over our driveway. He often fixed people's cars for extra money. I didn't like it when he did that. Brenda and I always had to clean his tools and clean up the mess. I hated the smell of oil and gas. I wasn't a tomboy like Brenda. I often wondered if that was why Dad tended to favor Brenda.

After we ate and did the dishes, we all piled into the Ford T-bird and headed to Grandma's house. She was ready and waiting to go. Grandma didn't have a phone of her own, but if anyone needed to get in touch with her, they would call her next door neighbor, Mrs. Lewis, and she would relay the message. Brenda slid to the middle of the back seat, Grandma got into our car, and we made the 15-minute drive to Dr. McNabb's office.

Dad, Brenda, and I waited in the car while Mom and Grandma went into the doctor's office. Dr. McNabb lived in large three-story home. His office consisted of three small rooms at the east side of his house. There was a sidewalk that led from Logan Street to the entrance of the porch. The door opened into the waiting room.

It seemed as though Mom and Grandma were in Dr. McNabb's office for a long time. Finally, they came out, walked across the tree-lined street, and got inside the car. Dad leaned forward and started the engine. As he did so, he asked, "How did it go?"

Grandma said nothing, so Mom answered, "I told him about her losing weight and the lump on her side."

Dad looked over at Mom and asked, "What did he say?"

"He took her back into the examining room, and when they came back, he sat and talked to both of us. He thinks the lump is some sort of problem, so he scheduled an examination for her with Dr. Thompson next Friday at three o'clock."

I looked at Grandma upon hearing that. She appeared as though in a daze. She quietly said, "He said I'm probably going to need an operation. You know what that means, don't you?" Everyone was silent. "I'll probably come out of there in a pine box," she stated in a quiet, eerie tone.

That announcement had a tremendous impact on everyone, especially me. I had never encountered the death of anyone close to me. Truthfully, I really had never even thought about death, but I thought about it then. *Does Grandma mean she is going to die?* I wondered. I loved my Grandma, and didn't want her to die. I attended church, but really had no true concept of life after death. In reality, I wanted to believe it, but it was such an abstract idea. At eleven, I couldn't really grasp the concept. I thought, *This can't be happening. She can't really be going to die.*

The following Friday, Dad and Mom took Grandma to see Dr. Thompson. Brenda and I stayed with Grandma Eward, Mom's mother. Dr. Thompson was one of Lewistown Hospital's best surgeons. While Grandma was being examined at the hospital by Dr. Thompson, Brenda and I played jacks on Grandma Eward's sun porch.

Grandma and Pap Eward lived in Ewardtown, just a few miles from the Lewistown Hospital. Ewardtown had actually been named after my great grandfather Joseph Eward. Many of my relatives lived in Ewardtown.

Grandma and Pap had fifteen children. My mom was the thirteenth. She always said that made her unlucky. Ewardtown Road was a dead end. Their house was on top of a large hill at the end of the road. Three of my aunts lived in houses near Grandma's and Pap's house. Aunt Marie and her family lived in Great Grandma Eward's house at the bottom of the hill; Aunt Betty and her family had built a house beside Aunt Marie's house, and Aunt Dorothy had married the boy next door, Hank Marks, and lived in the house on the west side of Grandma's and Pap's house.

Unlike Grandma Bishop, Grandma and Pap Eward always had someone visiting at their house. Grandma Eward babysat for my Uncle Jim's daughter, Connie, because he and his wife, my Aunt Doris, worked at the Viscose, a rayon factory in Lewistown, and they had no one else to provide child care. Also several of Mom's brothers-in-law worked at Standard Steel, a large steel mill in Burnham, and her sisters would stay at Grandma Eward's when their husbands worked the night shift. Standard Steel was the largest employer in the area, and that is where Pap worked. The wages were higher there, and that helped Pap feed his large family.

Grandma never worked outside the house, but she worked long and hard at home. Mom told us how Grandma Eward baked bread and pies almost every day when Mom was a child. She said it took at least three chickens to feed the family. Mom's older brothers and sisters helped with the laundry, cooking, and caring for the younger children.

It was always such fun to go to Grandma and Pap Eward's house. Sometimes in the summer, I would stay for a month at a time. There were so many cousins to play with. I would also spend a night or two at my cousins' houses. We always had a great time. Brenda was more of a homebody. In fact, one weekend she insisted she wanted to stay at Grandma's and Pap's for the weekend, but before bedtime, she ended up in tears and Uncle Jim had to take her home. If I stayed at Grandma's with her, though, she would be content.

Two of my cousins, Gloria and Rick, stopped by Grandma Eward's house that day while Brenda and I waited for Dad, Mom, and Grandma to return from Dr. Thompson's office. We were discussing what game we should play, when we heard Dad's car pull up at the side of the house. Mom came in and said we had to get going, and then went in to talk to Grandma Eward for a few minutes. As we got into the car, I sensed something was wrong. Grandma Bishop seemed upset, and Dad was just staring out the window. No one said anything. Mom came out a few minutes later, and we started home. We completed the ten-mile ride home in silence. Again my thoughts turned to death. I began to pray:

Dear Jesus,
Please don't let my grandma die. Please let her get better.
Amen.

Dad dropped Grandma off at her house and said, as she was getting out of the car, "We'll be up sometime tomorrow. Don't worry about cooking supper if you don't feel up to it. Lucy and Betty can cook." Lucy was my mother and Betty was her sister. The next day would be Saturday, and we had a weekly ritual where my Uncle Jay and his family and our family would gather at Grandma's house for supper.

As Dad was driving back down to our house, he and Mom were quietly talking. Dad turned on his right signal light to turn down Lingle Valley Road, and said, "It sure doesn't sound good, does it?"

With a concerned glance at Dad, Mom replied, "No it doesn't. The doctor said the lump has to be removed. That's why she needs surgery."

"When are they going to schedule the operation?" Dad asked. "Have they set the date?"

"Next Tuesday at eleven," Mom replied. They hadn't mentioned this until Grandma was out of the car.

"I'll have to take off work to take her," he stated. " I still have some vacation time so that shouldn't be a problem." Mom just nodded in agreement.

That night I ate very little supper. I was so worried about Grandma. After doing the dishes, it was my turn to wash, I went to bed. In bed, I again prayed:
Dear Jesus,
Please don't let Grandma die. Please let the operation go well.
Amen.

I had heard Mom and Dad talking about how much the operation was going to cost. They thought Grandma's medical bills would be paid by the Welfare Department, but they had so many regulations that it was difficult for my parents to understand them. Mom and Dad had no spare money. They had difficulty scraping money together to pay all their bills. There was seldom any money left for extras. We lived from paycheck to paycheck. Dad was the only member of our family who was working. He worked at the Municipal Water Authority in Lewistown, which was approximately twelve miles from our house. He drove a backhoe, a claw-like tractor digger, and installed new water lines and repaired broken ones. He moonlighted as a self-employed automobile mechanic to earn enough money to remodel our house which they had recently bought.

They had bought our house from an old woman named Mrs. Muttersbaugh who lived next door. They had been renting for several years, but one day Dad approached Mrs. Muttersbaugh about buying the house, and she agreed to sell it. She was an odd old lady who had gone blind. Rumor was that she had cataracts and could have had them removed, but chose not to because she was too stingy. I don't know if that was true, but she sure was stingy. My mother did some household chores for Mrs. Muttersbaugh. Once while Mom was there, Mrs. Muttersbaugh told her she had gotten very hungry through the night because she had eaten only half of the six chicken wings she had boiled for supper. She said she only ate half of them so she could make two meals out of them. She wasn't rich, but she had three properties and money in the bank. She certainly didn't need to starve herself. She was always doing things like that.

Sometimes Mom made me go over to Mrs. Muttersbaugh's house and read the Bible to her since she was blind. I was afraid in her house. It smelled strange, and she looked creepy just sitting in her rocking chair staring straight ahead. Her hair was gray and came down to her waist, but she braided it and twisted it around her head. Sometimes I saw her brushing her hair in front of the window. I thought her hair was gross being that long and gray. Also it was thin, and you could see scabs on her scalp at times. She frightened me, so I avoided her as much as possible

Once, though, I had picked some of her flowers from her belly-button bush to take to my teacher and got up my nerve to go in and ask her if it was okay. I had already picked the flowers, and they were in my right hand when I asked her. She said she didn't want me to pick any of her flowers because she wanted them there for everyone to see. Since she was blind, she didn't realize I had already picked the flowers. I became so frightened that I ran and threw the flowers in the outhouse, and began crying because I thought somehow she would know, and I would get into trouble. To my relief, I never did get into any trouble.

Chapter 2

The next morning when I woke up, as I rubbed my eyes and stretched, I recalled the events from the day before. I again prayed for Grandma's well being:
Dear God,
Please let my grandma be okay, and please don't let her die.
Amen.

I then swung my feet around and sprang out of bed. It was Saturday and there was no school. I quickly slipped on a pair of jeans and a sweatshirt and bounced down the stairs heading for the kitchen. I was ready for breakfast. Everyone was on their own at our house. We never had a cooked breakfast where we all sat down to eat at one time. I usually had some kind of cereal. Oatmeal was my favorite. Mom was in the kitchen washing dishes from the following night's snacks.

"Will you make me some oatmeal?" I asked.

"Sure," Mom said, and she took her hands out of the dishwater and dried them on her apron. I walked to the other side of the kitchen and slid into my seat at the kitchen table.

"What's Dad doing?" I asked Mom as she measured the water for my oatmeal.

"He's out in the garage changing the oil in the car," she answered. Dad was a fanatic when it came to cars. The oil got changed every 2,000 miles and not a mile over that. He also constantly bought cans and cans of STP oil treatment to add to the oil. He swore by that stuff. The manufacturer should have hired him for a commercial because no one else could have believed in STP more than Dad did.

I watched Mom as she prepared my oatmeal. After several minutes, I asked, "Mom, what's wrong with Grandma? I heard you and Dad say she had a lump on her side."

Mom scraped my oatmeal into a dish and went to the refrigerator to get the milk. She sighed, hesitated, and then said, "The doctor just said there is a lump on her side that shouldn't be there. They have to remove it so she can get better."

"What made the lump?" I asked with a mouthful of oatmeal.

She simply replied, "They don't know."

I continued eating in silence as I thought about that.

After I finished breakfast, I went outside and got my bike out of the garage. Dad was still messing with the car. "I'm going up to Grandma's," I said as I jumped on my bike.

"Okay," Dad replied, "but don't stay long. I want you and Brenda to cut some weeds over by the creek today. Tell Grandma we'll be up for supper."

"I will," I called as I pedaled out the road.

To get to Grandma's house, I had to cross Lingle Valley Road and go up the dirt alley past Cathy's house and then up the hill in between Jane Carson's house and Cathy's grandparents' house. Generally, I couldn't pedal the whole way up the hill, so I would get off and walk my bike the remainder of the way up the hill and across Route 322. Crossing the road was the only dangerous part of going to visit Grandma. Route 322 was a two-lane highway, and as the trucks came off the mountain, they often surpassed the speed limit. When the coast was clear, I ran my bike across the road to Leeper's store.

Leeper's was the neighborhood hangout: a small green house with a cement front porch. Mrs. Leeper was a widow. She lived in the back of the house with her daughter, Carole; the front of the house was a two-room country store. Supplies were kept in the back room. In the front room was an enclosed glass candy counter on the right side, a meat counter on the back wall, and a soda cooler along the two side-by-side windows in the front. The soda sat in extremely cold water inside the cooler. Hires Root Beer and Nehi Orange were my favorites. There were several shelves in the center of the store that displayed bread, rolls, and canned goods and shelves along the left side wall that displayed cakes, pies, and chips.

My friends and I loved to purchase the penny candy from the candy counter. Mrs. Leeper would get upset with us for making her open and close the two sides of the counter as our candy choices jumped from side to side. I liked licorice best, but I also liked Black Jacks, Mary Janes, Tootsie Rolls, Teaberry Balls, and Sugar Daddies. Brenda was wild about Mallow Cups. She saved the cards and sent for a free box of candy bars when her cards totaled 500 points. It took months for her to earn them.

I continued up the road beside the store. It turned to the left several hundred feet beyond the store in front of Suloff's Kennels. I was then on Pine Street. Mrs. Suloff was the school nurse. Her husband, Mr. Suloff, had a number of coon hounds he raised and sold. Occasionally, Mr. Suloff would go down Lingle Valley Road past our house running his dogs alongside his old Chevy pickup. They would howl the whole way out the Valley.

After the left turn at the Suloffs' house, you could see the end of the road straight ahead. Approximately one eighth of a mile up the road, it intersected with another road that went to all the houses "up back" as we called it. Grandma's house was straight ahead at the end of Pine Street, which was a dead end road.

When I got to Grandma's house, I parked my bike at the side and went in the back door. You couldn't use her front door because whoever built the house had not put stairs up to it. The front door opened into her living room, and it always remained locked since it was approximately an eight foot drop from the door to the ground.

"Grandma," I called since she wasn't in the kitchen. "Where are you?"

"I'm in here," she called, and she came walking out from her bedroom pushing through the flimsy blue cotton curtains that hung between her kitchen and bedroom.

"What are you all doing today?" she asked. Even after so many years, Grandma still had a southern drawl.

"I just thought I'd come up to visit you," I answered.

"Oh you did? That was nice," she said as she walked over to the kitchen table, pulled out a chair and sat down. "What do you want to have with the fried chicken tonight?" she asked.

I smiled and replied, "biscuits." Her biscuits were the best. I could eat them every day and not get tired of them. Dad didn't care for them very much, though. He said that when he was growing up, many times when Pap was out of work, all they had for supper was gravy and biscuits. But he loved the rest of Grandma's cooking.

"Dad said to tell you they'll be up tonight, and if you don't feel well, Mom and Aunt Betty can do the cooking."

Grandma snorted and said, "I'd hate to eat the fried chicken those two would cook!"

I just giggled. Grandma didn't think any "Yankee" could cook. I liked to visit her. She would tell me stories about what it was like for her growing up in the South. She loved the song, "Oh Susanna" by Stephen Foster because it mentioned Alabama.

I felt sorry that Grandma had never gotten back to Alabama. Our family just didn't have money to go on vacations or trips. My uncles could have taken her, but two of them didn't talk to her, and the other one was too stingy. Uncle Jay never went anywhere that you had to stay overnight. As we sat down at the kitchen table, Grandma asked, "How are you doing at the new school?"

"Okay, I guess," I replied. Grandma always made me feel special. I proceeded to tell her all about high school. "The school is really big, and sometimes we get lost. The bell rings when it's time to go to another class, and you only have three minutes to get there before the bell rings again. Of course, there is no recess; I sort of miss that. We have to take gym this year, too, and they make you take showers. All the girls are in one big shower at the same time."

Grandma huffed and declared, "That's indecent! Young girls should have privacy."

"I know," I agreed and continued. "We have lunch in a big cafeteria, and a lot of older kids eat at the same time we do. They have four lunch periods, too. If anyone gets in trouble at lunchtime, they have to stand up by the book racks along the back wall. It's real noisy in the cafeteria."

"Do they have good lunches?" Grandma asked. She was always concerned about food.

"Yeah, pretty good. The same things they had at the elementary school. I like pretty much everything. I especially like the hot pork sandwiches." I was the opposite of Brenda; she liked very few of the school lunches. She was happy bringing Lebanon Bologna and potato chip sandwiches from home.

"You kids these days are lucky. Back in my day a lot of people didn't get to go to school, or if they did, they would only go for a short time and then have to quit to help with the work at home. I went to school for a while. We only went to eighth grade back then," she reminisced. As Grandma was talking, I noticed she did look different. She seemed tired and that wasn't Grandma to me. Generally, she was full of energy and always working on some project. Once she taught Brenda and me how to make a little nine-square patchwork quilt while she was working on her own quilting project. It was a lot of fun. Other times, she allowed us to help while she made candy or baked cookies. The entire time she would tell us stories about the "old days," when she was a child in Alabama.

After we visited for a while, I said, "Well, I better get going. Dad wants me and Brenda to cut some weeds over in the woods before we come up here tonight." Dad had a bad temper, so I didn't want to risk making him angry.

Grandma stood up and said, "Hold on a minute." She then disappeared on the other side of the curtain into her bedroom. When she returned, she handed me two dimes and said, "Here, stop at Leeper's and buy yourself something on your way back home." She almost always gave me some change so I could stop at the store.

"Gee, thanks," I said and called, "Bye," as I scooted out the kitchen door and hopped on my bike.

Going home was always faster because it was downhill. I rounded the corner at Suloff's and skidded into the parking lot at Leeper's, which consisted of a gravel space big enough for two cars parked side-by-side. I leaned my bike on the porch and went in.

Mrs. Leeper came out of the back room and stood at the counter where the cash register was. I picked up a five cent bag of Middlesworth's chips and pulled a Hires Root Beer out of the cooler. I spent the remainder of my twenty cents on penny candy. I had to tell Mrs. Leeper which kinds of penny candy I wanted. I chose Black Jacks, Mary Janes, and black licorice. After she filled my order, she asked, "What are you going to do today?"

"Just hanging around for a while, then I have to cut some weeds for Dad," I replied.

"That sounds like a lot of work," Mrs. Leeper said as she took my money and put it into the cash register.

"Yeah," I said. "I hate to cut weeds. There's a bunch of poison ivy in the woods, and I'll probably catch it."

Mrs. Leeper just chuckled.

I gathered my feast and went out and sat down on Mrs. Leeper's porch to devour it, watching the traffic go by on Route 322. A few minutes later, Betsy came out of her house from across the road and waved. Her house was next door to Anne's and Bud's, Cathy's grandparents.

"What are you going to do today?" she yelled across the road.

"I have to cut some weeds and then we're going up to Grandma's tonight," I shouted back.

"Cathy' s coming over later to hang out. If you get a chance, come up," Betsy invited.

"Okay," I called, and Betsy disappeared back into her house.

Betsy, Cathy, Brenda, and I spent many, many hours on Betsy's front porch watching the traffic go by. There were four chairs lined up along the banister. Betsy always got the first chair because it was her house, and we all considered it the best chair. The rest of us would argue about who got the other chairs. Usually, though, whoever got there first got the chair next to Betsy.

Betsy also had a playhouse in her back yard. Her father had built it for her and her sister, Francie. It was a one-room, ten-by-ten wooden cabin with a small window in front. The roof was slightly tilted upward so the rain would run off. Inside, there was a large chest built into the right side of the wall, filled with an assortment of clothes accumulated from Betsy's family and neighbors.

When we were younger, we used the clothes to play dress-up. There was one particular pair of black suede spike heels we all fought over. They had been Cathy's mother's. Her feet were very small, size five. Even at our ages, we had to squeeze our feet into the shoes.

Betsy had a swing set beside her playhouse. We all enjoyed doing acrobatic stunts on the bars. Skin-the-cat was fun; I was good at that. I was extremely flexible, and loved gymnastics at school. From the swing set, you could see down over the hill into Lingle Valley. Standing in front of the swing set and looking down the hill, Cathy's trailer and Havice's swimming pool were about fifty yards away. You could also see Mrs. Muttersbaugh's house that was in front of our house.

After my feast was finished, I retrieved my bike from the side of the store and again crossed Route 322 and backtracked my earlier path. When I arrived home, Brenda was in the living room eating cereal and watching TV. She always seemed to need more sleep than me.

"We have to cut weeds today," I informed her when I entered the house.

"I know," she whined.

"I'm going to get mine done. Betsy and Cathy are going to hang out later," I related as I went through the living room, the sitting room, and out the back door. Dad was done changing the oil, and he was getting the lawn mower ready to mow the backyard. He was always working on some project, and I had grown to hate Dad's projects because he often got very angry while completing them.

Once when I was in second grade, and we lived in Shreader, Dad had decided to re-wallpaper the living room even though we only rented the house. He had never papered, but like all his other projects, he had decided that he could do it. The paper was beige and had huge leaves on it; I think they may have been oak leaves. Our living room was large, fifteen by twenty feet.

There were only two large rooms downstairs in that house: the living room and kitchen. The staircase was in the center of the house, just inside the front door.

Before the wallpapering was half-completed, the problems began. I believe Dad was getting tired. The paper would bunch up in spots, and he couldn't smooth out the wrinkles. The more frustrated Dad became, the more wrinkles he created in the paper. Finally, he reached his boiling point, and angrily tore the piece of paper he was working on from the wall, bunched it into a ball, and threw it toward the other side of the room. Since it was only paper and wallpaper paste, it did not travel very far. He then violently pitched the wooden handled wallpaper brush against the wall, and it fell to the floor in two pieces. That made him even more angry, and he instructed me to, "Go down to John's and tell him I need to borrow his wallpaper brush."

It was a Friday evening in February, so it was already dark outside. My Uncle John lived about a half mile down the road. I would have to walk past an old lime quarry and factory. At that time, I was only six, and I was terrified to carry out Dad's order, but I knew I had no choice. My mother began protesting, and that made my father angrier. I whispered to Mom that it would be okay as I went into the hallway to put on my winter coat.

I ran the whole way to my uncle's house. It seemed like an eternity, but in reality it probably was less than fifteen minutes. When I arrived at Uncle John's, I asked to borrow his wallpaper brush. He asked, "Did your dad make you walk down here?"

"Yes," I answered, shivering as I became aware that I was cold. Prior to my arrival, I was too frightened to feel the cold.

"Let me get my coat and the brush, and I'll give you a ride back to the house," he said he disappeared down the basement stairs. I was so glad he was taking me back in his car. I thought he might then stay and help, and Dad would stop yelling at Mom, Brenda, and me.

It worked, for when we arrived at my house, Uncle John got out of his car and went into the house with me. By then, Mom had cleaned up the mess Dad had made with the torn paper and broken brush. Uncle John explained to Dad that everything he was doing was wrong, which I could tell irritated Dad, but at least he was able to finish wallpapering. Uncle John stayed and helped for a while. I was extremely relieved, as I'm sure Mom and Brenda were.

Many other similar episodes occurred throughout my childhood years. I became conditioned to hate and fear those projects. Inevitably, I would get in trouble some way and receive some form of punishment. It was always me who was yelled at the most, criticized the most, and generally punished more severely and more often. Sometimes I wondered if Dad felt that by punishing me, the oldest, he was somehow punishing his older brothers who were favored by his mother, my grandmother. He always maintained that he treated Brenda and me equally. Whenever he said that, I marveled at how he could say it, and apparently believe it, when the opposite seemed so obvious.

"Where's the sickle?" I asked as I entered the garage.

"Hanging up there," he replied and motioned to the back wall.

I took the sickle down and began walking toward the patch of woods directly across from our house. Dad had bought the one acre wooded lot from Mr. Stuck. Mr. Stuck was one of our neighbors who lived four houses down from us at the end of the dead end alley that went by our house. Dad purchased the lot so no one could build directly across from us, and we would also have a nice picnic area. We and our friends would often build campfires to roast hot dogs and marshmallows. The far boundary of the woods was marked by Lingle Valley Run. We all simply called it the "crick."

That was where Dad wanted me to cut weeds. I was always frightened of snakes. I had seen few snakes in those woods, but I knew they were there. Mom was constantly telling Brenda and me to, "watch for snakes." The gnats were always bad, too. As I slung the sickle, I worked up a sweat and the gnats were swarming around my head. It took me about half an hour to finish what I considered to be my half of the weeds. When I finished, my hair was pasted to my head, my sweatshirt sleeves were pushed up above my elbows, and I was itchy all over. I thought by wearing long sleeves, I would be less likely to catch poison ivy or oak. I practically ran out of the woods. I laid the sickle on the front porch, and went into the house. Brenda was just getting ready to go outside. "I'm done with my half," I announced.

"I bet," she said. "You better have half of them cut."

"I did," I said emphatically. After I washed and dried my hands and face in the bathroom, I went to the kitchen for a drink of cold water and found Mom wiping the shelves in the refrigerator. As I filled my glass with water from the faucet, I informed her, "I'm going up to Betsy's house."

"Okay, but be back here by three," she replied.

I quickly went out the front door. I didn't usually ride my bike to Betsy's because I cut through two of her neighbors' backyards as a shortcut. When I arrived, Cathy and Betsy already had their behinds parked on the front porch. I would take the third chair in the lineup.

"Hi, guys," I called as I approached the porch. "What's going on?"

They both turned in unison, and Betsy said, "Nothing much. We're just hanging out."

"How do you like the high school?" Cathy asked as she rocked her chair back and forth by pushing her right foot against the banister.

As I took the chair beside Cathy, I replied, "I love it, but I still get lost, and I hate the older kids making fun of us."

"I do too," Betsy agreed as she, too, rocked back and forth on her yellow metal porch chair.

We continued talking about school and just about everything else the remainder of the afternoon. Betsy told us about a real cute boy she had already noticed. His name was Chet, and he was in eighth grade. She believed he lived in Reedsville. I confessed that I thought Ed Fryer, a boy in my English class, was cute, too. Our discussion then moved on to all the boys we found attractive and what classes we had with them. Cathy declared that it wasn't fair that we had so many cute boys at our school, and there weren't many cute boys in her school.

As three o'clock approached, I stood up, yawned, and said, "I've got to get going. We're going to my grandma's tonight for supper. See you guys Monday if I don't see you tomorrow."

"Yeah, see you," Cathy said.

Betsy simply said, "Yeah."

My thoughts returned to my grandma as I took the shortcut back to my house. I wondered what that lump could be. I hadn't said anything to Cathy or Betsy. No one really knew anything yet.

When I arrived home, I entered the house through the back door. Mom yelled, "Your dad's getting a shower, and then we'll be leaving."

"Okay," I called in response. Then I flopped down on the tangerine colored vinyl couch in what we called our sitting room.

Originally, that room had been the living room, but when Dad purchased the house, he completely changed the layout. Previously, there had been four rooms: kitchen, living room, and two bedrooms. There was no indoor bathroom. We had an outhouse attached to the left side of the garage. When I was in elementary school, Dad cut an opening into the ceiling of the living room, built a stairway, and made two bedrooms upstairs. He then moved the kitchen to Brenda's and my old bedroom, the living room to his and Mom's old bedroom, and the bathroom to the old kitchen since it was the smallest room in the house. He had to add a wall and make an entranceway by the back door so it wouldn't open into the bathroom. That left the sitting room. You would walk through the back door into the entranceway, turn right into the sitting room, and then go through the sitting room to get to the living room. You would then turn left to go to the kitchen.

I liked it when Dad was building the upstairs. Brenda and I would climb up a ladder into the partially finish rooms. Everything smelled like new wood. On several occasions, Dad allowed us to sleep upstairs with our pillows and blankets. We thought that was great. Mom was concerned, though, that we would fall down the opening. To her amazement, we survived.

Finally, Dad finished showering and was ready to go to Grandma's house. "Come on, kids," he called as he went out the back door. Brenda had gone back into the house and was parked in front of the TV. She reluctantly stood up and walked over to turn the TV off. Mom came out of the kitchen, locked the front door, and followed Brenda and me out the back door. Mom then locked the back door.

She always locked the doors. Many of the people in the neighborhood didn't, but Mom was always concerned that a prisoner might have gotten loose. Sometimes the Forestry Department took prisoners out Lingle Valley to work on the road. That terrified Mom because once a prisoner had escaped. He was soon apprehended, though, and returned to prison without anyone being harmed.

Eventually, we were all in Dad's green Thunderbird heading to Grandma's house. As we went up Lingle Valley Road and turned left onto Route 322, he told us: "Now Grandma's upset about having to go to the hospital on Tuesday to get that lump removed, so don't say anything to her about it."

Mom instructed, "And don't say anything to Carol." Carol would be with her mother and father, my Aunt Betty and Uncle Jay. "She can't seem to keep her mouth shut about anything," she added.

"We won't," both Brenda and I said at the same time.

When we reached Grandma's house, Aunt Betty, Uncle Jay, and Carol were already there. Grandma was busy in the kitchen cooking away. As we entered the kitchen, we felt a heat wave hit our faces. Grandma's cook-stove was fired up. Chicken was frying in a skillet and biscuits were in the oven. Brenda, Carol, and I went into the living room to watch TV; Dad and Uncle Jay went back outside and sat on the side porch, while Mom and Aunt Betty began to help Grandma finish preparing supper and set the table.

Back in the living room, while *American Band Stand* was playing on the TV, Carol, Brenda, and I were engaged in a whispered conversation. Carol asked, "Did you know Grandma has cancer?"

"She does not!" I exclaimed in a loud whisper.

Brenda asked, "What is cancer anyways?"

"You're really stupid," Carol continued. "Everybody knows it's a very bad disease, and you die from it. That's what's going to happen to Grandma Bishop." Carol was two years older than I, and she thought she knew everything about everything. Aunt Betty and Uncle Jay actually encouraged that behavior by continually bragging about Carol's abilities and grades.

"You're a liar!" I insisted. "She just has a lump, and they're going to take it out."

"Sure she has a lump. That's what cancer is," Carol said.

"Liar! Just shut up!" I screamed in a loud whisper. We didn't want the grown-ups to hear us. We knew we would be in big trouble if they did. Mom's warning about not saying anything to Carol was too late. She must have already heard about Grandma from Aunt Betty and Uncle Jay.

As the evening progressed, the argument between Carol and me continued. I had no idea if Carol was right or wrong. I didn't want to believe that Grandma was going to die. I wasn't sure what cancer was, either, but I believed it was a disease you died from, just like Carol had said. When Aunt Betty and Mom were washing dishes and Grandma was outside talking with Uncle Jay and Dad, I heard them quietly talking about the operation scheduled for Tuesday.

Aunt Betty said, "Jay doesn't think Sallie looks good."

Mom replied, "No, she doesn't. She's been losing weight for quite some time. Dr. Thompson said the lump may be cancerous. They won't be able to tell until they open her up and do a biopsy. It's a huge lump, too."

"How is she going to pay for all of this?" Betty asked.

In a somewhat agitated tone, Mom said, "They told us at the hospital that her welfare card should take care of it."

"I hope so because Jay can't afford to spend any more money. He already has to pay for her," Aunt Betty whined. She really resented that Uncle Jay and Dad's other two brothers were court-ordered to pay parental support, and Dad wasn't. It didn't matter to her that Uncle Jay, Uncle Clarence, and Uncle John all made much more money than Dad. All three of them worked at Standard Steel, the local steel mill, and their wages were almost double Dad's.

Aunt Betty continued, "Who's going to take care of her when she comes out of the hospital? I sure can't. I'm not well myself, and we don't have anywhere to put her."

Mom snapped, "You have as much room as we do, but I suppose Werdna (that was Dad's middle name and Mom's family always called him by that name) will have to take her to our place."

"Well, he should do something since he doesn't have to pay anything," Aunt Betty countered.

Aunt Betty was Mom's sister, and Uncle Jay was Dad's brother. She made me so angry; she was selfish and stingy. Her family always drove a brand new car, and had built a new house on land they had gotten from Grandma and Pap Eward. They really had no financial worries. I wanted her to be concerned about Grandma's health, not worried about who was going to pay, and who was going to keep her. All I cared about was Grandma. I didn't want her to have cancer, and I didn't want her to die. Again I prayed:

Dear God,
Please don't let Grandma have cancer, and please don't let her die
Amen.

The next two days we continued in the same old routine. On Sunday, Brenda and I went to church--the Milroy Methodist Church located on Main Street. Dad and Mom didn't attend, but they made it mandatory for us to attend. When we were very young, Mom had taken us to her home church in Burnham. Dad never attended church, but claimed to be a believer. Dad said he didn't have the proper clothing to go to church, and Mom didn't want to go to a new church without him. While in church, I again prayed for my grandma.

The following Monday, we returned to school. Each evening while in bed I prayed the same prayer:

Dear God,
Please don't let Grandma have cancer, and please don't let her die
Amen.

Tuesday morning I got up before Mom called me. I had feelings of anxiety. I knew that was the day Grandma was having her operation. I quickly dressed for school and rushed downstairs. Mom and Dad were in the kitchen eating.

"You're up early," Mom said. Dad just looked at me but made no comment as he continued eating his raisin bran cereal.

"I couldn't sleep. What time does Grandma go to the hospital?" I asked as I poured myself a dish of corn flakes.

"She has to go in at eight o'clock to be registered, and the surgery begins at nine thirty," Dad responded.

"How long will the operation take?" I asked, and suddenly my cereal no longer held any appeal for me.

"We don't know. Probably a couple of hours, though," Dad said. "Why?" he asked, his eyes following me from the table to the kitchen counter where I carried my partially eaten cereal.

"I just wondered," I said, then emptied the cereal into the special container Mom had on the counter to save leftovers for the dogs.

"You shouldn't waste food like that," said Dad.

"We should be back home by the time you and Brenda get home today," Mom informed me.

"You know we may have to bring Mom back here to stay for a while after her operation. She might not be able to take care of herself for a while. If we do, we'll set up a bed in the sitting room along the stairway wall," Dad told Mom and me.

"I thought we might. Betty's already moaning she won't," Mom said. Uncle Clarence (Fat was his nickname) and Uncle John hadn't spoken to Grandma since the court ordered them to pay parental support.

"I know. We have to bring her here. She has nowhere else to go, and she's my mother," Dad sadly commented. It seemed ironic to me that Dad could be so compassionate with issues related to Grandma when at other times he could be so cruel to me, sometimes for no apparent reason.

Brenda was just coming down the stairs. Mom urged, "You better hurry. You're going to miss the bus, and we don't have time to take you to school."

As I continued down the back steps, I couldn't make out Brenda's reply. I went around the garage, crossed the board we had laying across the ditch, and climbed the hill between our two dog boxes. Both Spot and Brownie pulled at their chains, trying to get a pat on the head as I charged through their territory.

Since Grandma was having her lump removed that day, I was worried about her, but I knew Jesus wouldn't let her die. After all, didn't he promise that our prayers would be answered if we just believed? I believed. Again I prayed:

Dear Jesus,
Please don't let Grandma have cancer, and please don't let her die.
Amen.

The school day dragged. I was preoccupied all day with thoughts of Grandma. At eight o'clock, I thought, *she should be at the hospital now*. At nine-thirty, I thought, *the operation should be starting now*. At lunch time, I wondered if the surgery was over. Several times throughout the day I repeated my prayer:

Dear Jesus,
Please don't let Grandma have cancer, and please don't let herdie.
Amen.

Finally, it seemed like an eternity later, the last period bell rang, and the school day was over. I picked up my books and returned to homeroom. Later, on the way home, I continued thinking about Grandma. I exited the bus when it pulled in front of the Walters' house, then I ran down the hill and took the shortcut between the dog boxes. Brenda's bus would come later. As I came around the garage, I saw Dad's Thunderbird parked in the driveway. They were home; I didn't know if that was good or bad.

When I entered the house through the front entrance, Mom and Dad were both sitting on the rose-beige sectional that wrapped around the far corner of our living room. I could tell that I had interrupted their conversation.

"How's Grandma?" I asked.

Dad looked at me with his deep-set, sad, blue eyes and said, "She's still in the hospital. They weren't able to remove the lump. They just sewed her back up. The doctor said there is nothing else they can do. She'll have to take about thirty radiation treatments to try to shrink the tumor, but that's it."

As my dad talked, my heartbeat got faster and faster. I was having difficulty breathing. I forced the question out of my mouth: "How long does she have to stay in the hospital?" I asked. But that was not what I was thinking. I wanted to know if she had cancer. Tumor sounded so much more terminal than lump. I wanted to know if she was going to die. Also, what the heck were radiation treatments?

"She'll probably get out in about a week. She won't be able to go back to her house for a while, though," Mom said.

"Where will she go?" I asked. I had heard them plan before to bring her to our house, but I needed to hear it again.

"We're going to bring her here until she's able to go back to her house," Dad responded.

"Oh," was the only reply I could manage. I was shocked. I had been certain God was not going to let her have cancer. I couldn't accept it. Initially, I was in denial. *This can't be true,* I thought. I believed that Jesus wouldn't let her have cancer. This has to be some kind of mistake. Maybe the tumor isn't cancerous. Again, I prayed:

Dear Jesus,
Please let this be a mistake. Please don't let Grandma have cancer, and please don't let her die.
Amen.

Grandma was released from the hospital a week later. Dad had set up a folding cot in our sitting room against the staircase wall. The couch was moved to the other side of the room. Brenda and I shared the small, light green bedroom at the top of the stairs. Mom's and Dad's bedroom was behind ours. They had to walk through the middle of our bedroom to get to theirs. There was a dark, walnut-varnished wooden door separating the two rooms. Their bedroom was painted sky-blue.

Dad held Grandma's right arm to help steady her, and she held onto the large white wooden post with her left hand as she walked up the two steps to get onto our front porch. Dad led her across the porch and through our front door into the living room. Grandma sighed as she eased herself down onto the end of the couch at the side of the room.

She looked at Dad and said, "I told you, Werdna, that I would be coming out of that place in a pine box, and I was pretty much right."

"Now, Mom, don't give up. They're going to start your radiation treatments in two weeks. They think that will shrink the tumor," Dad attempted to encourage her.

"I don't think so. I just feel it in my soul that I'm dying. I'm ready, though. I'm not afraid. I'm just too tired to go on living," Grandma stated matter-of-factly.

"Mom, you shouldn't think like that. That's not going to help you," Dad said as he looked at her and slowly shook his head back and forth.

"I'll just be in the way here," she proclaimed.

"You can stay here as long as you want. You're not in the way," Dad said, trying to give her some comfort with his words.

"Your brothers don't want me, do they?" Grandma asked with tears in her eyes.

"I called John's and Fat's houses and told their wives you were having an operation, but neither one called back. Don't worry about them. They'll pay for the way they're treating you someday," Dad said and then paused. After several seconds that seemed like minutes he continued, "Jay said Betty wouldn't be able to take care of you because she hasn't been feeling well, herself. You know Betty. She always thinks she's sick. I really don't think there's anything wrong with her."

"Me neither," Mom added. "It's just an act so she can get some attention."

I couldn't listen to any more of it. I quietly crept out the back door. Brenda was sitting on the back steps.

"What's going on?" she asked.

"Grandma's talking about dying. I know she's not going to die," I insisted.

"What makes you think so?" Brenda asked.

"I just know it," I said as I grabbed my bike that was leaning against the garage and took off out Lingle Valley Road.

Whenever I was sad, I headed for the bridge that crossed Lingle Valley Run. I liked to sit on the large stone steps that extended from the top of the bridge to the bottom of the bank right at the water's edge. The bridge itself was made of wooden planks, and it had two inch cracks between each plank. The railing was made of nine inch diameter trees stripped of their bark. There were two rows of railing running the length of the bridge on both sides. When you crossed the bridge, you were able to see the water beneath you because of the cracks between the planks.

I sat down on the top stone step, my favorite spot, and stared down into the water. The motion and roaring of the water had a calming effect. Whenever I was upset about something, I would go to that spot. There was a large, bushy mulberry tree three feet away from the stone step I was sitting on. Brenda and I had picked the berries from that tree for many years.

As I stared down into the water, tears began to roll down my cheeks; I was beginning to accept the fact that Grandma had cancer. I reasoned that it must be true if those doctors were going to give her radiation treatments, whatever they were. Surely they wouldn't do that if she didn't have cancer. Soon my silent tears turned to sobs as more and more despair settled onto me. I found myself again praying what I now thought of as "Grandma's Prayer." Now, though, I was bargaining with Jesus:

Dear Jesus,

I know Grandma must have cancer, but I don't know why. Since she has cancer, please just don't let her die.

Amen.

I probably sat there for over an hour after my sobs had subsided. I silently stared at the water and allowed it to calm my soul. I had nothing to wipe my nose on, so I just wiped it across my sleeve. Eventually, I got back on my bike, crossed the bridge, and rode out the dirt road away from my house to the corner. That was where the road turned sharply to the right to go up around the state-owned land. Tears again flowed down my cheeks as I thought about Grandma. I then sharply turned my handle bars to the right as I turned my bike around and headed back to my house, allowing the breeze on my face to finish drying the tracks of my tears.

Chapter 3

Grandma's radiation treatments began on Monday, October 5th. Those treatments were supposed to stop the tumor from spreading and kill the tumor cells. That therapy was chosen since Dr. Thompson had determined it was too late to surgically remove the entire tumor from Grandma's body. He had transferred Grandma's case to Dr. Kinsey, the oncologist at Lewistown Hospital.

It was decided that Grandma would have thirty-nine radiation treatments. Mom and Dad were told that about sixty percent of cancer patients required that kind of therapy. They administered treatments Monday through Friday. No treatments were given on the weekends or holidays. Since Mom didn't drive and Dad worked through the day, it was difficult arranging for these treatments. Dad was able to work some night shifts because at that time, the Lewistown Municipal Authority was operating a pump house that had to run twenty–four hours a day due to a drought situation. Grandma's neighbor, Mrs. Lewis, helped the remaining times that Dad couldn't rearrange his work schedule. Dad had attempted to get his brothers to help with providing transportation, but they refused. It was hard for me to comprehend how my uncles could be so cruel to their mother; it must have been even harder for Grandma to understand.

Skin breakdown at the entry site of the radiation beam is often a major side effect of radiation treatments. Grandma was fortunate in that regard. She had no skin breakdown from her treatments. She did experience fatigue which was another common side effect. She was very tired, and I remember she was always cold. Dr. Kinsey warned that later into the therapy, vomiting and diarrhea could occur.

My anxiety didn't seem as great while Grandma was receiving her radiation treatments. I had hope because something was being done, and I felt certain Jesus would heal Grandma from that horrible disease. I made certain I didn't miss repeating Grandma's prayer one single night throughout the entire nine month period. She had to get better! Jesus wouldn't lie.

Getting Grandma ready to go for treatments was taxing for my mom. She had no help providing personal care for Grandma. Of course, Dad would feel uncomfortable helping with bathing her, and Grandma would, too. None of our relatives volunteered to help or to provide Mom and Dad with any caretaker relief. Mom thought Brenda and I were too young to be burdened with helping.

Mom would awaken Brenda and me for school, fix us some breakfast, and then make Grandma something to eat. She usually tried to come to the table for her meals. Initially, she could do that, but as time progressed, she had to take her meals more and more frequently in bed.

When her treatments began, she was still very weak from the surgery, and the treatments also made her tired. Mom would have to help bathe and dress her. She would go along with Grandma when Dad or Mrs. Lewis transported her to the Lewistown Hospital.

Grandma moved very slowly and Mom had to help steady her when she walked down the two steps from our front porch to the sidewalk. The sidewalk then extended twenty feet to the edge of the alley where Dad or Mrs. Lewis picked her up. They would back out of our driveway, then pull up to the sidewalk and open the passenger door right in front of Grandma. Mom would then assist Grandma in easing herself into the front seat of either vehicle.

At the hospital Mom would escort Grandma to the Radiology Department. The entire treatment process took only about thirty minutes. They rarely kept Grandma waiting once she arrived. Dr. Kinsey had told Mom to rub Vaseline on Grandma if she got any burned areas from the radiation. She never did.

When I returned home from school the first day of Grandma's treatment, I rushed into the house through the back door to find out how it went. Grandma was lying on her side in her bed. I asked, "How are you Grandma?" as I sat down in the tangerine-colored, vinyl chair beside her bed.

"I'm okay, sweetheart," she weakly answered.

"Do you feel any better?" I asked hopefully.

"Not really. It's probably too early to tell any difference yet," she said as she pulled herself higher and repositioned her pillows.

"I prayed for you today," I softly stated as I fidgeted with my bottom sweater button.

"That was real nice, honey," she said, and reached over and patted my leg.

Brenda came through the back screen door at about that time, dragging her yellow windbreaker behind her. It was the beginning of October, and we were having an Indian summer. Mom had opened the back door, and I could hear the sparrows chirping in the apple tree in our back yard.

"Hi, Grandma," Brenda said as she wandered through Grandma's room and on to the kitchen for a drink. She stopped at the coffee table in the living room to deposit her book bag and windbreaker.

"Hi," Grandma answered.

I sat there for a little while not knowing what to say. Grandma had closed her eyes and was just lying there with her hands folded on her belly. My eyes began to fill with tears, so I quickly stood up before they overflowed and took my jacket to the closet to hang it on one of the brass hooks.

I heard Mom in the kitchen ask Brenda, "How did school go today?"

Brenda responded with the usual, "Okay."

"Do you have any homework?" Mom asked, rattling something in the refrigerator.

"No," Brenda answered and passed me when I was going into the kitchen.

Brenda went over to the sectional in the living room and flopped down to watch TV. It was already turned on. Mom usually had it turned on in the afternoons so she could watch or at least listen to her so-called "stories." She kept up with most of the soap operas on the two TV channels that we received. *As the World Turns* was her favorite. We had antennas in our backyard so we could get TV reception from Altoona and Johnstown. They were the closest television stations.

Many times Dad would send Brenda or me outside to turn one of the antennas in an attempt to get better reception. Our TV reception was never what, by today's standards, would be considered good. The picture was fuzzy--we referred to that as snowy--and sometimes, you could hear static. We still enjoyed watching television, though.

Through the opened front door, I could see Elmer, a boy my age who lived two doors down the alley from our place, go by on his bike. Elmer always had a big wad of cotton stuffed into his left ear. His mother Polly said he had to keep the air out so he didn't get ear aches. Cathy, Betsy, Brenda, and I secretly called him "Elmer Fudd."

Mom had sat down at the kitchen table, preparing salmon cakes for supper. I asked, "What are we having with the salmon cakes?"

"Fried potatoes," she replied.

That sounded great to me, and I let Mom know by saying "mmm."

Brenda yelled "Yuck!" from the living room.

As I sat at the table watching Mom, I heard Dad's tires on the gravel in the alley. I got up and went out to sit on the red oak swing that hung on the right side of our front porch. The swing had been a gift from my Uncle Jim who was married to Mom's sister, Daisy. Dad had done some repairs on his car and refused to take any payment, so Uncle Jim made us the swing. He had a small wood shop in his basement where he made wooden items for extra income. I loved the swing. We had a flowered lounge chair on the other side of the porch, but I always preferred the swing.

When Dad came around the side of the porch, he asked, "How's your grandmother?" Dad was a big man, over six feet tall, with blue eyes and dark brown curly hair that he wore slicked back. He looked like a mixture of Matt Dillon from *Gunsmoke* and Elvis. In fact, he loved telling the story about how once when he was in the hospital, a few of the nurses thought he *was* Elvis.

"She seems tired," I answered as I pushed the swing in motion with my right foot.

Dad had his silver aluminum lunch box in his right hand and his jacket tucked under his arm. I looked at his big, laced work boots as he came onto the porch, opened the front door, and disappeared into the living room. Dad seemed to be in a good mood. Whenever he was in a bad mood, he frightened me.

The kitchen window beside the swing was pushed opened about six inches. I heard him put his lunch box on the kitchen counter beside the sink. He then asked Mom, "How was the treatment?"

I peaked through the window and saw Mom place the salmon cakes in the big black cast-iron skillet, as she answered, "Okay, I guess. They really didn't tell us anything new. It's too early for any side effects based on what they told us before."

Dad left the kitchen and went in to talk with Grandma. I continued swinging and uttered Grandma's prayer:
Dear God,
Please don't let her die.
Amen.

My family ate earlier than most of my friends' families. Dad worked the seven to three shift, so he got home shortly after Brenda and I did. Mom always liked to eat around four o'clock. Of course, that meant we would be hungry again before bedtime. One of our favorite snacks was a bowl of cereal before bedtime. If I skipped breakfast, which I did occasionally, I said I had eaten my breakfast before I went to bed. Mom always said that didn't count. Another snack Brenda and I often ate was ketchup bread. We would squeeze ketchup into a saucer and then dip pieces of bread into it and eat it. It sounds disgusting now, but we liked it then.

When Mom was finished preparing supper, she called, "Linda, time to eat."

"Okay, I'm coming," I said and quickly went in and sat at my place at the kitchen table. Brenda and I sat at the back because it was easier for us to get behind the table. When we weren't eating, the table was pushed against the wall so we would have more space in the kitchen. None of the rooms in our house were very big, and we needed to conserve space wherever we could.

Brenda had her usual hamburger that night for supper. She didn't like salmon cakes, either. Dad told Brenda and me to say the prayer. We said the same prayer at every mealtime:

"God is good, God is great, and we thank him for our food. By his hands were are fed. Give us Lord our daily bread. Amen."

As I was eating my salmon cake and fried potatoes, I watched Grandma. She nibbled at her food and said very little throughout the meal. When she was finished, she had eaten only about half of her salmon cake. No one mentioned the treatments while we were eating.

Throughout October, Grandma's treatments continued. She appeared to be getting weaker each week. The doctor said she was still losing weight. Her appetite was not improving. I worried about her most of the time. While in school, I often would think about her being at the hospital. I sometimes got tears in my eyes, and had to desperately try to keep from crying. Sometimes I didn't manage to do that, and tears would find their way down my cheeks. I would quickly wipe them away and hope no one saw me.

As Grandma's treatments continued and no progress was evident, I found it harder and harder to concentrate, especially in school. Even when I was having fun, sometimes it would suddenly occur to me that Grandma was sick at home. I felt guilty for having fun at those times. My relatives were whispering that she was dying, but I didn't believe that. I knew Jesus could do anything. I wondered, *Why don't they believe it, too?*

Chapter 4

As Grandma entered her second month of treatment in November, she began to have episodes of vomiting and diarrhea. That made her weaker and weight loss continued. Dr. Kinsey had prescribed codeine for her pain. I don't believe morphine was legal at that time. I never heard Grandma say she was in pain, but I believe she was. She would gasp occasionally as if a wave of pain had consumed her. Also, she was beginning to groan in her sleep. Since my bedroom was right at the top of the stairs from her room, I would lay awake at night and listen to her sounds. Any indications of pain would make my prayer more urgent:

Dear God,
Please don't let her die. Please take the pain away.
Amen.

Throughout the radiation therapy period, Grandma often mentioned Uncle Clarence and Uncle John. Mom had called them, so they knew she was receiving treatments for the cancer, but they never called and never visited. Barbara, my cousin, who was Uncle Clarence's daughter visited occasionally, and neighbors sometimes dropped in, but the remainder of the relatives from Dad's side of the family stayed away except for Uncle Jay's family. Mom and Dad never left Grandma alone. They were afraid something would happen to her while they were away. Still, no one offered to give them any caretaker relief.

At the end of November, Dad talked to Grandma. I remember that he said, "I don't think you should continue to pay rent on your house since we don't know how long it will be before you can return there." I was in the living room at the time, but I could still hear their conversation in Grandma's room.

Grandma replied, "You mean you don't think I'll ever be returning?"

"Now, Mom, you can't think that way. You have to have hope," Dad said.

My heart had begun racing. I thought, *Why does she think she's going to die? She has to trust Jesus.*

Grandma continued, "Werdna, you know they can't do anything and I'm dying. You may as well move my things." I then heard her crying. Between her quiet sobs, I heard her say, "Your brothers don't want me, and they won't even come to see me. I've done the best I could for them all my life, and now I just don't matter. I'm a terrible burden to you; you may as well just put me in the poorhouse."

I didn't know what the "poorhouse" was, but it sounded like a horrible place. I didn't want them to send my grandma there. Later, I would learn that the "poorhouse" was a county home where the poor and sick elderly were placed when they had nowhere else to go. It was a forerunner to nursing homes.

Dad said, "Mom, you are welcome here as long as you want to be here. I would never send you away. I don't know what's wrong with the rest of them. Just don't worry. We'll take care of you. We'll pack up your things and put them in the garage." Dad continued, "Just don't worry."

It seemed ironic to me that Dad was the only son helping Grandma. Prior to Grandma's illness, she made it no secret that her eldest sons were her favorites since she considered them to be Southerners. All three were born in Alabama. Dad was born in Pennsylvania after Pap and she returned to Pennsylvania with their family. Grandma always referred to Dad as her "Yankee" son.

The following Saturday, Dad borrowed his friend Harry's truck, and we moved Grandma's belongings to our house. She didn't have much furniture. It all fit easily into the garage. The remainder of her personal belongings were moved into our house. Grandma looked sad as we carried the few meager boxes of things that she had accumulated over her lifetime into her room. I think she knew that she was in the final stage of her life. I didn't, though; I still believed Jesus would heal her. Mom and Dad never talked directly to Brenda and me about Grandma dying. We heard them talking to each other, and we overheard other people, relatives and neighbors. Of course, sometimes we overheard one of them talking to Grandma about death. I particularly remember Dad discussing life after death with her; he described what he believed heaven to be like: a beautiful, wonderful place. Whenever someone stopped by, there were whispers about death. Brenda seemed to ignore it. She and I rarely discussed what we heard the others say. I still refused to believe it. It was my belief that their faith just wasn't strong enough since they were saying she was dying.

Grandma had an occasional good day. During these times, she would go outside and sit on the porch swing or watch some TV shows. It was 1964 and the news covered many Civil Rights issues. The summer of 1964 was known as the "Freedom Summer." On June 6th, Negro churches were burned in Mississippi. Then three Civil Rights activists were killed in Mississippi the same month. In the North, Negro uprisings were occurring in Harlem, Brooklyn, and Rochester.

The Viet Nam war was also dominating much of the news reports. On April 27th, approximately 25,000 marched on Washington in an attempt to end the war in Viet Nam. The same month, at least that many troops were in Viet Nam. Other demonstrations regarding the war were occurring throughout the United States.

Grandma would watch these reports and complain about the state of the country. The racial issues upset her the most but, like many other people, she didn't understand the Viet Nam war.

As Grandma's health declined, I was finding concentration at school becoming more and more difficult. When her radiation treatments were completed, it was almost Thanksgiving. That year at Thanksgiving, I was more aware of the blessings we had than any time in the past. I guess when you're faced with the threat of losing something precious, you take a mental inventory of all you do have.

Mom had made a traditional Thanksgiving meal, but Grandma missed doing the cooking. She just didn't feel well enough to cook that year. She also wasn't able to eat much Thanksgiving dinner. She was gradually losing her appetite. I could see that she was losing more weight. She had weighed 180 pounds prior to her surgery. Her clothes were now hanging on her. I was still convinced, though, that she would get better. My prayers continued.

I recall the first day Grandma wasn't able to get out of bed at all. It was shortly after Thanksgiving; I was still off school for Thanksgiving break. Whitetail deer hunting was a popular sport in our area, and we had no school the Monday and Tuesday following Thanksgiving Day because many students went hunting. Deer season had opened on Monday.

Tuesday morning when I went downstairs, Grandma was still in bed. She was awake, but I could tell she didn't feel well. She was curled in the fetal position and coughing. "Grandma, are you okay?" I asked as I walked up to the side of her bed. There was sunlight filtering in the windows through the lace curtains. It created a pattern that was moving across her pink chiffon bedspread. The two windows of Grandma's room were located side-by-side on the back wall, and they looked out onto our back porch. The porch ran the width of our house and blocked some of the light from entering the room. There was a white iron rod loveseat and chair on the porch with flowered brown and white cushions.

The porch overlooked our backyard. The backyard extended to meet the bottom of the hill where Lingle Valley Road descended. The garage was on the right. It blocked the view of our dogs and their dog boxes. You could see the fifty-five gallon barrel Mom and Dad used for our burn barrel on the other side of the ditch. That was before the existence of burning ordinances in our community.

Grandma whispered in reply to my question, "No honey, I'm not. Could you get me a bucket? I think I'm going to throw up."

I ran outside and found Mom hanging clothes on the green plastic clothesline beside our driveway. Dad had placed a pole at each end of the far side of our driveway and strung the clothes line between the two.

"Where's the bucket?" I asked with an urgency.

"Down at the bottom of the steps," Mom answered as she fastened a pair of Dad's work pants to the clothesline with wooden pinchy-type clothespins. I ran over to the stairwell entrance and hurried down the steps as Mom asked, "What do you need it for?"

"Grandma thinks she's going to throw up," I said, grabbing the bucket and running up the inside cellar stairs that led into the corner of our living room. I barged through the door, slammed it shut behind me, and rushed around the corner to Grandma's bedside.

"Here's the bucket," I said.

"Thanks; just set it down. I think I'll be needing it," she said and winced. I set the bucket near the top of Grandma's bed, went into the living room, and turned on the TV. As I sat there watching *The Beverly Hillbillies* rerun, I heard Grandma vomit into the bucket. Before too long, the smell of vomit evaded the living room, so I went outside to escape it.

Grandma threw up on and off all day. Once she missed the bucket, and Mom had to clean it up. She used Lysol to help eliminate the odors, but you could still smell vomit mixed with Lysol. When Dad got home that night, we had supper. Mom had made vegetable soup, but Grandma wasn't able to eat. Mom couldn't eat, either, because she was nauseated from cleaning up Grandma's vomit. I remember the anxiety I felt at the supper table. I barely ate anything myself. Generally, I had quite a healthy appetite.

I was worried about Grandma. While eating my soup, I noticed that my hands were quivering. After supper I tried to complete my homework, but I kept thinking about how sick grandma was. Trying to concentrate on my social studies homework, I heard Grandma throw up again. I was in the kitchen sitting at the table, but I could still hear almost everything that happened because our house was so small. I would have gone somewhere else to do my homework, but there was nowhere else to go.

Dad was lying on the sectional in the living room watching *Dragnet*. He didn't say anything. Sometimes he would just stare at the ceiling instead of watching TV. When he did that, I wondered what he was thinking. I would never dare to ask him; I was actually afraid of him most times.

I heard Mom helping Grandma go into the bathroom several times during the evening. Previously, she had been able to go herself, but she was too weak that night. I overheard Mom tell Dad, "I sponge bathed your mother today because I was afraid she wouldn't be able to get in and out of the tub."

He replied, "That's a good idea. She might have fallen as weak as she is."

Grandma was in her bed again. I guessed she was sleeping. Dad told Mom, "Tomorrow when I get home, I'm going to make her a portable potty since it's getting harder for her to get to the bathroom."

"How are you going to do that?" Mom asked.

"I'll take one of her old kitchen chairs and cut a hole in the center. Then I'll put a shelf underneath, and we'll be able to set a metal chamber pot on that. I'll pick up a regular commode seat from Claster's to put on the top," Dad explained. Claster's was a local building supply store.

"That should work," Mom replied.

In the kitchen, I had finally finished my homework. After gathering my books in a pile, I left them on the corner of the kitchen table and walked back into the living room. I sat beside Mom on the couch and watched the remainder of *Dragnet* with Mom and Dad. Brenda was in the bathroom, and Grandma was asleep.

When Brenda finished in the bathroom, it was my turn. After I finished bathing, I dressed in my blue and green plaid flannel pajamas, threw my dirty clothes into the yellow vinyl clothes hamper, and went upstairs to bed. I made certain that I again said my prayer for Grandma.

Dear God,
Please make Grandma get better and please don't let her die.
Amen

The next morning, Mom was standing at the bottom of the stairs calling me and Brenda. I hopped out of bed. The floor was cold; our upstairs was not heated. Dad had hung a pair of green fiberglass drapes at the top of the stairs to keep the heat from going upstairs to conserve oil. I quickly went downstairs and into the bathroom. I heard Grandma vomit. She had been sleeping when I went by her on my way to the bathroom. I heard Mom assisting Grandma to get cleaned up. Then I heard her call, "Linda, are you about done in there?"

"Yes," I replied as I placed my toothbrush back in the silver holder mounted to the wall underneath the medicine cabinet. Our bathroom was green and yellow. We had an avocado green tub, commode, and sink. There were yellow four-inch square tiles four feet high on the walls and green textured paint the rest of the way to the ceiling. The bathroom was L-shaped. The toilet was located behind the wall from the sink, and the tub was on the back wall.

I wrapped a towel around me, gathered my things, and went back upstairs to dress. The odor of vomit struck me as I went through the room. I could hear Mom helping Grandma into the bathroom. Brenda was still sleeping in her bed across from me. I said, "Grandma is sick and in the bathroom, and you're going to miss the bus if you don't hurry up."

"Oh no," she said as she jumped up, gathered her clothing and rush downstairs as I finished dressing.

Our household routine continued almost unchanged over the next several weeks. On December 12th, we celebrated my birthday. I turned twelve that year. I always felt I got cheated because my birthday was so close to Christmas. Each year, Mom baked me a cake, but we never got big birthday gifts. In fact, we rarely got birthday gifts at all. My sister and I had never had a birthday party, either, where we could invite all our friends and classmates. Mom and Dad just couldn't afford the expense. Cathy had a big party every year. Her birthday was in July, and for the past few years, she had been having pool parties at her grandparents' pool. I would have liked to have a party, but it wasn't meant to be. This birthday, I chose a chocolate cake with peanut butter icing; that was my favorite. I was glad Grandma could share my birthday cake with the family.

After my birthday passed, it always seemed as though Christmas was upon us in no time. But this year, the Christmas season was not as festive as usual. In the past, we had placed our Christmas tree in the corner of the sitting room against the stair wall where Grandma's bed was now setting. This year, we put the tree in the corner on the other side of the room across from her bed. We didn't have space in our living room because there were four doorways and the sectional took up most of the other space in that room.

Several years before, I had taken over the decorating of the tree. Brenda really had no interest. Mom and Dad saw it as more of a chore than a privilege. I, on the other hand, loved to decorate the tree. My family said I was a perfectionist and had to have everything just right.

We generally didn't get a large tree. Usually, our tree was about four feet tall, and Dad would set it on a sheet of plywood placed on top of two saw horses to make a platform. It would take me hours to decorate the tree. Each bulb and light had to be placed the same distance away from each other. Each icicle was hung separately. I couldn't stand it when Brenda would just take a handful of icicles and throw them on the tree. I liked to place each one individually in a particular spot.

After the tree was decorated, I would place sheets of crepe paper under the tree on the platform, and Dad would set up his electric train set. Over the years, Brenda and I had made papier-maché houses and trees for school projects, and these were placed under the tree. We also had a manger, wise men, and animals that I would set up at one end of the platform. There was a white light at the top of the manger that lit up for the star. After the whole village was placed under the tree, I would sprinkle plastic snow over everything. I just loved to turn off the room lights and look at the tree with just the tree lights turned on.

That year, Brenda and I looked through the *Sears Catalog* and picked out clothes we wanted. I remember choosing a navy blue jumper and a plaid skirt with a big pin on the side that I did receive. We also got a game or two, a new nightgown, and, of course, underwear. Mom always got us underwear for Christmas. Mom and Dad never bought each other any gifts when we were young because they used all their money for our gifts. Grandma got a couple of new nightgowns. It was a nice Christmas, but, of course, I worried about Grandma.

Christmas Day and the week following was a visitation week for my mom's family. Relatives would visit each other in the evenings and look at the gifts everyone had received. They came to visit us, but we were unable to go anywhere because Grandma couldn't be left alone. Uncle Jay came to visit Grandma, but her other two sons did not. I was sad because I knew that made her sad.

Grandma got sick some during the holidays, but it wasn't too bad. She was too weak to go anywhere during that period, though. I missed visiting my other grandparents and all my cousins.

On New Year's Eve, I sat up and watched 1965 ushered in on TV as the ball dropped at Times Square in New York City. Some of our neighbors would go outside at midnight and shoot their guns into the air. We could hear the gunshots echo throughout the valley. Dad never did that even though he had numerous guns since he hunted.

That night, as I climbed the stairs to my bedroom, I saw Grandma lying in her bed staring at the ceiling. I simply said, "Good night, Grandma."

"Good night," she replied.

After I jumped into bed and pulled my quilt up to my chin, I said another prayer for Grandma:

Dear God,
Please let Grandma get better.
Amen.

It was Monday, January 4th, and we had to return to school. In a way I was anxious to get back to school to get it over with, so when I heard Dad getting ready for work at five a.m., I got up myself. I had chosen to wear my new navy blue jumper that I had just gotten for Christmas. In less than an hour, I was ready to go. I sat in the living room watching *Captain Kangaroo* until it was time to go to the bus stop. There was news on the one channel. I preferred *Captain Kangaroo*.

As the new year was beginning, thoughts of Grandma were occupying more and more of my time. At school I would find myself thinking about her and realize I had heard nothing the teacher had said. Sometimes I would become overwhelmed with emotions and struggle to keep back the tears.

All the constant stress of caregiving was beginning to show on my mother. She appeared to be exhausted all the time, and I worried about her, too. My dad was staring at the ceiling more as the weeks passed. I wasn't sure what he was thinking about, but I could tell he was deep in thought. Sometimes I thought I saw tears glistening in his eyes, but I would never dare mention it. We didn't talk about emotions in my family. My sister seemed to be unaffected by any of the changes that were occurring in our lives. Maybe that was just her way of dealing with the family crisis. After all, it's not every day that one of your loved ones is dying.

That was both my and Brenda's first close encounter with death. Distant relatives had passed away before, but that was different. When Pap Bishop had died, we were both toddlers; neither of us could remember. We were older now, and Grandma had been an eternal presence in our lives. It was hard to even imagine life without her. She had always been special to me. I was able to talk to her about things that were important in my life. She never criticized me, and she made me feel loved. I could tell that she listened closely to what I said and valued me as a person, regardless of my age.

Not only was I struggling with coming to terms with my own mortality, but I was in the middle of puberty and caught between being a twelve-year-old child and a young woman. Just weeks before, everything had been so simple; now life was extremely complicated. I was going to a different school; many of my old friends were lost in different sections, in different parts of the building. My hormones were raging and causing all kinds of emotional and physical changes. But most devastating of all was my fear for my grandma's life. Perhaps in the recesses of my mind, I knew she was dying, but I couldn't admit it to myself. I didn't want it to be true; I simply didn't want to lose someone I loved so much.

I continued with my prayers for Grandma; however, they were subtly changing. In the beginning, I had asked God not to let her have cancer and not to let her die. Now, I was no longer asking that she not have cancer. I suppose I had acknowledged that she did have the disease, but I still wanted to believe she wouldn't die.

Once I had heard on television that if someone's cancer stayed in remission for five years, their chances of survival were very good. I begun asking God to allow Grandma to live five years so she wouldn't die from the disease. That was the new hope I hung onto. Cancer was far less frightening if you had a chance of beating it.

When I look back, I wonder what Grandma's thoughts were. She spoke very little about her condition. Surely, it must have been hard for her to believe she was dying. Don't we all want to deny things we can't accept? It must have been very hard for her to be at that stage of her life. She knew she was sick, but no one ever told her she had cancer. That seemed so deceitful to me. I contemplated why everyone should know but her; after all, it affected her more than anyone else. I'll never know for certain if she knew anyway, but I believe she did. She mentioned dying occasionally, but no one ever confirmed it. I imagine she could sense her own impending death.

Not only did she have to deal with facing death head on, but she had to deal with the rejection of her own children. How heartbreaking that must have been. It would be impossible for her not to think of her children. She had given birth to them, sacrificed through the years for them, and then at the end of her life cycle, she saw two of them reject her totally. She must have felt intense emotional pain. To be forced to make her children support her because they would not do so of their own free will must have hurt beyond words. My uncles' refusal to visit her when she was dying most likely speeded her death. What a very, very sad ending to her existence.

    I wanted to strike out at my uncles. It seemed a natural progression to me for a parent to care for a child, and then when the parent ages, they reverse roles and the child cares for the parent. Grandma had taken care of them; now it was their turn to take care of her. I asked myself over and over again, how could my uncles be so cruel?

    Perhaps Grandma was making her own deal with God. Perhaps she was asking Him to return her sons to her before her death. I knew she had asked for them several times. If she was praying, why wasn't God answering her prayers?

    When I would return home from school, Grandma would be there lying in her bed. It was so sad to just see her lie there. She rarely got up anymore. Her eyes were all sunken in, and there were big black circles around them. Grandma's skin had a yellow cast. Often her nightgown would slip over her shoulder, and you could see her collar bone protruding. She was extremely thin. It was very sad to see her so sick.

Chapter 5

We managed to get through January and February with little change in Grandma's functioning. The vomiting was sporadic, but occasionally, Grandma would have a good day.

Sunday, March 7th, Grandma was having just such a day. It started out like any other typical Sunday at our house. Brenda and I attended the Milroy Methodist Church. Dad and Mom would watch Rex Hubbard, a religious church service, on television and then Mom would cook Sunday lunch. Sometimes Brenda and I would ride to church with Cathy and her mother; other times Dad would take us and return to pick us up.

When we returned from church, Mom was in the kitchen frying steak, and she had begun mashing potatoes. I loved Mom's steak and mashed potatoes. She always made gravy, too. One of my favorite vegetables to have with that meal was peas. I liked to make a pond in my mashed potatoes and fill it in with peas. I then would take hot cauliflower juice and pour it over the peas. If we had tomatoes, I would garnish the top with a slice of tomato. I would pour gravy on a slice of bread, and then cut it into nine squares before I ate it. Brenda thought that all was totally disgusting, but I truly enjoyed it. That was the way I ate my food that day.

Grandma was having a good day, too. She joined us at the kitchen table and ate a good size portion of everything. That was very unusual for her since her sickness. Dad, Mom, and Grandma were discussing numerous topics while we ate. I recall them discussing America's involvement in the Viet Nam war. The day before, the first Americans set foot on Viet Nam battlefields. They also discussed the Civil Rights protests going on in the South. In February, Martin Luther King and 770 others were arrested in Selma, Alabama, for picketing at the county courthouse to end voting discrimination. Also, on February 21st of that same year, 1965, Malcolm X was shot and killed in a Harlem auditorium.

When lunch was over, Brenda and I helped clear the table, then she washed and I dried the dishes. After we were finished, we both got our bikes out of the garage and rode around the neighborhood. During our journey, we ran into Cathy and Betsy out by the water pump.

The water pump was on the right side of Lingle Valley Road 400 yards from our house. When we moved to Mount Pleasant in 1961, the residents of the community told us the water pump had at one time been used as a communal water source. It was no longer used, and, in fact, didn't even work. The kids in the neighborhood, however, now used it as a meeting place. It was one of the best hangouts, along with Betsy's porch and the porch on Leeper's Store.

That day Cathy, Betsy, Brenda and I decided to have a bicycle marathon to see who could ride in circles round the water pump the longest. We all dropped out before Betsy. She rode for more than two hundred laps. You would think that would have made her dizzy. Betsy and Cathy both had English bicycles with handbrakes. Brenda's and my bikes were the big clunky type with fat tires, and they had footbrakes. We both wanted English bikes, but we didn't get them.

We had spent several hours with our friends before returning home late that afternoon. I had some homework for math class that I had to finish early that evening. Brenda told Mom that she didn't have any homework. I usually procrastinated until Sunday evening before I did any weekend homework; Brenda was worse than me.

Prior to Grandma's illness, every Sunday evening our family would go to Grandma and Pap Eward's house and spend the evening. Many of my relatives would do the same. Dad would usually go down over the hill and visit his brother Jay. The other men, my uncles and Pap, would congregate in the living room and watch television. The women, my aunts and Grandma, would sit in the parlor, as Grandma called it, and talk.

I have many fond memories of visiting Grandma and Pap Eward. When it was their anniversary or birthdays, all my relatives on Mom's side would meet there. They would make ice cream in hand-cranked freezers. If it wasn't nice outside, they would make the ice cream on Grandma's and Pap's sun porch. All the kids, me included, would stand in line behind the ice cream freezers to get our turns at cranking the ice cream.

My aunts would prepare the ice cream mix and place it in the metal containers that came with the freezers. Then they would place the lid on top and put it inside the freezer. My uncles would begin layering chunks of ice with rock salt around the pans. The crank of the freezer would fit on top. I don't recall how long we had to crank the ice cream before it was frozen, but it seemed like a long time. That Sunday, I was longing to again attend one of those parties at Grandma's and Pap's house. There were always plenty of homemade cakes, too. Of course, I usually chose my favorite: chocolate with peanut butter icing.

My mind always wandered like that when I did my homework, and like most children, I welcomed any interruption. Later that night, there was another interruption. Grandma had gone into the living room with Dad and Mom to watch some television since she was having an okay day. I'm not certain what they were watching, but I heard an announcer on television say: "We interrupt this program to bring you a special report." I then heard my Mom say, "Oh no! Now what's happening?"

That caught my interest so I went into the living room and sat beside my mother on the couch. What I saw confused me greatly. I saw policemen firing tear gas into a group of black people and beating them severely. Some of the police officers were on horseback. They had clubs and were batting the people. Dad and Mom were exchanging comments of outrage. More frightening than that, though, was my grandma's reaction. Nothing in my twelve years had prepared me for that transition.

My grandma, a sweet, little old lady, whom I loved dearly and who was very sick and most likely dying, became a wild, angry, raging stranger before my eyes. She started cursing and screaming at the television set, saying things like, "Those damn Yankees just have to cause trouble. They won't let my people be. God didn't intend niggers to be equal with whites. Now listen to those damn reporters acting like my people are bad!"

Dad said, "Now calm down, Mom. You know what they're doing is wrong."

"Don't you dare say that to me!" Grandma shrieked. "You got their crazy ideas, too, because you were born and raised in this Yankee territory!"

"It has nothing to do with that," Dad continued. He, too, was in an extremely emotional state. "It's not right for anyone to beat another human being like they're doing. They didn't do anything wrong; they just want to vote and be treated like us. They're just as good as we are. Why shouldn't they have the same rights?"

As the violent clips on television raged on, Grandma stomped her foot and yelled, "Your grandparents would turn in their graves if they heard you say a nigger was as good as they were. You don't understand. Those are our people. They're defending their way of life. No outsiders should interfere. Especially

Yankees! You should be defending them. They're your kin. You just take after your Yankee father."

I was terrified. I really didn't understand what was going on, but I knew that what I was seeing was wrong. I later learned that the clips we saw were taking place in Alabama as demonstrators crossed the Edmund Pitters Bridge in an attempt to march from Selma to Montgomery. The march had been organized to protest the killing of Jimmie Lee Jackson, who was shot during a march from the church to the jail in Marion, Alabama, on February 17th. Jackson was black and a Viet Nam veteran. There were also fifteen to twenty other people injured in that demonstration against the killing of a state trooper in Marion. No wonder Grandma was so upset. Marion was her hometown. That episode became known as "Bloody Sunday."

Grandma and Dad continued arguing on and off all through the news clips and the commentaries that followed. Finally, outraged, Grandma stood up and insisted, "Just think about what you're teaching your children."

Dad responded, "I am thinking about that, Mother. It's wrong and the Civil War has been over for a long time."

Grandma just snorted and stomped into her room in disgust. For a moment, I had forgotten how sick she was. I hadn't said a word throughout the entire ordeal. I was afraid to. I didn't know what to think. I loved my grandma dearly, but I agreed with my dad about that issue. I just felt within my being that the behavior I had just witnessed was wrong. I couldn't understand why Grandma couldn't see that it was wrong.

In later years, I would come to realize that my grandma was a racist. While watching those Civil Rights news clips again, and others, for a "reaction paper" I was required to write for school, I felt shame for my country and shame for my race. I had learned, though, that Grandma was a link in the chain of racial hatred that began long before her birth. I was glad my dad had broken that chain of racial hatred in our family. He was far from perfect, however. He had battles of his own to fight.

Regardless what Grandma's faults were, I loved her, and I didn't want her to die. My prayers for her continued each and every day. I felt she had to get better. I also felt she would eventually change her mind about racial issues. I had the true optimism that only a child possesses.

Chapter 6

Uncle Jay contacted Dad about the first week of April and informed him he would like to take Grandma to his house to stay for a while. Dad told him it would be fine with him. Uncle Jay planned to pick her up on the following Friday. Mom packed some of Grandma's clothing and personal items, and Uncle Jay and Aunt Betty picked her up at four-thirty that evening.

I was sad to see her go, but I thought it might cheer her up to know another one of her sons wanted to help care for her. That was the first break my mother had since Grandma returned to our house from the hospital. I was surprised that my Aunt Betty was going to take over for Mom.

On Saturday evening our whole family was able to go shopping together. That was a treat. It had been six months since our whole family could go out together. We stopped at Town and Country and Grants; both were department stores in Lewistown's only strip mall. People's drug store was also in the mall. I liked the restaurant that was a part of Grants. It was called the Bradford Room. I rarely went out to eat, but I thoroughly enjoyed it when I got to go out with my friends.

I thought things must be going well for Grandma at Uncle Jay's house, for we didn't hear anything. In the third week of April, while we were visiting Grandma and Pap Eward, Grandma Eward said, "Lucy, why don't you and Werdna take Sallie back up to your place?"

Mom replied, "Why would we do that? Jay wants her to stay with them."

Grandma Eward said, "I just think you should take her back up with you."

Mom didn't say anything else about it then, but later that evening I heard her talking to Dad. They were speculating on why Grandma Eward said what she did. They really didn't know, though.

Later in the month, it became pretty obvious there were problems. On Saturday, April 24th, Mom and Dad were working on cleaning out the garage while Brenda and I were playing in the backyard. While we were throwing our red and yellow striped rubber ball into the air playing the game *Russia*, I saw Uncle Jay's car coming down the hill. I ran over to the garage and yelled in to tell Mom and Dad. They both walked around to the side of the house while Brenda and I followed. We were just in time to see Uncle Jay's car go back up the hill. He must have turned around in Mrs. Muttersbaugh's driveway.

There stood Grandma on the porch crying. Dad continued around the side of the house and walked up beside her. He said, "Mom, what's the matter?" Mom, Brenda, and I had followed Dad to the porch.

"They don't want me," she sobbed. "No one wants me."

"What do you mean they don't want you?" Dad asked in a confused tone.

"They fought the whole time I was there. I was just in the way," she said as she wiped her eyes on one of her embroidered handkerchiefs that Brenda and I had given her for Christmas.

Dad was shocked. He said, "Mom, don't cry. You're always welcome here." As he opened the screen door and took her arm to lead her through the door, he said, "Come on in here and sit down."

Uncle Jay had packed her clothes into cardboard boxes and left them on the porch. While she was at his house, he had her mailing address changed so everything would be forwarded to him. I never knew for certain, but I wondered if he thought Dad was benefiting financially by keeping Grandma, and he decided he wanted that advantage for himself. Grandma Eward had also implied that they might not have been buying her all the medicine she should have had. I would like to think that wasn't true because that would be more cruel than all the other things that had happened to Grandma.

I felt so horrible and sad inside that I had to fight back tears. Grandma looked like a walking skeleton. Her dress was just hanging on her. It looked like it was at least three sizes too big. Her eyes were even more sunken into her head, and there were larger black circles around them. I could tell my dad was upset because once while comforting Grandma, I heard his voice crack with emotion.

After Grandma had settled down some, Dad and Mom went out on the porch and carried her belongings into the house. It was heart wrenching that her life's accumulations were in those old, worn boxes. I went back outside to play because I was afraid I would cry. Uncle Jay didn't need to come unannounced and drop Grandma off like he did. Dad would have taken her back with open arms, regardless. He often got angry while working around the house, but he had a big heart. After that, Uncle Jay and Aunt Betty stopped visiting Grandma. I guess they must have been embarrassed about what they had done. If they weren't, they certainly should have been.

A few weeks later, Dad spoke with Jay on the telephone about why they brought Grandma back to our house. Jay told Dad that Betty was too ill to care for Grandma any longer. Mom and Dad didn't believe this, but they said nothing to avoid any further trouble.

May 2nd was my dad's birthday. Mom baked him a pineapple upside-down cake. That was his favorite. He seemed surprised when he got home, and Brenda and I presented him with the cake. Later that evening, I also had a surprise-- my period began.

I was both happy and frightened. I knew what was happening because when I was in sixth grade, all the girls in my class were taken to the auditorium, and we were shown a movie explaining menstruation. I remember how it was such a big deal, and my teacher, Mrs. Headings, acted like it was a big secret. She told us not to discuss the movie with the boys in our class. Of course, when we got back, several of the boys asked us where we had been and what had happened, even though they were instructed not to. We just told them that we were not allowed to talk about it. That night, I told Mom about the movie, but she really didn't discuss it with me.

A few of my girlfriends already had their periods. I was glad I wouldn't be the last one. It symbolized growing up to us, and no one wanted to be the last one to "grow up." That change in my life brought all kinds of new problems with it. Suddenly, I was concerned about all kinds of scenarios such as: What would happen if blood ran through my clothing at school? What if I got it and didn't have any pads? What if I had it in gym class? And on and on.

My mom rarely talked to me about any of the changes I was experiencing. That's how my family was. Her mother had never talked to her about it. They felt those things should not be discussed. She did give me a book to read, though. She had sent for it through some mail order place. It was supposed to explain "the facts of life" to me. I had eagerly read the book, but most of what was in it, I had already learned from my peers.

Sometimes when I saw parents who were openly affectionate, I wondered what it would be like if my parents were like that. Maybe from time to time, I just needed a hug and to have someone tell me they loved me. My dad had a bad temper, and sometimes when he was angry, he was even abusive.

Often, I wished things were different, but we all know, you can't always get what you want. So I just accepted it because that was the way it was.

All of those hormonal changes I was experiencing were wreaking havoc on my emotional state. I would be extremely happy one moment and in tears the next for no apparent reason. I didn't understand the extreme mood swings. There was no one to talk to about them; I had to adjust the best I could.

Chapter 7

As the weeks passed in May, Grandma was vomiting more often. She was almost totally bedridden now. Her cries in the night became more frequent, too. Each time I was awakened at night, I desperately prayed for God to help her get better. I kept thinking she was getting closer to the five year survival date, and then she would recover. I needed to believe that; I didn't want to lose her.

She no longer got dressed; she always wore a nightgown. She talked very little. Occasionally, I would slip into the chair beside her bed and just sit with her. We rarely spoke. I didn't know what to say, and I don't believe she felt well enough to speak. She looked so old and frail. On her better days, she would reach over and pat my hand.

Sometimes after visiting with Grandma, I was so upset, I needed to visit my special spot. I would ride my bike to the bridge and sit there quietly and pray Grandma's prayer. Being there along the water's edge made me feel closer to God. After my prayer was over, I would feel a calm come over me. I knew Jesus was with me at those times.

By the end of May, Grandma could no longer retain any medications, so her doctor prescribed suppositories for her. My mom was the one to administer those. Now, when Grandma would cry out in pain, my mom would insert another suppository.

Grandma ate very little by that time. Mom kept trying to get her to sip some kind of juice. Apple juice seemed to stay down the best. She vomited almost every time she ate. I don't believe they had dietary supplement drinks like Ensure back them; if they did, we didn't have any for Grandma. She continued to lose weight dramatically.

It was extremely difficult to watch Grandma waste away to nothing. I desperately wanted to believe she would get better, but it was harder and harder to deceive myself as I couldn't help but see her decline in health. I always had butterflies in my stomach, and more and more often, I would begin crying no matter how hard I tried not to. I had withdrawn from my peers gradually throughout the school year as Grandma's condition progressively worsened. Often I was unaware of what was going on around me, for I was too absorbed with thoughts of Grandma and the fear that she would die. My peers were beginning to perceive me as different, and I was too depressed to care. I was glad when school was out, for concentration for me was practically nonexistent. I was thankful summer had arrived, but not excited about it as I always was in the past. The future was too dark and frightening.

Once I was wandering in the yard by the side of our garage, and I paused to watch my dad. He had the two small windows in the back of the garage pushed open, and he was standing there staring up at the hill with his arms resting on the window sill. Grandma was having a particularly hard day; she was vomiting black stuff that smelled horrible. I wondered if he was praying for her. I dared not intrude in such a private moment, so I quietly slipped up the stairs onto the back porch.

Over the few previous months, Dad had become very quiet. More and more I would find him staring at the ceiling with his arms over this head as he lay on the end of the couch where he usually watched television. That tended to upset me even more. Mom looked worn, and sometimes she would cry when she thought no one could hear her. Before Grandma's sickness, Mom looked very healthy. She never wore makeup; she had a natural beauty. I thought she looked like a movie star in her high school graduation picture. Then she had shoulder-length dark brown hair and green eyes. She had gotten her hair cut since then, but her clear complexion and smile were the same. Brenda was the only one who seemed unchanged. It was hard to tell what anyone felt, however, because we never discussed feelings in my family.

There seemed to be no escape from Grandma's illness. Inside the house, I thought I could smell death even though I refused to acknowledge it was there. Throughout the night, I would awaken numerous times to Grandma's cries until I thought I could bear it no more. Sometimes I would put my index fingers inside each of my ears and attempt to block the sounds. At the same time, I would pray for it to end, not in Grandma's death, but in her recovery. I could not be realistic; my heart was unwilling to accept what my eyes told my mind was happening. Regardless of my desires, hopes, and prayers, the end was approaching as death came closer to grasping my grandma.

It was a humid summer night, June 14th, 1965. Inez, our neighbor, came down to visit Grandma that night. She lived across Lingle Valley Road, in the second house on the right in the alley. My friend Cathy's trailer was the next house past Inez's on the left. Inez was in her seventies and lived alone in her tiny four-room cottage. She didn't drive, so Mom would do her grocery shopping for her, and they became good friends. She knew Grandma was ill, and that was the first time she had visited.

Brenda and I were sitting on the swing on our front porch since it was so hot inside when Inez walked down our lane. "Hello, girls," she called as she came up the sidewalk in our yard.

"Hi," both Brenda and I answered in unison as we continued gently pushing the swing with our feet.

"I came by to see your grandma," Inez informed us as she stepped onto the sidewalk and came toward us.

Mom heard her through the screen door and came to meet her. "Come on in," she invited, as Inez passed Brenda and I as she went in the front door. We could hear her talking to Mom and Dad as she went through the living room to reach Grandma's room.

Approximately ten or fifteen minutes later, I heard Inez talking in the living room again. "Jim, your mother is dying. She's already turning blue. You need to take her to the hospital so the girls don't see her like this," I heard her tell him.

Dad had wanted to keep Grandma at home because she didn't like hospitals. Apparently, though, Inez had frightened him. I couldn't make out what he said, but then I heard Mom on the phone calling the Milroy ambulance.

I was frightened. Why was the ambulance coming? Grandma was going to get better; I knew she was, but Inez said she was dying. What did she mean Grandma was blue? She hadn't looked blue to me.

Brenda and I remained on the front porch swinging. We were silent. I was afraid to go into the house; Brenda must have been, too. The screeching of the swing's chain against the porch roof seemed to be deafening. In fact, the volume of all the summer sounds around us seemed to be amplified. I could hear the crickets and the katydids chanting in the woods across from us. I could even hear the water rushing in Lingle Valley Run on the other side of the patch of woods in front of our house. On the outside, everything seemed as it should be, but that was a big deception.

As I sat there absorbing all the sounds around me, uncertain what to do, the red and yellow station wagon style Milroy ambulance rounded the curve and turned left off Lingle Valley Road onto our lane. It appeared huge and threatening to me as I watched it inch its way toward our house. I didn't want it there, but I couldn't make it leave. The driver continued moving forward ever closer to our house. When he was parallel to our front porch, he stopped and called out his window, "Do the Bishops live here?"

"Yes," I said, and he continued forward and pulled into our driveway. The driver, a big, stocky man about fifty years old, got out and closed his door. On the other side of the ambulance, another younger man got out. He was approximately five-feet ten-inches tall and much thinner. They walked to the back of the ambulance, opened the door, and pulled out a gurney. Both of them raised the collapsed legs on the gurney, carried it to the sidewalk, and pushed it to our front porch. They then lifted it and carried it up the steps.

Mom came to the door and said, "Come in through here. She's in the next room." The two attendants finished carrying the gurney up the two steps and pushed it through the living room door. Several minutes later, they pushed it back out the door, only that time Grandma was lying on it. I could see that she had her eyes open as they pushed her by us, but she said nothing. I said nothing, either; I just sat there and watched them take her away. I wished I would have said good-bye. She still didn't look blue to me, and I wondered what Inez had meant. Dad and Mom came out the door behind Grandma and the attendants. The attendants had proceeded to the ambulance, opened the back door, and slid Grandma in.

"You ride in the ambulance with Mom, and I'll follow in the car," Dad instructed Mom.

"Okay," Mom answered, and she crawled into the back of the ambulance and sat beside Grandma.

Dad looked at me and Brenda and said, "You two stay here. It will be better that way."

We didn't answer, but Inez was standing on the porch now, and she said, "You go along, Jim, they'll be fine. I'll stay here with them until you get back."

Dad then got into his Thunderbird and followed the ambulance back out the lane and turned right onto Lingle Valley Road. Both vehicles disappeared up the hill. Brenda and I hadn't left the porch swing throughout the entire ordeal. We just sat there staring at the road where they had been. Inez was chattering away in an attempt to distract us from what had just happened, but I can't remember anything she said. We both just stayed on the swing as if afraid to get up.

In my mind, I kept repeating Grandma's prayer. Only this time I added: *Please let the people at the hospital make Grandma better. She has to get better*, I thought. God didn't lie. He said, "ask and you will receive." That's what all of my Sunday school teachers had told me throughout my twelve years.

Eventually, as we sat there, Brenda and I began responding to Inez's small talk. It had been approximately an hour since they had left; it seemed more like an eternity. As we were talking, Dad's car rounded the corner and I saw him and Mom in the front seat. I stretched my neck upward in an attempt to see Grandma in the back seat, but she wasn't there. I wondered why she was not with them. Why had they left her at the hospital?

Dad parked his car in our driveway, and he and Mom got out and walked up to the porch.

"They're going to keep her," Mom told Inez. "They got her settled in a room, and she told Werdna that she wanted a drink. It took him quite a while to find a nurse to take her some water. He was getting mad."

Inez replied, "I'm sure that was frustrating, but it's good she's in the hospital. They'll be better able to take care of her now."

Dad came onto the porch as Mom and Inez talked, leaned over against one of the four white posts that supported the roof, and ran his fingers back through his hair as he responded, "I hope so, but they just don't seem to care about anything."

"It might seem that way, Jim, but I think they really do." There was a long pause, then Inez stood and started down the porch. "Well, I better get up the road," she said.

"Hold on a minute. I'll get you a flashlight," Mom said as she went into the house.

"You girls better go in and get ready for bed pretty soon," Dad instructed Brenda and me.

As we were entering the house, Mom passed us exiting. She handed our big red flashlight to Inez. "Thanks," I heard Inez say. "I'll see you get it back."

Mom replied, "Thanks for staying with the girls."

"Any time," Inez answered as she continued out our sidewalk and headed toward her house.

I hurried up the stairs to my bedroom to get my pink cotton nightgown out of my dresser drawer and went back down the stairs and into the bathroom to bathe. For some reason, I felt such an urgency. I could hear Mom in the living room calling Dad's brothers. She said to each, "We had to call the ambulance to take Sallie to the hospital. She was beginning to turn blue." There it was again. *What did they mean?* I wondered. I didn't listen to the remainder of the telephone conversations. I didn't want to hear. I couldn't hear how they responded either, but I was sure it wasn't an appropriate response.

After Mom was done making the necessary calls, I heard her talking to Dad, and from what I could gather, Uncle Jay wasn't going to visit Grandma that night because it was so late. Apparently, Uncle Clarence and Uncle John weren't going at all, but then why would they? They hadn't bothered before. My hatred for them was growing.

After I finishing dressing, I quietly returned to the living room in my nightgown. Mom was just sitting on the sectional focusing on the television, but I wondered if she saw anything. Dad was lying down on the other end of the couch with his arms above his head, hands clasped together, looking at the ceiling. Brenda was out in the kitchen. I sat down beside Mom and looked at the TV. *Alfred Hitchcock Presents* was on. I don't know how long we sat there pretending to watch the program before the phone blared in the corner of the room. We only had the one big, black dial-type telephone in our house. At that moment in time, it seemed like some kind of monster. It was then that everything began to move in slow motion. It appeared like Mom had great difficulty progressing toward the phone. When she finally made it to the corner, she sat on the arm of the couch, picked up the receiver, and said, "Hello?" We couldn't hear the other side of the conversation, but Mom started sobbing and said to Dad between sobs: "Your mother died... They want to know what funeral home should be contacted."

Dad remained lying on the couch and responded in a trance-like manner: "Have them call Heller's in Burnham."

Mom again placed the receiver to her ear and said, "You're supposed to contact Heller's in Burnham."

I didn't hear anything else. It occurred to me that Grandma had died. How could that be? There had to be some kind of mistake. God didn't lie. He should have made her better. He always answered prayers. That's what everyone had told me. I felt like I couldn't breathe. I had to get out of that room. In a fog, I moved through the living room. Brenda had left the kitchen and was standing in the doorway. As I stumbled through Grandma's room, my eyes sought out her bed and verified that she was not there. I proceeded up the stairs to my bedroom. I silently slipped into my bed, pulled the blankets

up to my chin, and allowed the tears to begin to flow down my cheeks. Again I prayed:
Dear God,
Please don't let this be true. You don't break your promises.
Please bring her back here.
Amen.
That would be my last prayer for many years.

I have no idea how long I lay in bed. Time had stopped for me. I could hear sounds downstairs, but they were just background noises. Reality, as I had known it, had ceased to exist that night. Eventually, I fell asleep. It was not a restful sleep, though. Several times during the night, I was awakened by fragmented bizarre dreams. In the most frightening dream, Grandma was an angel standing before me all in white with her arms outstretched. When I reached for her, she turned into a skeleton, and the bones turned to dust before me. I was terrified when I awoke. I was even more terrified when I realized Grandma was really dead. Again I cried into the night until I finally went back to sleep.

Around nine thirty the next morning, I awoke. The reality of the night before again struck me with tremendous force. I could hear my parents stirring downstairs, and Brenda was asleep in her bed across from me. My eyes hurt and were swollen from crying so much throughout the night. I threw back my blankets, swung my legs to the right, and sat up on the edge of my bed. I dreaded going downstairs because I knew Grandma's empty bed was at the bottom of the stairs. Still, I couldn't believe God had betrayed me like that. I stood up, stretched, and reluctantly began my descent down the stairs. The empty bed was there just as I knew it would be. Visions of Grandma throughout the past nine months flashed through my mind. A nauseated feeling came over me, and I quickly sat down on the vinyl couch to regain my composure. After the feeling passed, I stood and continued into the living room.

Mom and Dad were both sitting there discussing plans to go to Heller's Funeral Home to make burial arrangements. All three of Dad's brothers agreed to meet him there at three o'clock that afternoon. None of them had to work due to a death in the family. Fate seemed doubly cruel as I realized they were going to assist in making her burial arrangements even though they had refused to see her when she was alive. I thought I could never forgive them for hurting her so much. I truly hated them.

I didn't realize it then, but not only was I angry with my uncles, I was angry with God. He, too, had been very cruel. It seemed as though he had abandoned my grandma and me. I didn't care that people were saying it was a blessing because now Grandma wasn't suffering. God could have stopped her suffering and her death…if he wanted to. How could I continue to pray to a God who didn't care? That was the question I kept asking myself.

Grief has a way of destroying your appetite. I wanted no breakfast. After I went back upstairs and dressed in a two-piece shorts outfit, I slipped out the back door, walked around the side of the house, and continued out Lingle Valley Road. I stopped at the bridge and watched the water as it splashed and trickled over the stones and rocks on the bed of the creek.

I pondered why the circumstances of our lives were sometimes so painful. Was that necessary? A twelve-year-old didn't think so. Would anything ever be "normal" again? I didn't think so.

After about an hour or so had passed, I returned to our house. Brenda was awake then and sitting in the living room. It struck me odd that my family wasn't discussing Grandma's death. It was as if everyone was pretending it hadn't even happened. Dad was folding Grandma's roll-a-way bed to remove it from her room. It was a portable cot that folded at each end. After he had it folded and fastened it in the center, he and Mom rolled it through Grandma's room, into the foyer, and out the back door. They carried it down the back steps and stored it in the garage. I couldn't watch them remove it. I felt that I was losing another part of my grandma. My heart was so heavy; grief consumed me. I wanted to cry for help, but I believed no one would hear.

Around two o'clock that afternoon, all four of us climbed into Dad's Thunderbird and headed for Heller's Funeral Home. That had been the first time since Grandma returned from my Uncle Jay's house that we all left the house at one time. In a way, that again confirmed her death to me.

Heller's Funeral Home was located in Burnham right beside the Borough Police Hall. The Burnham YMCA was directly across First Avenue. On the left side of Heller's stood the J & B Bar. Behind the bar was the entrance to Standard Steel along Walnut Street. The bar attracted many of the steel workers as their work shifts ended.

Dad pulled into the funeral home parking lot. The funeral home itself was a large three-story house with gray siding and white trim that had been converted. Prior to being a funeral home, several local doctors had used it for their offices. Uncle Jay's and Uncle John's vehicles were already there. Dad and Mom got out of our car, and Dad instructed Brenda and me to wait in the car. A few minutes later, Uncle Clarence pulled in, parked his bright red Chrysler, and went inside.

It didn't take Brenda and me long to get bored with waiting. It seemed like hours before we saw the door finally open, and my Uncle Clarence stormed out the door, jumped into his Chrysler, and squealed out of the parking lot. A few minutes later, Uncle John, Uncle Jay, Aunt Betty, Dad, and Mom exited. Uncle John, Uncle Jay, and Aunt Betty got into their vehicles and left. Dad and Mom got into our car. Dad started the engine, put the vehicle in gear, and pulled out of the parking lot. He said to Mom: "Can you believe the scene Fat made in there?"

"That was ridiculous," Mom replied.

"Our mother's body isn't even cold, and he's complaining about the funeral costs," Dad continued. "He just wanted to get her the cheapest funeral he could," he said with disgust. "I just wanted to punch him in the mouth."

Mom quietly said, "That wouldn't do any good, Werdna."

"I'll borrow the money if I have to; she's going to have a decent burial," Dad said, his voice breaking as he drove out of Burnham and toward home.

They continued talking about Uncle Clarence's behavior the rest of the way home. All I could think of was how much I hated my uncles. I wanted to tell them to go away. I wanted to tell them I didn't want them to go to Grandma's funeral. In the end, I would tell them nothing. Dad never would have permitted it.

Chapter 8

It was Wednesday, June 15, 1965, the day of Grandma's viewing. A private family viewing would be held at two p.m. The public viewing was scheduled from seven p.m. to nine p.m. Mom had ironed dresses for Brenda and me to wear, and they were hanging on the door of the closet in the bathroom. Both were sleeveless sundresses we wore to church. I was worried about seeing Grandma. After all, I had never seen her dead before. I had never even been to another viewing. I didn't know what to expect.

During the morning, some friends and relatives came by and dropped off casseroles, cakes, cheese platters, and other assorted food items. It was nice of them because I was certain Mom didn't feel like cooking. At lunchtime, I went into the kitchen and picked at some of the foods. No one was eating much.

Shortly after lunch at about one o'clock, we began getting dressed for the private viewing. Mom had said, "You girls can put your dresses on now because we may not come back here before the viewing tonight. Your dad and I are wearing our same clothes, too."

"Okay," I said as I started toward the bathroom to get my dress. Brenda was following me, but she said nothing.

About forty-five minutes later, we all were dressed, in the car, and on our way to Grandma's viewing. I remember thinking that it was odd how life just moved forward as if nothing had happened. Grandma was *dead*. Why didn't the world recognize that? Stores were still open, people still worked, and life continued all around us as if nothing significant had happened. I wanted to scream. I wanted to blame someone. I wanted to run away. I did none of these things; I just sat there in silence as Dad continued to drive to the funeral home.

When we reached Heller's Funeral Home, Dad pulled into the parking lot and parked beside my Uncle Jay's brand new Dodge. Dad's brothers all had fairly new model vehicles. Dad couldn't afford one. He had two vehicles, though. The 1953 two-tone blue Desoto was his favorite. He usually drove his newer Thunderbird; but today he drove the Desoto. He always said he was going to keep the Desoto until it was an antique because it was in excellent condition. I personally never cared for that car. The seats were fuzzy, and the car had a musty smell.

We all got out of the car and followed as Dad led us through the front door of Heller's. We then took the first door to the right that led into the viewing room where Grandma was laid out. Uncle Jay, Aunt Betty, and Carol were already seated inside the door on the right hand side. Dad sat down next to Uncle Jay, and they began talking as Mom, Brenda, and I took our places in chairs next to Dad's. Before long, all of the remaining immediate family members arrived and took their places. All three of Dad's brothers were there: Uncle Clarence, Uncle John, and Uncle Jay.

The funeral director, Mr. Heller, came out of his office and was talking to Dad and his brothers, but I couldn't make out what he was saying. He then walked to the other end of the room and opened a set of white, wooden folding doors. There lay Grandma. My heart started racing. A wave of disbelief struck me. Grandma was wearing a blue gown Dad and his brothers had picked out for her. He walked to the edge of the casket and motioned for us to come up. As I approached, I saw that there was a white blanket pulled up little higher than her waist, covering the bottom portion of her body. Grandma's hands were folded over her stomach.

The casket was dark mahogany brown and had a white ruffle lining. Bouquets of pink gladiolas were on each end of the coffin. Inside the lid, a small spray of pink carnations lay with a card reading, from her grandchildren. There were numerous other baskets of flowers from friends and relatives placed around the edge of the room.

I looked at everything in the room except Grandma's face. I deliberately tried to avoid looking at it because I felt I could not bear to do so. Finally, I felt compelled to look. At that time, I realized it was my precious grandma lying there. Suddenly, I felt as though I could not breathe. The emotional pain I felt was overwhelming, and I could not contain it. The tears began to flow almost immediately, and moments later, sobs followed. I didn't want to cry. I knew my family viewed tears as a weakness, but the harder I tried to stop the tears, the more they increased. I sensed everyone in the room was staring at me as I made my way out into the lobby. I couldn't bear to turn around and look at anyone. I had no tissues, and I remember someone pushing several into my hand. I took one, wiped my eyes, and blew my nose. As I turned around, I saw the podium with the container of Grandma's memorial cards. I picked one up. It seemed that if I had something to hold onto, I would not shake as badly. My legs felt like jelly.

The card was white, trimmed in gold, and there was a cross with flowers centered on the front below the words: In Memory. Inside, on the left flap, were lilies centered and beneath them it said: "God is our refuge and strength, a very present help in trouble." Psalm 48:1. On the right side, it read: *In Loving Memory of Sallie I. Bishop Date of Birth, July 11, 1892 Passed Away June 14, 1965 Services held at Heller Funeral Home Thursday, June 17 at 1:00 p.m. Clergyman: Rev. Melvin F. Warntz Place of Interment: Mount Rock Cemetery*

Absorbing the words as I read them instigated another flood of tears as the reality of Grandma's death struck me again. I struggled for about another ten minutes, trying to get my emotions under control. I then glanced into the viewing room. I was horrified that I saw no tears. She deserved tears. Why weren't they crying? Worse yet, some were carrying on conversations as if she didn't lie there in her coffin.

That made me very angry. Grandma was gone and would never return. Surely, my relatives knew that. I felt isolated and alone in the middle of all of Dad's family members. I believed I must be different from them. How else could they show no emotions? They all just stood there chatting and ignoring Grandma. It was bad enough that some of them rejected her in life; but I couldn't bear to see them reject her in death, too. "Grandma, I love you," I whispered as I looked at her one last time before my family and I walked into the hall and made our way to the front door.

While leaving the parking lot, Dad said to Mom: "We may just as well go up to your parents' place until the viewing tonight."

"I thought we might," Mom replied.

Grandma and Pap Eward lived only four miles from Heller's. Uncle Jay, Aunt Betty, and Carol lived at the bottom of the hill. Dad walked down the hill to visit with Uncle Jay until it was time to go back for the public viewing. Brenda and I stayed on the sun porch while Mom went in to visit with Grandma and Pap. I hadn't cried since I left Heller's, but my emotions were still raging right beneath the surface. Brenda and I didn't discuss the viewing. Perhaps she was struggling with her emotions, too. We were playing jacks when Aunt Betty and Carol came in. Aunt Betty went through the sun porch and into the living room where Mom, Grandma, and Pap were sitting. Carol had changed into shorts. She sat down on the cement step where we were playing.

"I heard you crying," Carol proclaimed as she looked directly at me.

"You did not," I snapped back at her.

"I did too, and I saw you, too," she said.

"Shut up," I retorted.

"Yeah, shut up," Brenda added in my defense.

"Well you shouldn't do that. People aren't suppose to cry in public. You made a big scene," Carol continued.

"Oh shut up," I repeated, but what I wanted to ask was, "Why didn't you cry?" She was just a brat, and I was angry at her, too. I wanted to tell her so, but I knew I would get into trouble. I just tried to ignore her and continued playing jacks. Eventually, she left and went inside with the others. Brenda and I kept playing our game until Grandma Eward called us in to eat a sandwich. She had made us each a Lebanon Bologna sandwich and gave us each a glass of milk. Mom had said she didn't want anything. Carol and Aunt Betty had returned home to eat.

Shortly after we had eaten our sandwiches and returned to the sun porch, Dad arrived from Uncle Jay's and said to me, "Go get your mother; we're leaving." It was after six o'clock. We all climbed back into our Desoto and once again returned to Heller's. Mom and Dad sat talking for a while before they got out of the car.

I felt exhausted as we made our way toward the front door. It seemed to me that day would never end. Once more we followed Dad into the building. When friends and relatives began arriving, Dad stood in the back of the room near the casket. Brenda, Mom, and I sat on chairs located near where Dad was standing with his brothers. Carol, Aunt Betty, Bobbie, Barbara, Aunt Jane, Abbey, and Johnny sat on other vacant chairs as they arrived. Other more distant family members and friends filed by the casket, made comments to Dad and his brothers, and then made their way through the center of the room, stopping periodically to talk with different family members.

I tried my best not to look at Grandma. When the tears started to come, I pinched the skin on my right side as hard as I could so I would concentrate on the physical pain in an attempt to stop the emotional pain. I would use that technique to control my emotions for many years. It didn't always work, though. Sometimes the emotional pain was so overwhelming that I didn't even feel the physical pain.

As the evening wore on, friends and relatives began thinning. It seemed like everyone said the same things as they passed by Grandma. Comments such as: "Doesn't she look nice?"; "At least now she won't suffer anymore"; "How are the girls holding up?" etc. I thought it was strange they said a dead person looked nice. Their remarks about Grandma not suffering anymore made me angry. So what, she wasn't suffering any more; she was dead! Wouldn't it be better to be alive?

Several times that evening, I lost my battle to stop the tears. I was able to control the sobs, however. The tears came in silence. I remember I felt a void since I no longer prayed Grandma's prayer. I wondered why God hadn't heard my prayers anyway. I wondered why he had forsaken me. After all, the Bible said, "Ask and you will receive." I had asked and I hadn't received. Grandma lay there before me in her casket dead.

The next morning I awoke and immediately remembered it was the day of the funeral. I realized that day would be the last time I would see Grandma. Her funeral service was to be held at one p.m. at Heller's. Interment would be at Mount Rock Cemetery in Lewistown. She would be buried next to Pap Bishop's grave.

Pap's grave had no tombstone. There was a small metal marker that had been placed there when he was buried in 1956. I had heard Dad talking with Mom in the kitchen the day before. He had said, "I talked to Jay, and he said he would help pay for the tombstone for Mom's and Dad's grave. John might help, too."

"How much will it cost?" Mom had asked him.

"I don't know. We're going to get prices from Luck's Monuments on Valley Street," he had answered. "Fat said he wasn't going in on it," he added.

"That doesn't surprise me," said Mom.

That made me angry once more. I hated my Uncle Clarence and maybe my Uncle John, too. I wasn't too fond of my Uncle Jay, either. I wanted Grandma to have the best. I was glad my Dad was buying Grandma a grave marker. I was glad he was my father instead of one of his brothers. Tears trickled from my eyes as I thought about my uncles' cruelty. At times I thought Dad was cruel to me, but I felt certain his brothers would be worse. I got out of bed and went downstairs. Mom and Dad were in the living room. No one did much in the morning. I did manage to eat a bowl of Rice Krispies, although I really didn't taste them. Then I returned to the living room and watched some TV until it was time to get dressed for the funeral. Each time I walked through Grandma's room, which was often since I had to go through it to get anywhere in the house, I looked at the corner where she had been just days before. Usually, I would need to fight back the tears. Memories of her cries through the night and the emotional cruelty she suffered returned to me, and I felt as though I could feel her pain. *Grandma how I miss you!* I cried out in my mind.

By twelve-thirty, my family and I were on Route 322 on our way to Heller's Funeral Home. I knew that would be the last day I would see my grandma. I didn't want to forget her. Already, I couldn't remember the last thing I had said to her. Oh, how I wished I had said good-bye when they took her by me on her way to the ambulance. Now I would never be able to say those words. She was dead. I remember thinking it just couldn't be. Grandma had always been there.

I felt as though our Desoto was invisible as we floated down the highway and pulled into Heller's parking lot one more time. Life continued all around us, but I no longer felt I was part of it. Something had changed that would never be the same. The pain I experienced was excruciating. I didn't want to go to the funeral, but I knew I must. Grandma would want me to be there and besides, I didn't have a choice.

I followed my family into Heller's in a daze. If only I could have stayed like that, I would have felt no pain. I didn't want to feel the pain. I wanted to escape. To escape, I had to try not to feel anything. Absence of feeling was what I was seeking.

However, the moment my feet touched the thick, rich carpet in the lobby, my emotions again came to life. I fought desperately to control them. I had pinched my side so hard it was bleeding where my fingernails had dug into my flesh. Still, the physical pain lost the battle; the emotional pain was the victor.

As I took my seat in between my mom and Brenda, the sobs began. We were seated in the row behind Uncle Jay, Aunt Betty, and Carol. Each of Grandma's sons were seated in order according to their ages. Dad was the youngest, so we were behind the rest of the immediate family. *How unfair life is*, I thought. Dad should have been first. He was the son who took care of Grandma and loved her. The sons who had refused to visit her or hear her cries were seated first. I wanted to make my uncles leave. They didn't belong there. Grandma deserved better than them.

As Reverend Warnz began the service, I totally lost control. I was sobbing loudly and trembling violently. I wanted to cry out to God, but He couldn't hear me, I was certain.

Mom whispered, "Hush, stop your crying. You'll make it harder for your father."

I didn't want to make it harder for Dad, but I could not stop. I tried to keep my head down, but occasionally I caught a glimpse of Grandma, and once in a while, I heard a word or two the Reverend was saying. That only made me cry louder. I needed someone to wrap their arms around me and help ease my pain. My family members were not affectionate in that way, so I sat there alone in my overwhelming grief. I needed God, too, but refused to pray.

Reverend Warntz said many kind things about Grandma. His words made me cry harder. When he talked about her legacy, I wondered what my uncles were thinking. Did they have any shame?

I had gone prepared that day with a pocketful of tissues. It looked as though I might run out before the service ended, though. Mr. Heller asked if anyone cared to view Grandma's body for the last time. I wanted to go, but could not move physically, so I sat frozen in my seat. A few relatives went to the casket for the last viewing; then the ushers closed the wooden doors, and I would never again see my grandma.

They began to dismiss each row of relatives and friends separately, beginning at the front. As our row filed out, I whispered, "Good-bye, Grandma." They had already closed the wooden folding doors and most likely removed the casket. I hoped she could hear me wherever she was.

We went to our car and waited for the remainder of our relatives and friends to be dismissed and take their places in the funeral procession. I remember each car was lined up and had a little flag on it that said "funeral." I wondered how they stayed on the cars; later I learned they were magnetic and stuck to the metal. After everyone had exited and taken their assigned positions, the gray hearse with Grandma's body began the funeral procession to the gravesite.

I remember all the cars had their headlights turned on. We followed the hearse as it turned left onto First Avenue, went straight to the Stop sign, and then turned left again onto Walnut Street. We continued on Walnut Street across the intersection at Freedom Avenue, left on Spring Street, and left again on Oakland Avenue. Oakland Avenue ended at the entrance to Mount Rock Cemetery. The entire procession took approximately ten minutes for it was just a little over two miles.

While in the car, I had settled down somewhat. My nose had quit running;

however, my eyes were swollen and sore from so much crying, and my face was all blotchy. I saw myself in Dad's rear view mirror, and I realized I looked a mess. Dad and Mom were quietly talking in the front seat, but I didn't want to listen. Brenda sat beside me, and for a moment I wondered if she knew where she was. She didn't seem upset at all, and she hadn't cried at all during the service. It was then that I realized I had seen no one cry.

Why didn't they feel the pain I felt? Was there something wrong with them or something wrong with me? I remember being very confused as the cars made their way along the hemlock-lined lower road of the cemetery, turned left, started up the hill, and turned left again onto the middle road that went through the center of the cemetery. It was there that the hearse stopped. All the vehicles following stopped behind it. Everyone started to get out of their cars and walk toward the gravesite.

The attendants removed Grandma's casket from the hearse and the pallbearers--Dad, my uncles, and two oldest cousins--carried it to the gravesite. That, too, was upsetting since my uncles were part of the ritual. There was a sugar maple tree to the right of the open grave next to the corner of that section of the cemetery. The remainder of the trees were hemlocks. Grandma's gravesite was the first one on the bottom right of the middle section. Each section was divided by the single-lane, one-way road that surrounded the perimeter and went through the center of the cemetery.

As the casket was carried from the hearse and placed at the gravesite, everyone was silent and quietly made their way under the green canvas canopy placed over it. There were several chairs in the front, and my aunts sat on those chairs with their husbands, my uncles, standing behind them. Mom didn't take a seat. Dad stood beside her. The flowers from the funeral home had been placed around the gravesite, and their sweet fragrance drifted through the air. From that day forward, the smell of flowers would remind me of funerals.

I tried to walk slowly so I could disappear into the group and stand behind them. That way, I wouldn't have to look at the casket. My plan didn't work, though, because my mom turned around, sought me out of the crowd, and said, "Come up here, Linda." That forced me to move forward toward the front. I could see the casket and plainly hear the Reverend as I stood beside Brenda. I didn't want to hear him. Each word he spoke seemed like a spike driving a nail into Grandma's casket that would remain closed forever. I realized then that I would never see her again. Panic struck me as I struggled to remember what she looked like. My tears were released once more as I thought, *Please, please don't let her memory fade away.* Again I pinched my side as hard as I could, and that time it kept back the sobs, just not the tears.

Finally, the graveside service ended, and people began returning to their cars. I stumbled as I followed, wiping the remaining tears from my eyes. When I reached the Desoto, I again slid into the back seat and tried to shut out the world. I didn't want to think about the next day or the day after that. I didn't want to think at all; if I thought, the pain would crush me.

Over the next few weeks, the shock of Grandma's death dissolved and the true grieving period began. It was a real struggle for me because comprehension of death was initially beyond my grasp. It was the opposite of everything I knew. Thoughts of death unexpectedly evaded my mind numerous times each day. Prior to Grandma's illness, I don't recall ever thinking about it.

It seemed that the more I dwelled on those thoughts, the more distant I became. It was hard to have fun when it felt as though a large part of my life had vanished. I no longer saw the world through the same eyes. My innocence had disappeared, for the reality of Grandma's death removed the scales from my eyes. I now realized we all were mortal.

I frequently dreamed of Grandma throughout the next few weeks. She was always just out of my reach in my dreams. Usually, I would be moving toward her in various scenarios, but when I got close to her, I would reach out to touch her, and she would vanish, or I would wake up. I felt unsettled and fearful when I awoke from these dreams.

Often I would feel Grandma was with me. The first time I experienced that phenomena, I was frightened. It occurred the third day after her funeral. I had just gone up to bed, pulled back my blankets, and turned off the lights. I didn't have a bedside lamp. We had only the overhead light, and the switch was on the wall at the bottom left side of Brenda's bed. I was about ready to jump into bed, when I felt a chill come over my body, and I had the distinct feeling that Grandma had entered the room through the green fiberglass drapes at the top of the stairs. It seemed as though she was in my bedroom beside me. That startled me, and I didn't know what to make of it. I quickly jumped into bed and pulled the blankets over my head. In a few moments, the feeling passed.

That sort of thing began happening several times a week. Sometimes it felt as though she stood beside me and touched my hand. Dad had given me Grandma's gold signet ring that I constantly wore on my left hand. Part of me believed that she was somehow able to communicate with me through that ring.

Grandma had few possessions when she died, and even fewer valuable possessions. I considered her gold ring to be her most prized, valuable possession. It made me feel very fortunate to be the heir of her ring. I knew I would cherish it forever because to me, it was all that remained of my grandma.

Many times I had an urge to visit Grandma's grave. I couldn't, though, because it was about ten miles from our house. Dad probably would have taken me if I had asked. I didn't ask. We didn't discuss Grandma's death at all, and I was afraid it would make Dad sad if I asked to visit her grave. Also, I feared he might get angry with me.

Sometimes I wondered what it would have been like to touch Grandma's body after she had died. I didn't touch her at the funeral home. The sight of all the ruffles in the casket and the overwhelming smell of different kinds of flowers mixed together all seemed eerie in a way. Something about the scene frightened me, and I didn't want to touch her. I had never touched a dead body.

I had heard Dad talking to Mom before the funeral about Grandma's body being embalmed. I didn't completely understand that. Also, I wondered if they took Grandma's organs out if they embalmed her. That was before organ donations were popular, so her donating organs never entered my mind. I also wondered if she wore underwear underneath her gown and whether they put shoes on her. I didn't ask about that either. I wouldn't want to make it hard on my Dad.

PART TWO
JULY 1965-JUNE 1966
Time Line

July 1965 – National Coordination Committee to End the War in Viet Nam formed.

August 1965 – "Help" released by the Beatles; "Eve of Destruction" released by Dylan; Joan Baez's releases her first hit: "There But For Fortune."

August 6, 1965 – Lyden Baines Johnson signs Voting Rights Act.

August 26, 1965 – Last day getting married could improve your draft status.

August 31, 1965 – Lyden Baines Johnson signs law amending Selective Service Act to make draft card burning a federal offense.

Fall 1965 – Mini shirts in stores; the term "hippie" emerges; 'Ballad of Green Berets" tops the charts.

September 1965 – Linda begins 8th grade.

October 1965 – Viet Nam War protests in 80 cities; first draft card burning.

November 27, 1965 – "March on Washington for Peace in Viet Nam."

December 12, 1965 – Linda's 13th birthday.

December 15, 1965 – Gemini 6 and 7 rendezvous in space.

December 1965 – 184,000 American troops in Viet Nam.

June 6, 1966 – James Meredith shot while marching through Mississippi to encourage blacks to register to vote.

June 13, 1966 – Supreme Court "Miranda Case": suspects entitled to be informed of their rights when arrested.

June 29, 1966 – US starts bombing major oil facilities in Hanoi & Haiphong Harbor.

Popular Songs

"(I Can't Get No) Satisfaction," The Rolling Stones; "I Got You Babe," Sonny & Cher; "Unchained Melody," The Righteous Brothers; "Yesterday," The Beatles; "I Hear A Symphony," The Supremes; "Taste of Honey," Herb Alpert & The Tijuana Brass; "We Can Work It Out / Day Tripper," The Beatles; "Turn! Turn! Turn! (To Everything There Is A Season)," The Byrds; "Lightnin' Strikes," Lou Christie; "19th Nervous Breakdown," The Rolling Stones; "Good Lovin'," The Young Rascals; "Monday, Monday," The Mama's & The Papa's; "Strangers In The Night," Frank Sinatra

Chapter 9

As the weeks passed, my dreams about Grandma became less frequent. It was now the middle of July. Since the funeral, I had isolated myself from the world. I found I no longer enjoyed hanging out on Betsy's porch or at Cathy's grandfather's swimming pool. Most of the days I watched television and tried to avoid any human contact. That helped me to cope.

It was around that time that my headaches began. They were so severe that they would make me dizzy and nauseated. When at their worst, I would be forced to lie down for several hours which is usually how long it took for them to pass. During those periods, I couldn't eat anything but Popsicles. I felt I would throw up if I ate other foods.

In addition, I had trouble sleeping at night. That caused me to sleep some through the day, but I never felt rested. It was as if I had no energy. I would start to do something and then forget what I was doing. Sometimes I would just wander through the house.

Numerous times I would burst into tears for no apparent reason. I didn't want to leave the house. The thought of leaving would upset me. I especially didn't want to return to school. I felt I could never again fit in; I was a different person than the girl who started high school the previous year. I tried to hide my tears because my dad would get upset. He would say things like, "Straighten up." Or "What are you bawling about?" Of course, I couldn't straighten up, and I didn't know why I was crying. All I knew was I felt horrible inside. I didn't want to be around people most of the time, and I didn't feel that I could live the rest of my life like that.

At those times, I believed Dad was angry with me. Later, as years passed, I came to realize he wasn't angry; he just didn't know how to help me. He didn't know how to express his feelings because that was something he was taught he should not do. But, because I believed he was angry, I wasn't able to even attempt to explain how I felt. By having those feelings, I thought there must be something horribly wrong with me. I wanted to hide it and pretend I was "normal."

Sometimes Mom would ask me what was wrong, but I couldn't tell her even if I knew. I knew she told Dad everything. Then she made comments that made it worse, like, "Your dad doesn't know what to do with you." And, "You have to get over this." I remember thinking: *Get over what?* I didn't know how to get over whatever it was. My feelings were becoming more intense.

It's strange, but during that time I can barely remember Brenda being there. It's as though I blanked her out of my mind. It might have been because she was happy. Acknowledging happiness would have made me more aware of how unhappy I was. Also, it made me feel "abnormal."

Finally, in desperation, due to my continued tears and headaches, Mom and Dad scheduled an appointment for me to see Dr. McNabb, the same doctor Grandma had seen originally. My appointment was scheduled for Wednesday, July 7th at 4:30 p.m. In a way, I was glad I was going to see a doctor. I didn't want to have those feelings. Life was no longer fun and something to look forward to. Life was now painful and something I wished I could escape.

My parents could accept a physical reason for my behavior much easier than an emotional one, and I was well aware of that. So when my emotions triggered the tears, I would blame them on the headaches. "It just hurts too bad," I would say. That way I was less likely to feel "abnormal." At age twelve, no one wants to feel different. At that age it is important to be identical to your peers and blend in. I certainly didn't want to stand out, especially for something bad or weird.

The first day that I was scheduled to see Dr. McNabb, I awoke in my bed and squinted because the sun was streaming through the window at the top of the stairs in my bedroom. There were white sheer curtains on the windows, and a heavy dark green window shade was underneath that had been raised about half-way. I rubbed my eyes, stretched, and then got out of bed. I dressed in black shorts and a gray tank top and went down the stairs. That day seemed like any other that summer except that I would be going to see Dr. McNabb. I both dreaded and looked forward to the visit. Relief from the intense emotions I felt would be welcome. As I passed through Grandma's room, I looked at the spot where her bed had been. A wave of sorrow washed over me, and I hurried into the kitchen.

Mom was in the kitchen defrosting the refrigerator. She would always set a hot pan of water inside the freezer to speed the thaw process. There was one large door on the refrigerator that opened, and inside was a much smaller door at the top where the freezer was located. There was no self-defrosting then. Mom would break off large pieces of ice as the thawing began. As it became more difficult, she would chisel away at the ice with a table knife.

She didn't say anything as I entered the kitchen and got a box of cornflakes from the cabinet. The milk was already on the kitchen table along with everything else that had been inside the refrigerator. I took my bowl of cornflakes over to the table and sat down in Dad's chair on the left end of the table. As I reached over, picked up the milk, and began pouring it onto my cornflakes, I asked Mom, "What time is my appointment tonight?"

Mom took a break in her chiseling, pulled her head out of the freezer, and said, as she looked at me, "Four-thirty. We'll leave right after we eat. I'll wash the dishes when we get home." She again put her head into the freezer, and tried to remove the ice in the back. I finished eating my cornflakes in silence. Then I took the dish and spoon over to the sink, rinsed them, and set them on the right side of the sink where the dishes accumulated before they were washed.

I went into the living room, turned on the television, and began watching the remainder of the morning movie. The morning movie came on at nine o'clock, and I watched it often during the summer. Many times the feature was a science fiction film. I loved watching giant ants invading cities, aliens taking over the earth, and earthlings visiting other planets.

Those movies were very entertaining to a twelve-year-old. That particular day, a vampire movie was on. As I watched it, I looked at the clock on top of our floor- model Zenith television set. It was nine thirty-five. I calculated it was a little less than seven hours until my appointment.

As the movie continued, I watched it but wasn't aware of what was before my eyes because I was seeing with my mind's eye. Again, I was standing beside Grandma at the big oak tree in our front yard, and tears flowed down my cheeks. In a few moments, my grandma's image vanished, and I once again saw the vampires on the screen. I sniffed to keep my nose from running, and wiped my remaining tears with the palm of my hand. Again I glanced at the clock. It was nine fifty-five. A little more than six and a half hours until I would go see the doctor.

Throughout the day, I continued to periodically check the clock and calculate the time until I would see Dr. McNabb. Also, several times I began crying even though I had earnestly tried not to. Three-thirty eventually arrived, and

I bathed and changed into a newer shorts outfit. I went into the kitchen where Mom was cooking dinner. I saw that she was preparing fried red perch. Normally, I would have loved that meal, but I wasn't feeling very hungry that night.

Regardless of how I felt, Mom instructed, "Go get Brenda and tell her to come in. You two can go ahead and start eating. We won't have much time when your dad gets home."

I went out onto our front porch and called Brenda. She was sitting on Sammy Fleck's front porch. Sammy was an elderly man who lived about fifty yards from our house up the alley that ran parallel with Cathy's and Inez's alley. Many of the neighborhood kids would stop at Sammy's and sit on his porch with him. That was a time of innocence before children had to be taught to fear every old man.

Sammy was poor by the world's standards. He had no car, and he was a cripple. I never learned exactly what was wrong with him. I was told he had once worked for the Forestry Department, but he had to quit and go on disability because walking became too difficult for him. My dad visited often with Sammy. He took him his weekly groceries just like Mom did for Inez. Sammy never left his property that he had inherited from his father. It was barely more than a shack, but he seemed happy.

Once I heard Sammy and Dad discussing the astronauts. Sammy didn't believe anything about the space program. He definitely didn't believe that John Glenn had orbited the earth on February 20, 1962. Sammy thought the government had made it up in order to cover up what they were spending taxpayers' money on. Dad just couldn't convince him it was real.

I called Brenda and she got up from the wooden swivel chair, picked up her bike that was leaning against Sammy's left front porch post, and rode home. I returned to the kitchen and slid behind the table. Mom had already moved it out from the wall. She put the fried perch on the table and returned to the stove to take the French fries out of the skillet.

I heard Brenda come through the front door, and she entered the kitchen. As soon as she saw the fish on the table she moaned, "Oh, no!" Mom carried a small bread plate with a lid on it to the table and lifted the lid. Underneath was a hamburger.

"Good!" Brenda exclaimed as she slid into her seat beside me.

While we were eating our meals, Dad pulled into the driveway. Within a few minutes, he entered the kitchen and placed his lunch box on the sink. After washing his hands, he sat down with Brenda and me and began wolfing down his food so he could get me to Dr. McNabb's office on time.

Mom was eating her meal as she traveled back and forth between the stove and table as she served us and then cleared the table when we finished. As soon as Dad was done eating, we all went out the front door and got into the family car. I was anxious and wanted to get it over with. I remember wondering what would happen inside the doctor's office.

As Dad pulled in front of Dr. McNabb's office on Logan Street, I couldn't help but recall sitting there less than a year before, waiting as Mom and Grandma went inside the examining room. Mom reached over and opened her car door, then turned around, looked at me, and asked, "Are you ready?"

"Yeah," I said as I, too, opened my car door and stepped onto the sidewalk. I followed Mom across Logan Street after she had checked for cars coming in both directions. Dad and Brenda remained in the car. Mom and I went up the three steps to get on the porch and entered the door into Dr. McNabb's waiting room.

Inside was a small waiting room. There was a plaid couch along the far wall, several straight-backed wooden chairs and a deacon's bench scattered around the remaining perimeter of the room. Numerous still life pictures hung on the walls. I sat down beside Mom on the couch and awaited our turn. There was one other person in the room--an elderly woman who was leafing through a magazine.

Before long, an elderly gentlemen shuffled out through the door that I assumed was Dr. McNabb's office. He went over to the row of brass hooks on the wall to the left of the front door, picked up his navy-blue jacket, and slipped into it with some difficulty. He asked the elderly woman, "Are you ready, Marge?"

She replied, "Yes" and stood up, placed her magazine back into the wooden magazine rack, and followed her husband to the door. I noticed that she had not removed her jacket.

Several minutes after the old couple left, a nurse walked out into the waiting room, and called, "Linda Bishop."

Mom stood up, extended her right arm toward me, and said, "Come on." She walked behind me as I followed the nurse inside the door.

There was a small wooden desk, swivel chair, and two straight-backed chairs squeezed inside the tiny eight-by-eight room. The nurse seated herself on the swivel chair behind the desk, and Mom and I took the two vacant chairs in front of the desk. The nurse asked me numerous questions regarding my overall health. She then stood up and told me to step on the scale She marked down my weight: ninety two pounds. She also measured my height. I was five feet, two inches tall. The nurse then took my temperature and blood pressure. When these formalities were completed, she turned to me and asked, "Well now, what seems to be the problem today?"

I looked at her; then I looked at my mom. When Mom didn't respond, I said, "I don't know…Sometimes I get bad headaches."

"How often do you get these headaches?" the nurse asked as she scribbled notes in my medical record.

"A couple of times a week."

"How long do they last?"

"For one or two hours," I said, wiggling in my seat.

Mom added, "When she has a headache, she says she can't eat anything because it will make her sick."

The nurse looked at me and asked, "Is that right?"

"I can eat Popsicles, but I can't eat other foods," I replied.

"Do you have any other symptoms?" she went on.

"No," I answered.

Mom said, "Well she has been crying a lot lately. Her dad and I are getting concerned about this."

"Why does she cry?" the nurse asked and looked out over her glasses at Mom.

"Well, it seems as though she cries about everything, and sometimes there doesn't seem to be a reason."

The nurse looked over at me and said, "Make sure you tell the doctor about this. Okay?" I nodded that I would.

The nurse then stood up, walked to the right side of the room, pushed back the folding door between her office and the doctor's office and announced, "Doctor, we're ready now."

I entered the examining room, and saw Dr. McNabb standing near an examination table. He had gray hair and was clean shaven. He was wearing a white lab coat. I could see the end of a desk through another door at the far end of the examining room. Dr. McNabb looked at my chart and said, "Hello, Linda. How are you doing today?" .

"Okay," I said, not quite sure what I was supposed to do.

Mom was behind me. Dr. McNabb looked at her over his wire-rimmed bifocals and said, "Mrs. Bishop, you may take a seat right there." He motioned toward a single chair placed in the corner along the entrance wall. And…Linda, you hop up here," he said as he patted the end of the examining table. It had white paper on it that rattled as I faced forward, backed up against the table, and pulled myself up on the edge of the table.

Dr. McNabb glanced through my chart again then checked my heart with his stethoscope. He asked, "So you've been getting headaches?" He then looked into my eyes with his little light, turned my head and looked into my left ear and then my right.

"Yes," I said.

"How long have you been getting the headaches?" he asked.

After an uncomfortable pause, I answered, "I think about a couple of months."

Mom said, "She started getting them a week or so after her grandmother died.

"Were you close to your grandmother?" Dr. McNabb asked.

"She lived with us," I answered

"Do you miss her? he continued.

"Uh-huh," I responded with difficulty as my emotions began to stir.

"How did your grandmother die?" he asked.

"She had cancer," I said, tears forming in my eyes. I wondered why he didn't remember her.

I don't believe the tears went unnoticed by Dr. McNabb. "What grade will you be going into this year?" he asked. I was grateful he had changed the subject.

"Eighth," I said as I pushed myself further back on the table. It was difficult maneuvering my body on that paper.

"Are you looking forward to going back to school this year? Dr. McNabb asked as we looked eye-to-eye.

"I don't know…I guess so…I haven't really thought about it," I finally got out.

"Do you like school?" he pushed forward.

"Not really."

Mom added, "She loved school last year. She couldn't wait until it started. Now, she doesn't like to do much of anything. She just sits in front of the TV. She used to be out all the time playing with the kids in the neighborhood, or she would be riding her bike."

"Don't you like to do those things any more?" Dr. McNabb asked.

"I…I don't know," I answered. "I…I guess so."

"Is there something bothering you, Linda?" he pushed.

"No…not really," I lied.

"Why do you cry?"

"My head hurts real bad sometimes."

"Is that the only reason?"

"Yes. It just hurts and makes me sad."

"What makes you sad?"

"My headaches."

"Do you have any other pain with your headaches?" he asked.

"Sometimes my stomach hurts. That's why I can't eat...I'm afraid I'll get sick."

"Have you thrown up at all?"

"No...It just feels like I will."

Dr. McNabb paused and asked, "You get your period now?'

"Yes," I responded.

"Have you had any problems with it?"

"Not really...Sometimes I just get cramps real bad." I began fidgeting on the edge of the examining table; it was embarrassing discussing my period with a man.

"Is there anything else bothering you?"

"I...I don't think so," I said, but I was thinking about the nightmares and the feelings I had that Grandma was in the room.

"Okay, you can jump down," Dr. McNabb directed. "Go ahead out there and wait with my nurse. I'd like to talk with your mother for a few minutes."

"Okay," I said as I pushed back the door and entered the room with the nurse.

"Hi, Linda. Are you finished?" the nurse asked.

"Dr. McNabb told me to wait here," I quietly responded.

"Oh did he?" she replied. "Your mother will probably be out in a few minutes."

She was right. Mom came through the door a few minutes later with a small piece of paper in her hand. The nurse stepped back into the examining room to get my chart. She returned and said, "That will be five dollars for today."

Mom paid her, we left, went back into the waiting room and out the front door. When we passed through, I noticed there were two other people in the waiting room. After we went out the door, Mom and I went down the porch steps, crossed Logan Street, and walked to our car where Dad and Brenda were waiting. "Well, how did it go?" Dad asked as we opened our doors and took our original seats inside. "Did he say what was wrong with her?" he asked Mom as if I weren't in the car.

"He said he thought she is experiencing anxiety attacks, so he gave me a prescription for nerve pills," Mom explained.

"Nerve pills!" Dad exclaimed. "What the heck does she need nerve pills for?"

"He just said she exhibits signs of depression, that's all," Mom replied in her calming tone. Then I saw her give him her look that told she would tell him more later when I wasn't there.

"Where are we going to get the prescription filled?" Dad asked, changing the subject as he started the car engine and eased out onto Logan Street.

"I guess we should take it to Peoples drug store. That's where we usually go," Mom answered.

I sat in the backseat trying to absorb everything they were saying. Depression...what was that? Nerve pills! There must really be something wrong with me. I wondered what Mom's look indicated. Was she hiding something from me?

Mom and Dad never told me what kind of medication I would be taking, and it never occurred to me to ask because I wouldn't have known the difference anyway. Years later, though, I was told he had prescribed Atarax, a brand name of hydroxyzine. It was used to depress activity in the central nervous system to relieve anxiety. That was the beginning of my drug dependency that would occur sporadically throughout my teens and twenties.

Dad drove to People's drug store, and Mom went inside to have my prescription filled. I was to take one tablet in the morning and one in the evening before bed. That same night I saw the doctor, I took my first pill. I noticed in the morning it seemed more difficult for me to get up and move about, but I didn't wake up through the night. There were no nightmares either. That was a relief.

After I ate my breakfast, Mom gave me another pill. She guarded the pill bottle like it was her prisoner. I sure hoped those pills would make me better. I hated the sad feelings, the headaches, and all the tears. The tears were really embarrassing. That was part of the reason I didn't like to leave the house. Also, it was hard for me to get motivated. I just didn't feel like doing anything. It took too much effort. I was to continue taking the pills for two weeks and then go back to see Dr. McNabb for a checkup.

The beginning of the second week, I heard Mom tell Dad she had seen an ad in the help wanted section of the *Lewistown Sentinel* for production workers at Hanover Cannery in Centre Hall. They were paying $1.25 per hour. She said she thought she would apply. Dad said he thought it was a good idea because they could use some extra money to finish some projects around the house. So Mom called the following morning and was scheduled for an interview for that evening at six o'clock.

After supper that night, Dad told Brenda and me that we could stay home while he took Mom for her interview. That suited me fine because I didn't want to go out. Brenda and I washed and dried the dishes after they left.

It would take Dad and Mom about twenty-five minutes to get to the Hanover Cannery. They had to take Route 322 over the mountain toward State College, and then get on Route 144 to Centre Hall. They would then take a right onto Route 45. The cannery was five or six miles down the road on the right.

It was Brenda's and my job to do the dishes, and we took turns washing and drying. We switched at the beginning of each week. We both always wanted to wash, although now I can't understand why. That night I was washing and Brenda was drying. No one in our neighborhood had dishwashers.

When I finished, I went back into the living room and sat on the couch to watch television. Brenda finished shortly after I did and joined me, taking a seat on the beige rocking chair. We sat there watching *Donna Reed* before Mom and Dad returned.

The front door was open, so I heard the car's tires on the gravel in the alley and knew they were home. Dad came through the front door first and Mom followed. Brenda and I just looked at them, waiting to hear what had happened..

Dad walked over and sat on the couch. Mom did likewise. "Well," Dad said, "your mother got the job. She starts next Monday morning."

I didn't know what to think. Mom hadn't worked since I was in first grade, when Dad was laid off. She had only worked for about six weeks, then. Her working would be strange. I guess Mom was going through some depression of her own, and her way of dealing with it was to go to work. She must have felt she needed to get out of the house after being confined so long while caring for Grandma when she had been sick.

Dad said, "You kids will have to do more around here now since your mother will be working."

"Brenda asked, "Will we get more allowance?"

At that time, we each received one dollar a week. Dad said, "We might even double it."

"Good!" Brenda squealed with delight. I was glad about the extra money, too, but I couldn't muster up any show of excitement. I just sat there and thought about what he was telling us.

Brenda and I were to share the cleaning chores since Mom was going to work full-time. Mom insisted she was still in charge of the laundry. That was all right with me; I didn't want to do the laundry.

Mom started to work the following Monday morning. She worked ten hour days: seven to five. An old friend of hers, Dot Peters, from the Lewistown Heights, worked at the cannery, and she agreed to drive Mom to and from work. They were required to wear white uniforms and white shoes. They also wore hats and aprons. They removed stones, and bad vegetables from the conveyor belt as it passed them. Dot picked Mom up at six- fifteen to make sure they made it to work on time. Dad left for work about the same time. He liked to get there early so he could hang out with the guys before work started. Brenda and I would sleep in.

The first few days were fun for Brenda and me being on our own. The fun then began to wear off, and I again felt sadness. Mom left my pill out on the side of the sink in the morning. She never allowed me to have the bottle. I believe she thought that, if she did, I couldn't be trusted to take the prescribed dosage.

While Mom worked, I wandered through the house, picking at food and watching TV. I would stare at the clock and mentally calculate the hours until Mom would be returning. I enjoyed having her at home, and I missed her when she worked. We had daily chores assigned to us, but I found it more and more difficult to complete my share. Brenda would complain about that. She still hung out with Cathy and Betsy a lot. I did occasionally, but generally I liked to stay around the house that year.

Our neighbor on the south side of our house, Mrs. Lyter, had a granddaughter, Debbie, who visited her during the summer of 1965. Debbie was two years younger than I, but she was physically bigger. She was overweight, and her feet always smelled. Still, I liked to spend time with Debbie because I could be myself and know she would accept me no matter what I did or what mood I was in. That year I was very moody. Debbie was somewhat of an outcast; I believe that is another reason I befriended her.

Often Debbie and I would take my dog Spot for walks out Lingle Valley Road to the fork in the road. There you could take a left and go to Cooper's Gap or you could take a right to Alan Seeger, a local State Park. The fork in the road was approximately three miles from our house. We rarely explored beyond that point.

Sometimes we would climb to the top of the mountain where there was a huge pile of giant boulders. Mom thought it was dangerous for us to climb the mountain, but it wasn't a steep mountain. There was also a cave formed under the boulders. Debbie and I would go into the cave and plan how we would hide out there if the Russians ever invaded.

Other times we would build a fire on top of the largest flat boulder and cook our lunch. Of course, we never told our parents about the fire. Our favorite lunch was fried Lebanon bologna sandwiches and potato chips. We were able to see my house and Debbie's grandmother's house from our location on top of that giant boulder.

We also liked to talk about what we would do if there was a nuclear attack. It was scary, but many adults talked about bomb shelters at that time. I worried because we didn't have one, and I didn't know anyone who did. We also discussed bomb shelters in some of our classes at school. It hadn't been that long ago since the Cuban missile crisis. When I was in sixth grade, the Wagners, a family that lived along Route 322, brought their grandson up from Florida to stay with them until the crisis period was over. The thought of an atomic war was very frightening.

When Dad got home in the evenings, Brenda and I were expected to help him prepare supper. Dad and Mom bought sides of beef to save money, so we had many frozen one-pound packages of hamburger. If no meal had been planned and nothing was thawed, he would often take a sharp butcher's knife and cut a frozen block of hamburger into strips. He then fried them, and we would take several and make a hamburger sandwich. Brenda loved these, and I didn't think they were bad, either. Another favorite of his was baked T-bone steaks with powdered onion soup sprinkled on them. The soup mixed with the steak's juices to make a sauce. Brenda and I didn't care much for these. That amazed Dad. He would ask, "What's the matter with you kids? This is the best food you can get. I sure wish I could have had it so good when I was a kid." Brenda and I heard that so often that we began looking at each other and rolling our eyes when Dad started that particular lecture.

Often at the dinner table, we would have discussions about world events. It seemed that Dad and I had opposite views on just about everything. Sometimes the discussions became heated and turned into arguments. That was dangerous for me because if Dad's bad temper kicked in, he might stand up, reach over the table, and hit me across the head. When that happened, I would end up in tears, and Mom and Dad would argue. Mom always would yell, "Werdna, don't hit her on the head." I don't know why I would push it; I guess there was just enough rebel in me to defy logic.

I don't recall Dad ever hitting Brenda like that. She usually didn't argue with him, though. I felt I had to stand up for what I believed in. It was strange, though, that I didn't do that at school. I was more afraid of peer rejection than physical punishment.

Dad really did have a short fuse. I hated when he worked on projects around the house because if something went wrong he would become violent, and I was often the scapegoat. I actually feared him because I never knew when he might become angry and strike out at me. I didn't realize it then, but his treatment of me contributed to my overall depression. I didn't feel loved, and I needed the physical affection that was so obviously missing in my family. At twelve, I couldn't understand my strong emotions. I just knew that I hurt inside, and I was unable to express the pain in words.

I missed the hugs and kisses from Grandma, too. She had always made me feel loved. It was sad for me not being able to visit her in the evenings. I felt betrayed when God took her away.

Chapter 10

It was the beginning of August, almost two months since Grandma had died. I had decided to go up to the top of the hill to check for the mail. Our mailbox was at the edge of Cathy's old yard along Route 322 and the Lingle Valley Road. The mailman didn't go down Lingle Valley Road. I took the shortcut up over the hill in between the dog boxes. Spot had seen me coming and ran over for me to pat her head. I then proceeded up the hill, passed the corn crib, and got onto Lingle Valley Road. The Lingle Valley Sportsman Association had placed the corn crib at that location to store corn to feed the local deer. There was a four-foot chain-link fence on the other side of the road that ran from the crest of the hill to the bottom of the hill where Lingle Valley Road made a sharp left turn. The fence encircled Tate's cabins.

Mr. Tate was the owner of eight small cabins that he rented to hunters and tourists. The entrance to the units was along Route 322. Tate's house stood in front of the cabins, and his driveway was lined with large spruce trees. In fact, the whole three-acre area was heavily wooded. It was a very rustic, pretty setting.

That particular day, I noticed there was a blue station wagon parked beside the cabin that was closest to Lingle Valley Road. As I stood there looking at the cabin and the station wagon, a boy I immediately estimated to be about my age came out of the cabin, circled the station wagon, and opened the back hatch. That was when he noticed me.

"Hi," he called.

"Hi," I answered and continued standing there, staring.

He walked over to the fence, placed his arms on the railing, leaned toward me and said, "My name's Steve. What's yours?"

"Linda," I answered.

"Do you live round here?" he asked.

"Yeah. Right down over the hill," I informed him as I motioned in the direction of our house.

"Oh," he responded. "I'll be staying here the rest of the summer."

"Really?" I said. Steve was about my height and had straight light-brown hair. He was wearing jean cutoff shorts and a navy blue tank top. I thought he was cute.

"Yeah. My dad's an engineer, and he'll be here working on plans for the new highway. He brought us along for a vacation," he continued.

The state was planning on making Route 322 into a four-lane highway up over Seven Mountains from the west side of Mount Pleasant to Brownie's Bar on the other side of the Mountain before you got to Potters Mills.

"Where do you live?" I asked, suddenly realizing that I was standing in the middle of the road.

As I moved closer to Steve and off the road, he answered, "In Bellefonte." He then suggested, "Maybe we can hang out some."

"Maybe," I answered. "Right now I'm on my way to check for our mail."

"Is it okay if I tag along?" Steve inquired.

"Sure," I encouraged.

Upon hearing my response, Steve went back to the station wagon and closed the hatch. Then he returned, grabbed hold of the fence railing with both hands, and sprang over the fence, landing a few feet from me. Together, we started up the hill. At the crest of the hill, I saw two older boys playing basketball. The basketball hoop was beside the fence; however, it was owned by Mr. Workinger. He had gotten the hoop for his nephew Robbie who sometimes visited him.

One of the boys was tall and had fairly short dark hair, the other was shorter with longer dirty blond hair. I had never seen them before. It was a humid day, so both of them were perspiring. You could see beads of sweat around their hair lines, and their tank tops had wet circles under the arms. As we approached them, Steve said, "Hi, guys."

"Hi, yourself," the taller, dark haired one answered.

"What are you up to?" the shorter one asked.

"Just going after the mail," Steve answered. "This is Linda," he stated as he started an introduction. "These are my brothers, Bernie and Cecil," he told me.

"Hi," I said. Both boys appeared to be older than Steve. I thought they must be in their teens.

They both responded, "Hi," as we all checked each other out while they continued their game.

"See you guys later," Steve informed them as we continued our walk to my mailbox.

"What grade are you going to be in?" Steve asked as we moved away from his brothers.

"I'll be going into eighth grade this year," I answered.

"No kidding! Me, too." Steve exclaimed. "How old are you?"

"Twelve."

"I'm twelve, too," he said. "My birthday is October second. When's yours?"

"December twelfth," I stated. I had reached the mailbox, carefully reached inside and removed an Ames department store flyer and a phone bill from United Telephone. I pushed the mailbox lid shut with my right hand after switching the mail to my left hand.

Steve and I continued to chat as we walked back down Lingle Valley Road. When we reached his brothers, they were still playing basketball. They didn't say anything as we walked by.

Steve said, "They could play basketball for hours."

"Do you like to play basketball, too?"

"Sometimes, but not as much as they do."

"How old are they?"

"Bernie is sixteen, and Cecil is fifteen."

"Does Bernie have his driver's license?" I asked.

"Not yet. But, he has his permit," Steve informed me.

I was impressed! Sixteen seemed so old, and being able to drive would be great.

I decided against taking Steve on the shortcut that led through Brownie's and Spot's territory. It was hard to predict how they might respond to a stranger. Usually they were friendly, but they could become hostile at times. We walked on down Lingle Valley Road and took a left at the alley that led past Mrs. Muttersbaugh's house and on to my house. As we walked by Mrs. Muttersbaugh's house, I said, "The old woman who lives there is blind. Her name is Mrs. Muttersbaugh; she's kind of weird."

"No kidding," Steve said. "Has she always been blind?"

"No. I guess she didn't go blind until she got cataracts. People say she could see if she had them removed, but she won't. She's too stingy."

"If I couldn't see, I would do anything to be able to see again," Steve said in disbelief.

"Me, too," I said. "Being blind would be the worst handicap. I would much rather be deaf."

"Yeah. At least you could read lips to know what people were saying, or it could be written down for you to read," Steve speculated. "Not being able to see would be awful."

We had reached my front porch, and I took a seat on the edge of the porch near the steps. Steve sat beside me. I realized that he was really cute. Usually, I had difficulty talking to boys, but not with Steve. It seemed we could talk about everything, and I think we did. It was one o'clock when we first sat down on the porch, and we talked for hours, not realizing how late it had gotten.

At around three o'clock, Brenda came down the alley on her bicycle. She had been up at Betsy's house. She rode her bicycle into our driveway, got off, and leaned it against the clothesline pole because the kick stands on our bikes didn't hold very well in our dirt driveway. As she walked through the yard toward us, I said, "That's my sister, Brenda". To Brenda I said, "This is Steve; he's staying up in one of Tate's cabins for the rest of the summer."

"Hi," Steve said to Brenda as he leaned out around me to see her better.

"Hi," she answered and then took a seat on the porch swing.

Steve and I continued talking. We discovered that we both loved the Beatles. I told him about how Betsy and I had ridden the bus into Lewistown at around nine o'clock in the morning and waited in line until one o'clock for the movie *Help* to begin. We were the first ones in line at the Embassy Theater. It was located across the street from Murphy's Five and Dime store. Prior to the start of the movie, the line of people extended for several blocks. Friends of ours begged us to let them in line, but we told them it wouldn't be fair for the people behind us. After much harassment, though, we eventually did allow Dave and Jeff Ryan in line in front of us. Steve then told me about seeing the movie in Bellefonte. To this day, I cannot think of that movie without thinking about Steve.

Brenda contributed some to our conversation from time to time, but to me it was as if she wasn't there. I had a huge crush on Steve already. I never knew a boy like him. He was so easy and fun to talk to. Usually, I thought boys were boring and childish. The boys in my seventh grade class seemed so immature. They would have farting contests, and then sit and giggle about the noise and stink. I couldn't imagine Steve acting like that. I definitely liked that boy.

We were still sitting on the porch talking when Dad pulled into the driveway. "That's my dad," I said. I suddenly felt awkward because I didn't know how Dad would respond to Steve's presence.

As Dad walked around the side of the house carrying his lunchbox, Steve said, "Hi."

"Hi," Dad responded.

"This is Steve, Dad. He and his family are staying in Tate's cabins until school starts. They're from Bellefonte," I informed Dad.

"Is that so," Dad said. "How do you like it around here?" he asked Steve.

"We just got here today, but it seems real nice," Steve responded.

"You'll have to get the girls to show you around," Dad said as he went into the house.

"That's a good idea," Steve declared as Dad disappeared.

"I know," I said. "Maybe tomorrow we could go on a walk out Lingle Valley Road. I could show you where the reservoir is located and the cave on top of the mountain."

"That sounds great," Steve said with enthusiasm. "What time do you want to leave?"

"Well...it should be fairly early because it will take a while," I said very seriously.

"How's nine?" Steve asked.

"That's good, and I'll make some sandwiches. We'll have a picnic!" It was really beginning to sound like fun.

"Great! I'll bring some drinks," Steve added. He then turned sideways and asked Brenda, "Are you going to come along?"

"I don't know," Brenda answered as she continued pushing the swing with her feet. "Nine o'clock is pretty early. It depends on what time I get up."

"What about your brothers?" I asked.

"I doubt if they'll want to go. They're planning on Mom dropping them off at the Burnham pool for the day," Steve explained.

The Burnham pool was the closest public swimming pool in the area. Sometimes Betsy, Cathy, Brenda, and I went swimming there. They had a juke box that constantly blasted the latest music. On several occasions that summer, we had ridden the bus to my aunt's house and then walked down to the pool. Dad had picked us up on his way home from work. I hadn't been back to the pool since Grandma died. It was funny how her death always found its way into my thoughts.

Steve and I agreed to meet at my house at nine the next morning to begin our journey. After finalizing our plans, Steve said he had to go back to the cabin, and I told him I would have to help Dad cook supper. I was glad I had met Steve. He seemed very nice.

That night I could think of nothing but Steve. He had to be the friendliest, smartest, cutest boy I had ever met. I couldn't wait until the next day when I could spend more time with him. I was feeling emotions I had never felt before. I thought that he liked me, too. Suddenly, the world looked brighter, even with the gloom of Grandma's death still hanging over me. Things definitely seemed better.

At the supper table, Dad told Mom about our visitor that day. Mom asked a bunch of questions about Steve. When I told her we were going on a hike and having a picnic the next day, she was somewhat reluctant to permit it. "Please," I pleaded. "We already made plans, and he'll be here tomorrow at nine. I can't not go now!" I exclaimed.

Dad helped me out by saying, "Oh Lucy, I think it will be all right. He seems like a real nice kid, and he's Linda's age." Dad was like that, very unpredictable. Just when I was convinced that he didn't like me at all, he would defend me and my actions.

"Well...if you think it's okay, I guess it's all right," Mom said. "Are you going too?" she asked Brenda.

"I don't know yet," Brenda responded.

"Just be careful," Mom cautioned me. "And make sure you watch for snakes; they'll be out, as hot as it has been."

"I will," I promised, while thinking, *Why does she always have to mention snakes?*

I tossed and turned all night. It seemed as though morning would never arrive. That was definitely the most excitement I had felt in a long time. It seemed like I had lost the ability to feel since Grandma's death. Maybe I would be all right after all. Maybe the medicine was working.

The next morning, Steve arrived right on time, and knocked at the front door. I was all ready to go. Mom had fried the bacon for me before she went to work, and I had made us each a BLT and packed them in a brown paper bag. I also had some pretzels.

"Hi," I said as I opened the door, went out onto the porch with my goodies, and closed the door behind me.

"Hi," Steve said. "It looks like it's going to be a nice day."

"I know. I watched the weather this morning, and they're not calling for any rain."

"Great! I brought us each a can of Coke," Steve informed me.

"I brought BLTs. Do you like them?" I asked.

"Yeah, I really do," Steve replied as we excitedly began our trip, walking out Lingle Valley Road. I explained to Steve about the reservoir. It was operated by the Municipal Water Authority of Lewistown where my dad worked, and it was one of the reservoirs that provided the water supply for Milroy,

Reedsville, Burnham, and Lewistown. It was approximately one mile out Lingle Valley Road from our house.

When we reached the bridge that crossed over Lingle Run, we stopped to throw stones into the water. I told Steve, "This is my favorite place to think. I sit there on the stone steps and listen to the water."

He said, "I can understand that because it is peaceful and quiet here. There is just something about running water that makes me feel good."

On the other side of the bridge, the Thomas' farmhouse was on the right, and their barn was on the left side of the road. We had to pass through their orchard that lined both sides of the road. A stone wall served as the fence that separated the orchard from the road on both sides. There was a small herd of Black Angus cattle in the field on the right after we passed the orchard. As we approached the animals, I told Steve about the time Betsy, Cathy, and Brenda dared me to ride the bull we called Jesse. I took the dare and rode the bull, even though I was terrified. Steve thought that was hilarious. He kept asking, "You really rode it?"

"Yeah, I did." I said. I could hardly believe it myself. It was a miracle that I had not been hurt. My parents would have killed me if they had known.

We continued out to the corner where the road made a very sharp turn to the right and then another very sharp turn back to the left. At the first sharp turn, at the left, there was an archery range. On Saturdays and Sundays when the weather was nice, there were archery tournaments. Brenda and I sometimes walked through the range when no one was there, looking for lost arrows. I told Steve about some of the arrows we had found in the past. He said that looking for arrows sounded like fun. It was fun! We planned to do that before Steve left.

There were thick woods on both sides of the road after we passed the second turn. The woods extended for about half a mile to the reservoir road that was on the left. That, too, was a dirt road that went straight down the hill between rows of white pines on each side.

Often when Brenda and I walked out there with Dad, we would see white-tailed deer in the pines. At the bottom of the hill, there was a crystal clear stream that flowed quietly into the reservoir. It was a pretty scene. Thick green grass and wildflowers grew along the bank.

At the bottom of the hill, the dead end road ran parallel with the stream as they both stretched to the base of the reservoir. The dam was only about eight feet high, and the water flowed down over the dam into a large, shallow pool. Often Brenda, Dad, and I would walk Brownie and Spot to that spot, and they always ran into the water to get a drink. There was a path that entered the woods at the edge of the water; Dad had taken us for many walks on that path. That day, I had decided to share the path with Steve. "Follow me," I instructed as I led the way into the woods.

As Steve followed my lead, he asked, "Where are we going?"

"Just follow me," I called as I continued into the woods. It was a beautiful pristine setting. Mountain laurel lined the path on both sides, and eventually, the path led back to the water. A huge hemlock pine tree had fallen across the stream right where it snaked back to the left. Brenda and I had crossed that log many times. On the other side of the stream was a steep bank. The path continued at the bottom of the bank, and farther into the woods, it started up the mountain. If you followed the path to its end, you would be at the upper end of Milroy.

Steve caught up to me at the log. "Wow!" he exclaimed. "This is great. Can we cross the log?" he asked excitedly.

"Sure," I said. "But only if you're not afraid," I teased.

"I'm not afraid," he insisted.

"Okay then. I'll go first," I told him. There was a special technique needed to cross the log without falling off. When I was much younger, I would straddle the log and work my way across it. As I got older, though, I got braver and began walking across. When the whole gang came there, we would jump on the log and try to make each other fall in. We all had our turns at falling in. The log was only about four feet off the ground. No one got seriously injured.

I started across the log first. There were spots of moss growing on the tree that could be very slippery. Also, there were bare spots where the bark had fallen off that were slippery. "Watch out for the moss and bare spots," I warned as I reached the halfway point. When I got to the other side, I stopped, turned around, and waited for Steve to cross. "Come on," I called.

"Has anyone ever fallen in?" he asked.

"Sure, everyone I've ever been here with fell in at least once," I informed him. "Just watch out for the moss and the bare spots, and go slowly since this is your first time across." Steve slowly started across the log, placing one foot beside the other very deliberately. He eventually made it halfway across. "You're halfway now," I encouraged. "Keep coming."

He kept looking at his feet, refusing to look up at me. Once he almost lost his balance, but regained control. "I made it!" he exclaimed as he took his last step off the log and jumped down to the ground near me. "That was fun."

"Yeah, I liked it, too. Come on now. There's a nice spot up ahead where we can have a picnic. I don't think we have time to go to the cave. It's on the other mountain. Let's just follow this path today, and maybe another day we can go to the cave."

"That sounds good to me," Steve said. "Do you come out here often?" he asked.

"I used to come out here a lot with my dad and sister. Mom would even come along sometimes. Lately, though, I haven't been here much." Actually, I hadn't been out there since before Grandma had gotten sick, but I didn't know if I wanted to share that with Steve.

As we started on the first switchback on the mountain path, there was a large mossy area in a group of white pines that I suggested would be a perfect place for a picnic. Steve agreed. Neither of us had thought of bringing a blanket or a table cloth; after all, we were just kids, and kids didn't think about that stuff.

We both sat down on the moss and set up our feast. Food always tastes better outside. I took the sandwiches out of the bag and handed one to Steve. I then opened the package of pretzels and laid them between us to share. Steve pulled the cokes and a can opener out of his bag. He said, "I have a surprise, too." Then he pulled out two Mallow Cups. "Do you like Mallow Cups?" he asked.

I love Mallow Cups," I replied. We sat there for the next fifteen minutes or so devouring our feast. It was perfect in my opinion. Steve was just wonderful. He chatted as we ate and continued chatting when the food was gone. He never seemed to have any difficulty communicating. It was easy for me to talk to him, too. That was the most fun I'd had since before Grandma got sick.

Suddenly, a dark thought threatened to ruin the day, for I remembered that he would be leaving at the end of the month. I forced the thought from my mind because I didn't want to put a damper on our fun. Bellefonte really wasn't that far away, but to children with no transportation, it might as well have been on the other side of the world.

Eventually, we stood up and continued on our journey. When we came out of the woods, we could see Route 322. It had been so pleasant that I hated for it to be over. We still had to return home, but we would follow Route 322 back to Mount Pleasant. Somehow, it just would not be as wonderful as walking through the woods alone.

When we got back to Lingle Valley Road, Steve said, "This sure was a great day. The picnic was really nice. Maybe we can do it again before I leave," he added.

"I hope we can," I said. We had reached his cabin, and as we parted, I said, "See you later." He jumped the fence, and I continued down the road. That would be a day I would never forget. Steve would be a boy I would never forget.

Chapter 11

Steve and I saw each other every day for the next week. I could hardly wait to see him each day. I awoke when I heard Dad and Mom getting ready for work, but I continued to lay in bed until they had gone. When I was certain that they had left, I jumped out of bed, dressed, and watched TV until a respectable hour to go out to wait and watch for Steve. He would jump the fence and come down to our front porch after he had his breakfast. We discussed everything there on my front porch that August of 1965, and there was plenty to discuss. Brenda sometimes joined us, but most of the time, she went to Cathy's or Betsy's. I was still being treated for depression, but if you had asked me then, Steve was the best cure in the world. I just wished that August would never end

On Monday, August 9th, Steve and I had planned on climbing to the cave on top of the mountain. Summer wasn't the best time to be doing that because snakes might have been out, and my mother never failed to remind me of that. For that reason, I did not tell her of our plans to climb the mountain. Most likely, she would have forbidden it.

As usual, after Mom and Dad left for work, I got up. I was particularly nervous that day since I knew I was planning to do something my mother would not approve of. Steve knocked at our front door at about nine o'clock. I was ready to go. I answered the door and stepped onto the front porch with the lunch bag I had packed for us. This time I had made bologna sandwiches. In addition, I had two five-cent bags of Middlesworth chips. We would have a real spread. Steve, as he had promised, brought two cans of Coke.

"Come on," I said as I started out Lingle Valley.

Steve followed me off the porch, caught up to me in the alley, and walked beside me as we headed out on our journey. We stopped again on the bridge to throw in a few stones, and were on our way. It was very pretty in Lingle Valley that morning. As we walked through the orchard, we could hear robins calling to each other. We also could hear the buzz of honeybees as they flew from wildflower to wildflower that lined the dirt road on both sides. The Black Angus cattle were out in the field on our right.

It looked like a still life painting; it was absolutely beautiful. Neither Steve nor I spoke for several minutes as we drank in the sights and sounds around us. Finally, Steve asked, "Is it always this pretty out here?" It was more of a statement than a question, though, so I let it go unanswered. As we rounded the bend, I pointed up the hill and informed Steve, "That's where we'll be going--straight up that hill."

"Really!" Steve responded. "It looks kind of steep."

"It is steep," I informed him. "We can make it, though. It's the shortest way," I added as I began my assent up the hillside.

Steve followed close behind. The hill was known as "Dew Berry Hill" by the local kids, and many times we had ridden our sleds down that huge hill with half the kids from Milroy. It was great! Near the top of the hill, the white pine trees began getting denser. We worked our way through the branches as we continued up the hill. It was getting steeper as the hill turned into the mountain. The more we climbed, the steeper it got. We continued climbing in silence since we didn't want to waste our breath on talking. At last the trees ended, and there was nothing but huge rocks.

That part frightened me because my mother had done her job, and I was absolutely terrified of snakes. I couldn't even stand to look at them on TV or in books. So I cautiously jumped from stone to stone. I couldn't help myself when I warned Steve to "watch for snakes." I couldn't believe that came from my mouth; I really was my mother's daughter.

Steve wasn't frightened, though. "I'm not afraid of snakes," he announced. Well, at least he said he wasn't. I just hoped I didn't have to find out if it were true.

We continued upward over the rocks until finally, we had reached the top. The place I referred to as the top was a huge boulder where my friends and I had gone many times. I pointed out to Steve that we could see my house from where we were standing and a few of Tate's cabins.

"This is really neat," Steve proclaimed. "I feel like I'm at the top of the world."

We were both hot and sweaty. I wasn't accustomed to climbing in the summer. I was sure glad when Steve sat down beside me on the big rock and pulled out the two cans of Coke. As we both eagerly opened our cans with his can opener and gulped our drinks, we didn't even mind that it was lukewarm. After satisfying my thirst, I opened the lunch bag and pulled out our bologna sandwiches and chips. The salt in the meat and chips again made us thirsty, so we enthusiastically finished the remainder of our Cokes. When we finished, we packed all of our garbage back into the bag to take back down the mountain with us. Dad had always taught Brenda and me to keep the woods clean.

Steve and I continued sitting on the rock, admiring the scenery for quite a while. I told him about how Deb and I planned to come up here to hide out if we ever had a nuclear attack. That subject fascinated him, and we discussed all the different things that could happen if such a tragedy ever occurred. Steve said he would come to the rock, too, and bring his family with him. We planned how his family and mine would start a new world because everyone else would have been killed. That conversation led to the discussion about the cave.

"Come on," I said. "I'll show you where the cave is, but you have to promise never to tell anyone else. It must remain a secret."

"I promise," Steve stated with his right hand raised.

"Then follow me," I said as I led the way to the cave. I had misgivings about entering the cave because snakes might be in there, but I didn't want Steve to think I was afraid. Near the entrance I stopped and said, "There it is."

"Well, let's go in," Steve said excitedly.

"Go ahead," I said, stepping back. "I'll follow you."

Steve headed toward the cave. There were several smaller boulders near the entrance, and you had to jump from one to the other to get there. As I jumped from the one boulder, my foot slipped, and I partially fell until I caught myself with my hands on another boulder. Steve saw what had happened and made his way back to the boulder where I had slipped. He extended his right hand to me, and I reached out to take it. As our hands touched, I swear I could feel a current going through me. I never had a boy touch me like that. I felt as though I had floated up from the boulder. I wondered if Steve could feel it. As I regained my balance, I anticipated that Steve would drop my hand. I was surprised that he didn't. Instead, he held my hand tighter and pulled me toward him; then, as he jumped from boulder to boulder back toward the entrance, he gently pulled me after him.

As we made our final jump to the entrance, I fell against Steve's shoulder when he pulled me after him. I had never been that close to a boy. I didn't know how to act. I felt very strange and awkward. "I'm sorry," I said with embarrassment as he dropped my hand.

"That's okay. No harm done," Steve answered. We then explored the cave together and again talked about what a great hideout it would make. Something was different, though. I found it was more difficult for me to talk to Steve. I couldn't look straight at him any more. I guess I was afraid he could see how I felt. I wondered if he felt the same way.

Finally, both of us agreed that we better start back down the mountain. It was much easier going down than up. Steve helped me over the difficult obstacles the entire way down. It sure was nice having someone take care of me like that. I really liked Steve. He was the only boy I had ever felt that way about. I sort of did about Harold Eckley in sixth grade when he had my name written on his eraser, but it still wasn't like it was with Steve.

When we got back onto Lingle Valley Road, we talked and laughed as we continued to walk back home. At the alley, we stopped, and Steve said, "I have to get home."

"I do, too," I said. Neither of us had any idea what time it was, but we sensed it was late. "I'll see you later," I said as we separated and I walked toward my house.

"Yeah, see you later," Steve responded as he continued his walk up the hill.

As I approached our house, I could see the back of Dad's vehicle in our driveway. It was even later than I thought. I hoped it wasn't too late to help with cooking supper. When I stepped onto the front porch, I could smell something cooking in the kitchen, and I could hear Brenda's and Dad's voices coming through the open kitchen window as they noisily prepared supper.

When I entered the house, Dad looked into the living room and said, "It's about time you got here. Where have you been?"

"I took a walk with Steve and didn't realize it was so late," I answered.

"Well, you'll have to do the dishes all by yourself since I had to do your job now," Brenda declared.

"Okay," I said. That sounded like a bargain to me. I would be willing to do much more than that to spend a day with Steve.

"Just make sure you do, then," Dad added. They were cooking chicken and corn-on-the-cob. It smelled great, but I realized that I wasn't very hungry. All I could do was think about Steve.

When Mom arrived, we all sat down for supper. Mom and Dad were chatting throughout the meal, but I don't think I heard anything they said. My thoughts were on Steve. Boy, what a difference one person can make in your life. Suddenly, I felt that life was worth living again. It seemed like the terrible weight I had felt upon me had been lifted. My spirit was soaring. I forgot that I was also taking mood elevation mediation.

I continued to take my pills for depression, and they seemed to be helping. Whenever I started feeling sad again, I would think about Steve, and I would be happy again. I hardly saw Cathy and Betsy in August. I was too busy spending my time with Steve. Brenda and I were on our own during the day, so I don't think Mom and Dad realized how much time I was spending with Steve. Cathy and Betsy weren't interested in him; they liked his brothers. Brenda liked to hang out with Cathy and Betsy through the day, but she had no interest in any of the boys.

Steve and I made numerous trips out through Lingle Valley while I showed him all the sights in the area. He always seemed interested and had lots and lots of questions. I showed him where Brenda and I once saw a flock of wild turkeys cross the road in front of us, and told him how we followed them up Dew Berry Hill as they ran from us and escaped onto the mountain. He laughed as I told him they were taller than I was, but I believed they were.

I also took Steve to the spot where I had last seen Whitey; he was Brownie's brother. Dad had allowed Brenda and me to each choose a puppy from a liter of pups that Mid's dog had. Mid had been a neighbor of ours when we lived near Shreader. They were mutts, but we didn't care; we still loved them. When they were full-grown, Dad had taken them both rabbit hunting with him.

Once while we were walking out through Lingle Valley, Whitey chased a groundhog into his burrow on the side of a hill. We could hear his muffled barks inside the hill. We never saw him come back out. I refused to believe he had died in that hole. I insisted we just hadn't seen him come back out. For weeks, I would walk out through Lingle Valley calling for Whitey. He never came to me.

In addition, I showed Steve where the ground pine grew and told him how I gathered it at Christmas time to make wreaths. We visited where the raspberries and blueberries grew, too. Our tour included visiting "up back" where Grandma had lived. I even took him to her old house, and told him about playing on the cement walk and wall in back.

I showed him where the Lewises lived, and told him about Mr. Lewis' pet snakes that terrified Grandma. He laughed with me when I told him about how she threatened to hit Mr. Lewis on the head with a frying pan if he ever got the snakes near her. I related how she had once told me about Mrs. Lewis finding dead baby racer snakes behind a dresser in her bedroom. That's when she made Mr. Lewis move his snakes to the garage. I explained how he even bought snakes. He had someone bring him a glass snake from Florida. My mother, my grandma, and I thought the man was crazy.

Once after one of our trips, we stopped in at Leeper's store to get a soda and bag of chips. As we sat on the porch eating our snack, I reminisced, "Whenever I would ride my bike up to visit Grandma, she would always give me some money so that I could stop here on the way home."

"Really...What did happened to her anyway?" he asked.

His question shook me and made me feel as though a knife had entered my chest, for I felt a sharp stabbing pain. When the pain had passed, I quietly said, "She died."

Steve wasn't stupid; he immediately picked up on my sudden mood change. "I'm very sorry," he said. "You don't have to talk about it if you don't want to," he added as he gently placed his hand on my shoulder. His touch and compassion melted my heart. No one ever wanted to talk to me about Grandma's death. I was ready to share my story with Steve.

As we sat there on Leeper's porch that hot August afternoon, I began telling Steve all about Grandma's illness. "The trouble began when Grandma discovered a lump on her left side," I related. "Mom made an appointment for her to see Dr. McNabb. He told her she would have to go to the hospital for tests. After that, they told her she had to have an operation. After her operation, she was too sick to live alone, so she came to live with us. She had cancer."

"Did you like her living with you?" Steve asked.

"Yes, I was glad she came to live with us. I have three uncles who could have taken her, but they didn't want to. They wouldn't even help take her to the hospital for her radiation treatments," I said bitterly.

"That's mean," Steve commented. "What was her name?" he asked.

"Sallie Irene," I answered.

"That's a pretty name."

"She gave me this ring," I said as I showed him her signet ring on my left hand. He took my hand as he looked at the ring. "See, you can see the S, I, & M. Merrill was her maiden name," I said, feeling a rush of emotion from his touch.

"They are really fancy letters," Steve commented as he gently released my hand.

"Yeah, they are," I said, staring down at the ring. "Anyway, she just kept getting sicker and sicker. Her treatments didn't help her. Mom or Dad always had to stay with her because she couldn't be left alone. My one uncle, the least mean one, did take her for about a month, but then he brought her back and dropped her off without even telling us he was coming or talking to us when he brought her back. It was really sad because Grandma cried," I said, my voice beginning to crack.

"That would be sad," Steve said. "Your dad must be nice."

"He is," I said. "At least most of the time." I didn't want to tell him about Dad's temper.

"I'm glad he didn't act like his brothers. They even had the nerve to go to her funeral after they wouldn't visit her when she was sick. I just wanted to kick them out of there. I hope I never see them again," I announced.

"I don't blame you. That was terrible for them to do that. How did they act at the funeral?" Steve asked.

"That was the most disgusting part. They just stood around and talked about cars and stuff just like she wasn't even there. No one even cried, except me," I stated as my voice again cracked.

"I cried at my grandfather's funeral," Steve told me. "Lots of people were crying though, especially my mother. He was her father."

That information made me like Steve even more. He cried, too, and he didn't even think anything was wrong with that. After several moments had passed, I said, "I sure don't like funerals."

"Me neither," Steve said as he picked up his bottle of Hire's Root Beer and finished the last swig.

"Did you ever wonder where the dead people are?" I asked.

"Yeah...Where do *you* think they are?" Steve asked me.

"I'm not sure, but I hope they're in heaven like everyone says they are. Don't you?" I asked.

"Sure I do, but what do you think heaven is like?" Steve asked me as he looked upward toward the hazed August sky.

"It's hard to picture it. They say the streets are made of gold, and there are all kinds of jewels everywhere. All animals of all kinds will get along with each other, too, but I sure hope there aren't any snakes."

Steve declared, "There won't be. The snakes will be in Hell because they are evil."

"That's true!" I exclaimed. "The devil was a snake when he tempted Eve."

"Do you think people still have their bodies in heaven since we bury them?" Steve asked.

"No," I stated with certainty. "The Bible says we will get new bodies."

"That's good because most people who die are old and they need new bodies," Steve said.

"They say there will be no tears in heaven," I continued. "I think that's good." I was holding onto the banister while I sat there and leaned back and continued looking at the sky.

"Yes, that is good. There will be no more sadness, no murder or anything bad. I hope I will know who my grandfather is since he'll have a new body," Steve reflected.

"I think we will know the ones who die before us because if we didn't, we would be sad, and there will be no sadness," I reasoned.

"Yeah, that's right," Steve agreed.

"Did you ever touch a dead person?" I asked.

"No...Did you?"

"No. But I wish I would have touched Grandma. I wish I would have said good-bye to her, too, before she died," I added.

"I didn't tell my grandfather good-bye, either. I visited him in the hospital, but he was in a coma, so I didn't say anything. I used to spend the night at his and Grandma's house before he got sick. I never stay anymore because it's too sad," Steve informed me. "I miss him."

I had discovered that Steve and I shared many of the same feelings. Maybe I was normal, after all. I told him, "I miss Grandma, too. Sometimes I get so sad, I cry. I was crying so much that they took me to a doctor, and he gave me some medicine. It helps some, but I still get sad and cry, just not as much." It was just so easy talking to Steve. I wondered why it seemed so difficult to talk to others. How could I tell him so much?

Steve said, "Yeah, I get really sad, too..."

We both sat there for several minutes thinking about our discussion as the vehicles on Route 322 continued to whiz by us.

"Well, I guess I better be getting home. I have no idea what time it is," I said, as I jumped down from Leeper's porch and looked at the sky.

"Yeah, me too," Steve said. "Dad is coming home early today and we're going out to eat somewhere."

"You're lucky. We hardly ever go out to eat. I'll have to help cook supper since Mom's at work," I told him.

As we parted, Steve took a left and continued walking along Route 322 to Tate's cabins, and I crossed Route 322 and took the shortcut down over the hill by Cathy's trailer. I felt as though a burden had been lifted from my shoulders since I shared my feelings with Steve. He really was an incredible person. I would miss him so much when he returned to Bellefonte.

When I got home, I learned it was three o'clock. Dad wasn't home yet. As I entered the empty house, a wave of sadness washed over me. I never liked to enter an empty house. Brenda wasn't home, either. I assumed she was still visiting Cathy or Betsy. It was kind of spooky. I felt as though there were ghosts present. They weren't bad ghosts, but they were still scary. I wished Mom didn't work. I liked it better when she was home.

Before Mom worked, she always had supper cooked when Dad got home. Brenda and I never had to help. Her cooking was much better than ours, too. It wasn't as lonely then. I hated those feelings of loneliness. As soon as I began feeling that way, I would become depressed. Steve helped to take some of those feelings away, but Steve would be leaving soon. I wished he could stay forever.

I felt the tears come to my eyes. Mom would be home soon to give me my last pill for the day. I was so happy when I was with Steve; I wondered why I couldn't remain that way.

Chapter 12

As the end of August approached, my anxiety grew because I realized Steve would be leaving soon. We would be returning to school the day after Labor Day, so Steve's family was planning to leave sometime that holiday weekend.

On Thursday, the day before the holiday weekend began, Steve and I again planned to meet on my front porch before going off on a day of adventure. It was nine-thirty when I heard a knock at our front door, and I opened the door to find Steve standing there.

"Hi," he greeted me.

"Hi," I responded as I went outside onto the front porch.

"What do you feel like doing today?" he asked.

"I don't know. What do you feel like doing?" I asked.

"I have some money. Let's go up to Leeper's and get some candy," he stated.

"All right," I replied. "We can hang-out on her porch for a while," I suggested as we began walking through the alley.

We took our usual route, the shortcut by Cathy's trailer and between the Carsons' and Havices' houses. Inside Leeper's store, we had difficultly deciding what kind of penny candy to spend Steve's money on. We eventually ended up with quite an assortment of different candy. As we sat on Leeper's porch watching the traffic pass by, Steve shared the bag of candy with me.

He took a piece of black licorice out of his bag and handed it to me for he knew I loved black licorice. "Thanks," I said as I bit into the candy.

While my taste buds savored one of my most favorite tastes in the world, Steve reluctantly informed me, "We're leaving tomorrow."

No other explanation was necessary; those few words said it all. That was the moment I had wanted to postpone forever. For several minutes, I was speechless. When I could again speak, I spoke slowly and deliberately.

"I wish you could stay forever," I said with the most sincerity I had felt in my entire life. "We've had a lot of fun, and I'm really going to miss you," I continued as I struggled not to cry.

"I know. I'll miss you, too," Steve said, looking at his feet dangling over the edge of the porch to avoid looking into my eyes. "We can write. I'll give you my address before we leave. Who knows; we might come back next summer," he hopefully added.

I think we both knew, though, that our meeting the following summer would never happen. Bellefonte might as well have been on another planet as far as we were concerned; we couldn't drive, and our lives would move away from each other in different directions. I could not stand to think about it anymore, so I suggested, "Let's go look at the fish."

Rothrock's Tropical Fish store was right next door to Leeper's, so we walked over and entered the store. The bell attached to the door rang as we entered, and Mrs. Rothrock looked up from the book she was reading. She asked, "What can I help you with today?"

"We just want to look at the fish," Steve informed her.

"All right. Just don't touch the tanks," Mrs. Rothrock instructed.

For the next fifteen or twenty minutes, we studied the different species of tropical fish swimming in their varying environments of colored stones, glass bridges, and artificial plants as we stopped at each aquarium. There were guppies, swordtails, platy fish, black mollies, barbs, danios, rasboras, characins, cichlids, and, of course, goldfish. The main attraction was the piranha because that species was known as "man eaters." Steve and I stood looking at the piranha and speculated about how horrible it would be to get thrown into a river full of them.

Everything I did with Steve seemed fun and interesting. He made all kinds of comments about almost every fish there was. I sure would miss him. When we had visited each tank, we had completed the circle around the perimeter of the store that led us back to the door we had entered. As we exited, Steve said to Mrs. Rothrock, "Thanks for letting us look at the fish."

"Oh, you're quite welcome," she replied. "Do you have any tropical fish?"

"No, but I sure would like to get some," he said.

"Maybe you should ask your parents to buy some for you," she suggested.

"I might do that," Steve replied as we went outside, and he closed the door behind us.

There were two twenty-five gallon, in-ground tanks in the yard about twenty feet from the front door. Steve and I stopped at the tank on the left first to see if we could see the several large goldfish that Mrs. Rothrock kept in those tanks. The fish were there swimming around. After watching them for a few minutes, we moved to that tank on the right; there were still some goldfish in that tank, also. We watched them for a few minutes, too.

On two previous occasions that August, in the evening after the store had closed, Steve and I had gone to those tanks and attempted to catch those large goldfish in our hands while we lay stretched out on our stomachs on the ground with our heads and arms extended over the tanks. We had actually had one or two of the fish in our hands, but then they would slip away and fall back into the tank. I'm sure Mrs. Rothrock would not have appreciated our fishing expeditions. It was great fun for us, however. If we would have caught the fish, we were planning on releasing them back into the tank.

After leaving the fish store, Steve and I crossed Route 322 and walked down to the bridge over Lingle Valley Run. We both took a seat on one of the stone steps at the side; I sat on the top one, and Steve sat on the next one below it. He fished the candy bag out of his back pocket, and we finished eating the remaining candy as we talked about our adventures that summer. We sat there for a few hours laughing and reminiscing. Things then turned serious, as the time to leave approached.

"Linda, you've been my best friend this summer, and I will never forget you," Steve said as he continued to stare into the water.

"You've been my best friend, too. You're the only one I've been able to talk to about Grandma and my feelings. It's just so easy to talk to you," I told Steve, as I stared into the water, too.

Several moments passed before either one of us dared to speak again.

"I better get back to the camp," Steve said as he slowly stood up and finally looked into my eyes.

As he looked at me, I, too, stood up beside him and looked into his eyes. He was slightly taller than I was, so I had to look up because he had moved onto my step beside me. Steve reached out his right hand and took my right hand in his. "I'll come down tomorrow morning to say good-bye," he told me, still holding onto my hand.

"Okay," I managed to choke out of my mouth as I fought the huge lump in my throat. I moved on up the hill to get onto Lingle Valley Road. That forced Steve to let go of my hand as he followed me. We then walked side-by-side as he walked me back to the alley that led to my house. When we arrived there, he said, "Please write down your address for me, and I'll give you mine tomorrow so we can write."

"I will," I said as we parted, and he headed up the hill while I continued to our house. I was beginning to miss him already.

When I returned to the house, I noticed that Dad's car was in the driveway. I was becoming very emotional and didn't want him to notice, so I went around to the back porch and took a seat on the flowered cushioned chair. From that position, I could see the cabin where Steve was staying. Their station wagon was parked beside the cabin. No one was outside. I began getting depressed as I realized that after the next day, I no longer would see their car parked there; worse yet, I no longer would see *Steve*.

After I sat there staring at their car for about a half hour, I stood up, went into the house through the back door, and sat down in Grandma's old bedroom. I could hear Dad in the next room watching TV. It wasn't time yet to cook supper. As I sat there in the same spot where Grandma's bed had been, memories of her floated through my mind. I found myself wondering why we had to lose people we loved. I would have liked things to have stayed the same forever. I knew it wasn't realistic to think like that, but there was still enough child in me to want it just the same.

Throughout the evening, every time I thought about Steve, a great sadness would engulf me. I tried my best to block out the feelings, but I wasn't able to do it. Usually on Friday nights, I would stay up late watching the *Late Show* on television, but that night I wanted to be alone with my feelings, so I slipped out of the living room and went to bed early. When I was safely in my bed, I allowed my tears their freedom, and they flowed profusely down my cheeks. I missed Grandma terribly; I missed Mom when she worked, and I was going to miss Steve, too. That all was bad enough, but I also knew school would be starting for me in a few days, and I didn't want to go back.

So much had changed over the summer; I wasn't the same person. Since Grandma's death, I saw things differently. I had begun to see the cruelty all around me. I suppose I was growing up; I wasn't sure I liked it.

The next morning when I awoke, I quickly got out of bed and dressed in a two-piece baby-blue shorts outfit. Then I went downstairs to the bathroom to wash my face, comb my hair, and brush my teeth. I left the bathroom and went into the living room to find a pen and paper. When I located them, I jotted down my address and returned the pen to the drawer in the coffee table. I didn't want to miss Steve, so I went out the back door to make sure their car was still there; it was.

It was only eight-thirty so I sat on the back porch, waiting for Steve. I hadn't eaten any breakfast, but I didn't feel hungry. In fact, it felt like I had butterflies in my stomach. Shortly after nine o'clock, I saw Steve jump the fence and head down the hill. I called to him, "Steve, I'm here on the porch."

"Okay," he answered. "I'll be around in a minute," and he continued down Lingle Valley Road and then approached our house from the alley. He still didn't trust our dogs enough to take the shortcut through their territory. When he reached the back porch, he proceeded up the steps and walked over and sat in the porch chair beside mine. "Hi," he said as he handed me a slip of paper with his address on it.

I took the paper and handed him the one I had prepared for him. "My parents said I have to be back in a few minutes," Steve told me.

"Oh," is all I could manage.

We sat in silence, both wondering what to say. "Well, I better be going," Steve said, and he stood up and looked down at me.

I stood up, too, and looked at him for a few moments before I said, "I'll miss you."

"I'll miss you, too," he said, and before I knew what had happened, he leaned over and kissed me lightly on the cheek. "Good-bye, Linda," he said, then walked over to the steps and began his descent.

I walked over to the edge of the porch and said, "Good-bye, Steve. Have a nice trip home."

"Thanks," he called over his shoulder as he continued out our driveway.

Oh, my God! I thought. *He's really leaving.* I stayed on the back porch until I saw him again jump over the fence and return to the cabin. A few minutes later, he and his family came outside, got into the station wagon, and drove away. Tears rolled down my cheeks, and I thought my heart would break from the pain I was feeling. Even though I only knew Steve for a few weeks, he was the best friend I ever had. He would not be forgotten.

With Steve gone, I knew school would be starting in a few days. I didn't want to think about that, but I could not stop thinking about it. I wished Steve went to my school. It would be nice to have such a great guy at school as my friend. I wouldn't care what else happened as long as I knew Steve was there.

Eventually, I stood up and found my way back into the house. I couldn't shake the sadness that enveloped me. I wondered if it would ever leave again. I was still taking my pills, but I felt lonely and lost. I would learn that even though it felt as if I could not go on, life would indeed continue.

Chapter 14

The following Tuesday was September 6th, the day after Labor Day, and we were returning to school. I had taken one of my pills and was hoping I would make it through the day without any tears as I waited for the bus with the other kids. There were seven of us there that day. I was standing there with both arms wrapped around my new notebook; my weight all shifted to my left leg. That was the way I stood most of the time. There were three boys there: Elmer, Wayne, and Robbie. Elmer and Wayne had laid their book bags on the ground and were standing behind them in Walter's driveway, scuffing the gravel back and forth between their feet. Robbie had plopped his book bag on the ground when he had arrived, and he was sitting on it. Elmer's sister, Brenda, and my sister, Brenda, were standing there with stances similar to mine, just sort of staring at Route 322. They both were going to be in seventh grade, so most likely they were having their own feelings of anxiety.

As we stood there in somewhat of a daze, not quite awake that early in the morning, our bus, Bus 21, came over the crest of the hill beside Jane Carson's house and continued down Route 322, screeching to a halt in front of Lingle Valley Road. As the bus driver, Mr. Brindle, pushed the door opened, we all lined up single file and boarded the bus.

The previous year, I had sat with Betsy, but she wasn't on the bus today. *Maybe her older sister, Francine, drove her to school*, I thought. Cathy was on the bus, and Brenda sat beside her. I continued back the aisle and slid into last year's seat which was the third seat on the left from the back. As I settled into my seat and placed my notebook beside me, a wave of emotion engulfed me.

For no apparent reason, tears began seeping from my eyes. No matter how hard I tried, they continued. I had a small black purse I took with me to carry lunch money, my brush, and, thankfully, a pocket-size packet of tissues. As I slid my hand under the flap of my purse, I felt the plastic cover on the

Kleenex packet, and I pulled a tissue out from between the slit in the front of the packet. I quickly tried to blot the tears without drawing any attention to myself. Somehow I managed to get my tears under control, but I wondered for how long. It looked as though the day would be very, very long.

For the remainder of our trip to school, I struggled to get my emotions under control. I wished I had my pills so I could take another one to calm me down. I didn't want to go to school anymore. When we reached the school, the bus pulled in front of the double doors by the gymnasium and stopped. Mr. Brindle pushed the big silver handle toward the doors and it sprang opened. We exited the bus and headed inside to our homerooms. I was hoping no one noticed that the rims of my eyes were red from my tears.

As I turned left inside the corridor and headed to the stairwell, I remember thinking that I just wanted out of there. There seemed to be no escape. School attendance was mandatory. I still had a five-year sentence remaining. Kids flew by me on all sides. If only I could be like them; but I wasn't. When I reached the stairs, the entrance of which was located across from the home economics kitchen, I slowed because students were entering through the double doors to make their way up the stairs. In addition, other students coming down the stairs were yielding at the doorway and entering the flow of traffic toward the new wing of the high school. My homeroom was in the new wing, Room 181. Mrs. Bratton was my eighth grade homeroom teacher. She taught math. I sat in the first row, fourth seat back in front of Dale Cavanaugh.

My classes that year consisted of, English, reading, math, social studies, science, health, art, music, physical education, and home economics. The only class I liked was phys. ed. I especially loved gymnastics. My flexibility was very good, and I had high endurance. As far as academics, I found them boring. Science was my worst subject. My lunch break was from eleven a.m. until eleven-thirty.

I managed to make it through the first half of the day without any tears, but at lunchtime I felt the effects of my medication wearing off. It was difficult for me to make new friends due to my depression. Most of the time in my eighth grade year, I walked the halls alone.

That was devastating to a twelve-year-old girl when everyone had to belong to something. I believed I was on the outside of everything. The previous year high school had started out so happily, and I had such high expectations. I didn't know what happened.

I eventually made it through the first half of the day, and it was time for lunch. That day when I walked into the cafeteria, there were several hundred kids putting their books in the wooden slots that surrounded the room and taking their seats at the table. Groups of friends were gathering at different tables. There was a lot of laughing and joking, and it was pretty noisy. Tears began forming at the edges of my eyes again as I realized I didn't know where to sit. I lost contact with my grade school friends the previous year because we were in different sections.

I had been starting to adjust to the new school setting and all the social changes that went with it, then Grandma had gotten sick, and I just couldn't successfully make the transition. I was so worried about Grandma during seventh grade that I had never really noticed I was drifting further and further away from my peers. As I stood there considering where I should sit, I realized I didn't feel comfortable going to any of the tables. Finally, I placed my books in one of the book slots, took my place in the lunch line, and waited my turn to go through the kitchen to fill my tray.

They were serving hi-lo sandwiches with bologna, cheese, lettuce and tomato. Also, green beans, chilled peaches, and milk were served. After I passed through the line, I carried my tray over to a group of girls in my class. Deb Metzger was at the edge of the group, so I took a seat beside her. It was difficult for me to take part in the conversation because I was so self-conscious. I was thankful that Deb included me in their discussion about summer vacation.

I managed to make it through lunch and the remainder of the day without any more tears. Some of the rooms had clocks in them, and I found myself checking the time almost every minute. Most classes were fifty minutes long, so it truly did seem like an eternity when I watched the clock that closely.

When I returned home that night, Brenda and I had to help prepare supper before Mom got home from work. Dad asked me to go to the basement and get two cans of kidney beans, diced tomatoes, and tomato paste. We stored our canned vegetables in a white metal cabinet in the basement. Whenever Dad or Mom encountered sales on canned goods, they would stock up on the sale items. Dad also asked me to bring up a one-pound package of hamburger out of the white chest-type freezer in our basement. While I was engrossed in my mission, Brenda was setting the table.

After I gathered all of the items, I went back up the basement stairs, and returned to the kitchen. Dad had taken a skillet from the drawer underneath the stove and placed it on top of the black metal burner. We had a gas stove Mom and Dad had purchased from Suburban Gas Company. The company supplied the propane gas tanks as they were needed. We had two tanks, and when one was empty, Mom would call and have them deliver another tank.

Mom always claimed gas was nicer to cook with than electric because you had better control of the heat.

As Dad placed the hamburger in the skillet to thaw and brown, I opened the cans I had taken upstairs. After the burger was broken apart as it thawed and browned, Dad mixed in the vegetables. He then added some chili powder and garlic salt and allowed the chili to simmer until Mom got home.

Mom generally got home around five forty-five. As soon as she entered the house, she washed her hands in the bathroom sink, and then we would eat. Six o'clock was a late supper for us. Before Mom worked, we usually ate around four o'clock. Even though we were eating two hours later, our lunchtime at school remained the same.

Those two and a half hours between the time I got home from school and when Mom got home from work were lonely and often triggered tears. Dad got home shortly after Brenda and I did, but often he would lie down on the couch and take a nap. His job was physical and exhausting. I remember how isolated I would feel entering a quiet, deserted house. It was even worse when I went through Grandma's old bedroom.

Before we ate that night, Mom gave me another pill. I was glad because I felt I needed it. I was truly struggling to keep from crying, and I didn't know why. Time had become my enemy. It seemed to move so slowly at school, but at home it passed too quickly. I would periodically check the clock and mentally calculate how much time remained before I had to return to school. Logically, I knew that school wouldn't last forever, but emotionally, I didn't feel I could survive its completion. It was extremely painful for me.

How could I explain to anyone how I felt when I didn't understand? How could I tell my parents I didn't want to go to school? How could I tell them how awful some of the students treated me because they perceived me to be different? How could I tell them I didn't feel loved? How could I tell them any of this? I was certain that they would not understand. Those thoughts ran through my mind as the tears again flowed down my cheeks, and I once again looked at the clock on the kitchen wall to calculate how much time remained until I had to go back to my now personal torture-chamber known as high school.

I wiped my eyes on the sleeve of my shirt and hoped by parents hadn't noticed. I was sitting at the kitchen table waiting for everyone to take their seats. My pill hadn't had time to take effect As they sat down, they waited for Brenda and me to ask the blessing. I could hardly get the words out. I hoped they hadn't noticed.

TEARS FOR GRANDMA

    I had to pretend I was eating because I had great difficulty swallowing. I pushed my food around on my plate. I couldn't make it. I lost the battle, and the tears began to flow. I stood up and left the table. My parents said nothing, for they didn't know what to say. I went through Grandma's room on my way to the bathroom to get some tissues and wash my face. I returned to the living room instead of the kitchen, for I had no appetite. I again looked at the clock that set on top of the television set. It was six-fifteen: twelve hours and forty-five minutes until I had to be at the bus stop again. If only I could pray. If only I could find help somewhere.

Chapter 16

I continued to take my pills for the next week, then it was time for my follow-up visit at Dr. McNabb's. The pills helped some with the depression, but there were still tears. I just could not understand my feelings. Everything seemed so overwhelming. Kids in my class were going to the football games, hanging out at the drug store, and having a great time. I wondered why I couldn't be like them.

Thursday night at about five-thirty, we all got into Dad's T-bird and headed down Route 322 to Dr. McNabb's office. Approximately five minutes after we arrived, the nurse came into the waiting room and called, "Jodi Treaster." A middle-aged woman and girl who looked to be about six stood up and followed the nurse into the waiting room. They had the first appointment for the evening. Mom and I were left alone.

It seemed strange to me that Mom never asked me about how I was feeling or what my problems were. Sometimes when I cried, she would get upset and say I had to stop that. She didn't say it with anger; I think she just didn't know how to respond to my tears. I wondered if she knew I didn't feel loved. I was grateful, though, that she defended me when Dad was angry.

Soon the nurse came out and called, "Linda Bishop." Mom and I followed her into her office where she weighed me, took my blood pressure and temperature, recorded all three in my record, and told us to follow her into the examining room. "Linda, go ahead and hop up here," she said as she reached the examining table, and patted the paper that covered it. I did as I was told. "Dr. McNabb will be with you in a few minutes," she said as she turned and exited the room to return to her office. Several minutes later, Dr. McNabb came into the examining room from his office entrance on the other side of the room.

"How are you today?" he asked, as he checked my heart with his stethoscope, and then moved it around to my back.

"Okay," is all I said.

"How are things going?" he continued.

"Okay," I again responded.

"Everything all right at school?" he asked as he picked up his small penlight from the cart beside the table and looked into each of my eyes.

"I guess," I said as I squirmed on the table, making the paper rattle.

"Do the pills help you?" he went on. While he was asking me questions, he would occasionally jot down notes in my chart.

"I...think so."

"You don't sound too certain," he said.

"I don't cry as much," I said.

"What makes you cry?" Dr. McNabb inquired.

"I'm not sure...Sometimes I just get real sad, and I can't stop the tears."

"Are you happy, Linda?"

That question caught me by surprise. I didn't take time to think about my answer; I quickly answered, "no."

"Why aren't you happy?"

"I don't like to go to school. I would like to stay home." I had dropped my head and was looking at my feet. I didn't want to look at my mother.

"You know that you have to go to school, though, don't you?" Dr. McNabb asked softly.

"Yes," I answered and tears began. I tried my best to stop them, but I couldn't. Dr. McNabb handed me a tissue from the box on the table beside us, and I blotted the tears from my face and blew my nose.

"It will get better," he said as he reassuringly patted my leg. "You go back out with my nurse and your mother will be right out."

I did as I was told. Mom stood up as I was leaving. She hadn't said anything so far that visit. The nurse looked up as I entered her office and sat down in the chair across from her desk where Mom had sat earlier. She smiled at me, but said nothing as I continued blotting my tears.

Mom came out of Dr. McNabb's office about ten minutes later. I stood up and went into the waiting room while she paid the nurse. When she came out, we both exited the front door, went down the three stairs, and crossed Logan Street, backtracking our earlier path to where Brenda and Dad were waiting for us in the car. We both got into the car as Dad started the engine. "Well, how did it go?" Dad asked, looking at Mom.

Mom replied, "He said she should continue taking the medication. It will take a while to totally take affect, but it should help." Mom was rearranging items in her purse while she was answering Dad's question.

Dad was now driving up Logan Street, and we passed Standard Steel. He glanced over at Mom and said, "I hope he knows what he's doing. She doesn't seem to be getting any better." He was maneuvering the sharp left turn onto Derry Avenue as we continued toward home.

"Well, he found what was wrong with your mother," Mom replied.

They continued their conversation for the remainder of the way home, but I had tuned them out again. They always acted as if I wasn't there. I heard them and felt certain there was something terribly wrong with me. I recall looking at Brenda, and with concern she asked, "Are you all right?"

I nodded my head and fought desperately to keep from crying. Brenda turned and stared out the window. I think she had tuned our parents out, too.

The next few days were uneventful. I got up, ate breakfast, and took my pill. Then I went to school, returned home, took another pill, did my homework, and watched TV. Several times I was on the verge of tears.

Friday morning I again got up and began getting ready for school. I went into the kitchen and took my pill Mom had left for me on the counter. As I glanced at the kitchen clock to see what time it was so I could again calculate how long until school started, a wave of depression washed over me. Tears started flowing, and I began to sob uncontrollably.

Brenda wasn't yet out of bed. The house seemed so empty, and I was overwhelmed with loneliness. I walked through Grandma's old room on my way to the bathroom. That only added to my depression. Oh God, I missed Grandma, I missed Steve, and I missed Mom. It seemed as though no one cared what happened to me. The more I tried to pull myself together, the more uncontrollable my sobs became. I left the bathroom and returned to the living room. *Captain Kangaroo* was talking on television. I was unable to absorb what he was saying. Depression consumed me.

By that time, Brenda came downstairs and entered the living room still wearing her nightgown. "What's wrong?" she asked.

"I don't know," I sobbed in reply. "I just can't go to school."

"You better go to school, or you'll be in big trouble," Brenda warned.

Just what I needed, sibling compassion. "Too bad," I hissed. "I'm not going; I don't care what you say," I informed her.

"Well, do what you want, but don't say I didn't warn you when you get into trouble," she replied, then turned and headed for the bathroom.

I knew I could not go to school. I couldn't get my emotions under control, and worse yet, I couldn't stop the tears. Mom had left her work number for us in case of an emergency. I decided I would call her and tell her I couldn't go to school. I had never called long distance, so I was worried I would mess up the call, but some things worked in my favor I realized as the call went through. After the secretary got my mother on the phone, I began to explain why I was calling. "I can't go to school," I sobbed into the phone as soon as I heard her voice. I believe Mom was relieved because she expected worse news.

"Why not? What's wrong, Linda?" she asked.

"I don't know," I answered between sobs. "I just can't."

"Do you want me to come home?" Mom asked.

"Yeah," I answered as I continued to sob into the phone.

"Okay, just settle down. I'll get Dot to bring me home. I'll be there in just a little while," she said, attempting to calm me.

"Okay," I managed to get out before hanging up. I really wanted her to come home, but I realized I was probably going to get in trouble from Dad. I truly didn't know what was wrong. How could a twelve-year-old girl understand grief and depression?

Brenda had finished getting ready for school and left for the bus stop. I just sat there staring at the TV. Before too long, I saw Dot's car coming around the corner. Within a few minutes, Mom entered the front door. I began crying again as soon as I saw her. She laid her jacket and lunch bag on the coffee table and sat down beside me on the couch.

"What's wrong?" she asked.

"I don't know I sobbed," and I truly didn't.

"Linda, this has to stop. You can't keep crying like this. The doctor already gave you medicine, and you're still crying. We don't know what to do with you."

"I just can't go to school anymore," I got out.

"You have to," Mom insisted. "It's a law that you must attend school."

"I can't," I responded.

"Why not?" she asked. How could I tell her when I didn't understand it myself. I just knew I was even more sad at school than I was at home. At least at home, I could hide my feelings better because I could get away when I felt extremely sad. At school I could not. I didn't want the kids to see me cry. They already thought I was strange.

"I don't know," was all I could answer.

Mom sat there for a few minutes, then got up and made me some hot tea and toast. She never drank coffee; she was a tea drinker. Dad drank neither. I loved hot tea with a little cream. It had a soothing effect. Mom brought the tea and toast into the living room and set it on the coffee table. She then handed me one of my pills, and said, "I think you better take one of these." I did as she instructed.

After I drank my tea and ate my toast, I watched TV for a little while. *I Love Lucy* was on when I drifted off to sleep. The medication probably had something to do with that. When I awoke in the afternoon, I looked at the clock and realized it would not be long until Dad returned from work. I was dreading that. I was certain he would be angry about me calling Mom.

Around three twenty, Mom began cooking supper. We were having goulash. I liked goulash, but I didn't have much of an appetite. My anxiety was growing as I realized that Dad would soon be home. Brenda came into the house through the back door and walked into the living room. "Why's Mom here?" she asked me.

"I called her," I answered.

Brenda just shook her head and walked into the kitchen to see what was cooking. I could hear her and Mom whispering, but I couldn't make out what they were saying. They were still whispering when Dad's car passed by the living room window. My heart began racing for I knew I was in for it.

Dad came through the living room door and just stood there a few seconds looking at me and then continued to the kitchen. "What are you doing here?" he asked Mom. I blocked out the rest of their conversation because I didn't want to hear it. In a few minutes, though, he returned to the living room and said to me, "This has to stop. You can't be calling your mother home from work. Dot had to miss work, too, to bring her here. You have to stop your bawling all the time!" he commanded.

I thought *if only it were that easy*. I didn't want to cry; it was embarrassing and I didn't like getting into trouble. I said nothing, though. I only looked at the floor to avoid his stare.

When Dad saw I wasn't going to respond, he went to the bathroom to wash his hands and returned to the kitchen. I wished I didn't have to eat that night because I was expecting a lecture throughout the meal. I wasn't mistaken, either, because that is exactly what happened.

I put some goulash on my plate and pushed it around with my fork. I ate very little. Dad continued lecturing me and trying to force me to tell him what was wrong. How ironic! I wondered what he would have said if I said, "You are part of the problem." I wouldn't have dared, though. Even if I could have explained, I was certain they wouldn't understand, so I said nothing.

At least it was Friday, and I had the weekend to pull it together. I knew I had to go to school on Monday. Dad would go ballistic if I didn't. Throughout the weekend I continually calculated the hours that remained before I had to return to school. As Monday morning approached, my anxiety increased. I wished I could have extra pills. I thought they would help, but Mom would never permit that. She was afraid of me becoming addicted to my medication anyway.

I went to school the following Monday, and the weeks slowly passed as I continued my routine. I became a clock watcher. When I was at home, I calculated how many hours remained until I had to return to school, and when I was at school, I calculated how many hours remained until I could return home.

While at school, I attempted to blend into the woodwork. If the students didn't notice me, they wouldn't criticize me, was my theory. I never volunteered in class, and I participated in no activities that year. Just getting myself to school and getting my homework done was as much as I felt I could handle. Sometimes in the evening, I would go to a movie or bowling with my friends outside of school. I never did anything with my classmates because I felt alienated from them. Most of them never knew me before my depression. My friends remembered me as I had been.

Gradually, as the year wore on, I continued to work through the grieving process. Then slowly, very slowly, life again began to sometimes have meaning for me. I was still seeing Dr. McNabb, however, and there were still crying spells. Dad and Mom both seemed to be incapable of helping me through my depression. I really believe they just didn't know what to do.

I still hated coming home from school to an empty house. When Mom had been home, things seemed to have been better. Brenda and Dad just weren't very good company. Mom appeared to care about what I was doing. She would ask me questions about school and things; Dad never did. Generally, he would nap on the couch or work on his latest project in the garage. I hated to help with his projects, and I was lonely when he napped. Sometimes Brenda watched television with me, but we didn't have much interaction immediately after school.

Things at school still were not good, either. One dramatic episode I recall occurred when I was in Miss Foster's English class.

The night before, I had gotten my hair cut. Mom had taken Brenda and me to Minnie Murphy's home to have her cut our hair. Minnie lived in Yeagertown, and she cut hair in a room at the back of her house. I had just wanted the ends of my hair trimmed. She began cutting bangs, which I didn't want. Instead of stopping her, I just sat there and allowed her to cut them, but tears began running down my cheeks. I didn't think I should interrupt her while she was talking to Mom. Minnie eventually noticed and exclaimed: "My goodness! What's wrong?"

"I didn't want bangs," I said, as I sniffed and tried to stop the tears.

Minnie said, "I'm really sorry, sweetheart; I must have misunderstood. Don't worry, though. They'll grow back real soon." Mom and Brenda both thought it was funny. They were kidding me when we left Minnie's. That only made me angry and more upset. The worst was yet to come, however.

I already hated the bangs. Then what was about to happen at school was devastating to me. We had just gone into English class and I took my seat. The other kids were doing the same. Class would begin a few minutes later; the teacher wasn't there yet.

As Tracy Troskey took her seat behind me, she made the comment to Susan Sullivan who sat in the next row, one seat back from me, "Who's the flying Dutchman?"

Susan started giggling, and answered, "I don't know." She continued giggling, covering her mouth. Her entire body was shaking.

Miss Foster came into the room and closed the door. The giggles continued for another moment until the teacher said, "Obviously, something is very funny today. Tracy, would you mind sharing it with everyone?" Half the class now started roaring with laughter.

"No," Tracy said in her smart-ass tone. "Nothing's funny."

"I would suggest then that all of you stop laughing immediately," Miss Foster ordered. I was struggling to keep back the tears. Miss Foster had told everyone to open their books and was beginning to review the lesson. I was barely aware of what was going on around me. I was so humiliated and hurt. Tracy was like that, though. She thought that by belittling others, it made her look better. It occurred to me later that other kids may have gone along with her jokes to ensure that she didn't make them the next target. Knowing that, however, didn't make it any easier to deal with.

My tears were overflowing the rims of my eyes, and they appeared to be picking up speed. I kept wondering how I was going to make it through class. To leave, I would have to ask permission, and I didn't think I could do that because everyone would look at me and know I was crying. I sat there with my head bent over my book, reaching up to wipe away each tear as it slipped out. I would get them under control for a little while; then I would think about what had happened, and they would start again. Finally, the bell rang, and the students began to leave. I pretended I was searching for something in my purse so I wouldn't have to look up. When the room had cleared at last, I quickly exited and made my way directly to the girls' restroom. Once inside, I immediately went to an enclosed stall, sat down on the toilet with my clothing still in place, and released my tears.

I hated school! No matter how hard I tried, there was a group of cruel kids who refused to give me any peace. It was difficult enough trying to work through the depression I was experiencing since Grandma's death. I continued crying until the bell rang again, and everyone was in their classes.

I took that opportunity to quietly slip out of the restroom and walked quickly to the nurse's office. I had to take a left at the intersection and continue to the end of the corridor. The nurse's office was through a door located beside the gymnasium. I entered that door and took a seat on one of the wooden chairs lined up inside the door. I could hear movement in the next room, but I was quiet. A few minutes passed before the nurse, Mrs. Sulloff, walked by the doorway of her office. It was then that she noticed me sitting in the corridor. "Hello there," she said. "What seems to be the problem?"

I had stopped crying, but my eyes were red and swollen. I was certain she knew I had been crying. "I have my period, and whenever I get it, I get severe cramps. They're really bad this time," I lied. I couldn't possibly tell her what was really wrong.

"Oh, I think I have a solution for that," Mrs. Sulloff stated. "Come on in here with me," she instructed. I followed her inside her office. She took a cup and teabag out of her top left drawer. "Hot tea always helped me with that problem," she told me. She had a small hot-plate with a pot of water on the window sill behind her desk. She reached over, picked up the pot, and poured hot water into the cup onto the teabag. It was Lipton tea, the kind Mom always drank. Mrs. Sulloff asked, "Do you like sugar and milk?"

"I like sugar," I responded. She put a teaspoon of sugar in the tea from a white plastic container setting beside the pot, then placed the spoon in the cup. Next, she picked up the cup and set it on her desk directly in front of me.

"There...now when that is ready, just take out the bag and throw it there in my trash can," she instructed. "After you drink it, you may go on into the next room and rest on the cot. You should feel better in no time."

"Okay," I said as I removed the teabag, threw it in the trash can in the corner, and stirred the tea. I then asked with concern, "What should I do about not being in social studies class?"

"Oh, don't worry about that," Mrs. Sulloff said. "I'll give you a note to give to your teacher tomorrow."

"Thank you," I said feeling as if her kindness was too much to bear. I continued drinking the tea with difficulty since I was again struggling to keep back the tears.

As I finished my tea, she said, "Now go ahead in there and lie down until you start feeling better."

"Okay," I said again, then walked into the next room, removed my loafers, and lay down on the cot. Soon I became very drowsy and fell asleep. The hot tea on top of the medication had relaxed me so much that I could not stay awake.

When I awoke, I remember that I was startled at first because I wasn't certain where I was. When it came back to me, I panicked because I didn't know how long I had been sleeping. I sat up, slipped my loafers back onto my feet, and went into Mrs. Suloff's office. She was sitting at her desk doing paper work. "I fell asleep," I announced, somewhat embarrassed.

"That's the best thing that could have happened," she said. "How are the cramps?"

I hesitated a moment until I remembered what I had told her. "Gone," I replied. "What should I do about class?" I asked.

"School will be over in fifteen minutes," Mrs. Suloff informed me as she glanced at her big-faced watch. "You may as well wait here with me until the last period bell rings."

"All right, I will," I said with relief. When the bell rang, I gathered my things and returned to my homeroom. Fortunately, none of the troublemakers were in my homeroom class or on my bus. I would not have to face them until the following day. When the bell rang again, I made my way to my bus and found my seat. I settled in with my books and was glad I would be on my way home in a few minutes. I never told my parents about incidents like that one because I was certain they would not understand. It would be embarrassing, too.

Everyone always said, "All good things must end," but they never said, "all bad things must end." They do, though. Even my eighth grade year in high school came to an end, and none too soon as far as I was concerned. That year would not be one of my treasured memories. There had been too much pain.

Chapter 15

Later that year, our small community experienced a very frightening event. On May 6th, 1966, Little Mountain, one of the Seven Mountains, caught on fire. Little Mountain was where I had taken Steve to the cave, and it was very near my house and our neighbors' houses.

The Lewis family lived close to Sammy Fleck. There was a summer camp between Sammy's place and the Lewis'. Mrs. Lewis was Faye Pennepacker's sister which made her Cathy's aunt. On different occasions, I had stopped at their house with Cathy, and I came to know them quite well. Also, they had been at Cathy's grandfather's pool some of the times I was there with Cathy. They had two small children, Nancy and Scott.

I became quite fond of the children, and on numerous occasions, stopped in to visit them. Their basement had been refurbished and made into a large family room. I would go down there with them and watch TV, play games, and listen to records. They loved the Monkees and had some of their music. We also listened to some of their mother's music; I recall listening to "Moon River." Once in a while, Mrs. Lewis would ask me if I would stay with the children while she went to Milroy to complete some errands.

The Lewises also owned the house on the corner of Lingle Valley Road and the alley to their residence. It had been one of Mrs. Muttersbaugh's houses, and they had made three trailer rental lots at the side of the property that had been a large yard. Construction workers had moved their trailers onto these lots.

Mrs. Lewis had taught Bible School several years at the Methodist church Brenda and I attended. I recall singing in the children's choir with Brenda and Cathy, wearing our blue choir gowns and seeing the Lewises and Faye in the congregation. One particular Sunday stands out in my mind when we sang, "Fairest Lord Jesus." I liked singing in the choir and being in the church, but still I could not pray.

During that period of my life when I was visiting the Lewis children, our small community of Mount Pleasant experienced an event that I have always associated with their family since they played a central role in my life at that time. Mom, Dad, Brenda, and I were returning home from our weekly grocery shopping expedition when we saw a thick smoke at the edge of Milroy. It looked like dense fog, and the cars coming off the Seven Mountains had their headlights turned on so the drivers could see. Dad turned his on and continued traveling west on Route 322 toward our house. He said, "There must be a big fire up this way somewhere." No sooner had he said that when two screaming sirens blared from behind our vehicle, and he along with the other west bound traffic, pulled to the side of the road to allow the large red and white fire trucks to pass.

After they passed, Dad pulled back out onto Route 322. We were near Hartman Center, a United Church of Christ church retreat center. As we approached Lingle Valley Road, I could see flames on the mountain.

That was one of the most frightening experiences in my life. All sense of security was lost as I realized how threatening that fire was. The area of the mountain that I saw burning was where the large boulder and cave were located, and where I had taken Steve. Dad and Mom were concerned about the flames moving toward our house, and I could sense their anxiety.

When we got to our house, Brenda and I helped carry the groceries inside and put them away. When we finished, we went back outside to join the other neighbors who had gathered near the water pump to watch the fire and express their concerns.

Mr. Lewis was there when I arrived, and he told me how his son Scott had been frightened when he first learned of the fire and had asked for me. It made me feel good to know that Scott liked me that much. Mrs. Lewis had taken both children to Milroy, away from the smoke. Betsy was at the pump, too. She and I walked together up the alley by Sammy Fleck's house; Sammy was out on his porch. We continued past Bishops' camp, the Lewis' house; and on across the wooden bridge that led to Peg Frey's house.

During our walk, we talked about how we wanted to help fight the fire. It didn't occur to us that we had no equipment and certainly weren't dressed appropriately to fight a fire. As we started up the hill toward Mrs. Fry's house, we saw several bulldozers clearing a path through the woods. A group of firefighters were farther up the mountain. I later learned that they were making a fire line. When we got close enough for the men to see us, one yelled, "You girls get back down the mountain. This is dangerous and you could get hurt." Betsy and I were beginning to spend time together again. She knew I was depressed after Grandma's death.

Betsy called back, "We want to help fight the fire." The man who had initially yelled at us walked down to meet us. He wore a hard hat, and I noticed how dirty and sweaty he was.

He said, "I know you girls want to help, but the best thing you can do is return to your homes so we don't need to worry about you getting hurt."

Reluctantly and disappointed, we did as the firefighters had requested and turned around and left the scene. We both had so much energy, though, that we didn't want to return home. We decided we would go to Betsy's porch and watch the firefighters go by. On our way, we saw Cathy and Brenda in Cathy's front yard. Betsy called out to them, "Come on up to my porch. We're going to watch the fire trucks and stuff." Instead of going to her porch, however, we all stopped next door at Betsy's house and stood on Cathy's grandfather's sidewalk. We were able to see the fire from there. It felt good to be spending time again with our whole gang.

Well into the evening, we watched the events unfold around us. They had opened Route 322, and vehicles were again passing. The atmosphere became somewhat festive, and Betsy brought out a radio so we could listen to the news reports about the fire. In between, popular songs were playing. "Get Off of My Cloud" by the Rolling Stones still reminds me of the forest fire.

Eventually, Betsy's mother made her go inside, and the rest of us decided to go home. We walked with Cathy down over the hill to her trailer, and Brenda and I continued to our house. The news reporters were saying the fire was under control. Everyone was glad of that.

Later that evening when I climbed the stairs to my bedroom, I stopped and sat on the top step beside my window and looked out at the flames on the mountain. It was still frightening to see the fire, yet it was sort of beautiful, too, how the red flames lighted the night sky. That surreal image created another indelible memory that would forever be a part of me.

I learned the next evening in the *Lewistown Sentinel* that approximately 500 acres of mountain land were burned before several hundred volunteer firefighters were able to get the blaze under control. It further reported that the fire broke out around 4:30 p.m. on Friday in the vicinity of the Lewistown Municipal Authority's filtration plant.

The fire burned along the west ridge of Little Mountain for three-quarters of a mile along Route 322 and jumped almost 300 feet to cross the highway and ignite the other side. The Wright Construction Company was blamed for staring the blaze when their brush burning got out of control.

Firefighters had complained that hundreds of sightseers had hampered their efforts. Our gang enjoyed watching the sightseers drive by. It created an almost festive atmosphere in the midst of the danger.

The American Legion building was most endangered, and the blaze was brought under control just 100 feet from that structure. My home, along with others in Lingle Valley, were in danger, too. I believe, though, that we were so caught up in the excitement, that we had no time to think about the horror of what could have been until retrospectively. Fortunately, only two firefighters were injured, and their injuries were minor.

The summer of 1966 had arrived, and I was looking forward to better times. At least I wouldn't have to attend school for three months; and that alone made me happy. I had always thought that teenagers had all the fun. So far, my thirteenth year had not been a blast. I was hoping things were about to change.

Throughout June, Cathy, Brenda, and I made several bus trips to the Burnham pool. We rode the transportation bus to Burnham and walked to my Aunt Daisy's house until the pool opened. Aunt Daisy was Mom's older sister. Mom had seven sisters in all and seven brothers. Aunt Daisy was the third oldest. She was the only sibling of my mother's who had been divorced, but her divorce had taken place before I was born. Based on what I had heard, her first husband was in the service, and he had written to tell her he had met someone else and wanted a divorce. Their daughter Kathleen was just a toddler at the time. Later, Aunt Daisy married a man named Jim. He adopted Kathleen, and raised her as his daughter.

It was the first week in May, and May 2nd was Dad's birthday. Aunt Daisy knew that, so she made him a birthday cake, and we had a little party. Afterwards, I heard Dad tell Mom, that was the first birthday party he had ever had. Aunt Daisy and Uncle Jim lived at the top of the hill from the Burnham pool along Freedom Avenue. They lived in a one and a half story white cement-block house. Their back yard had a fence around it to keep their dog Penney inside. They also raised chickens in a small coup in the back.

On our visits there before the pool opened, Uncle Jim would be at work and so would Kathleen. She was five years older than I and had already graduated. Aunt Daisy would give us each a Coke, and Cathy, Brenda and I sat in her living room talking to her and petting Penney until the pool opened. When the pool opened at one o'clock, we would walk down over the hill, pay at the gate, and go inside and lay our towels on the grass near the edge of the pool. That month the juke box blared our favorite songs which included: "Red Rubber Ball," "Paperback Writer," "Hanky Panky," "The Pied Piper," "I Saw Her Again," and "Wouldn't It Be Nice." We spent the whole day lying in the sun, swimming, and flirting with the Burnham boys. Dad would pick us up on his way home from work. It was great fun. Things were definitely looking up.

I remember that year I purchased a two-piece black and white bathing suit at Bargain Town USA. Bargain Town was a discount department store located at the lower end of Lewistown. Often on Friday evenings, Dad would take us there to look for bargains before we headed to the Giant to do our grocery shopping. My bathing suit top was black and white checked. The bottom was also black and white checked, but it had a short all-white skirt that was attached to it. Cathy, Betsy, and Brenda all had two-piece bathing suits, too. We were self-conscious, however, and whenever we got out of the water, we would put our T-shirts on over our bathing suits before walking to the juke box or concession stand.

Many of the kids from Burnham went to the pool every day. When the pool was initially built, the community sold life-time passes for individuals or families. I believe those passes cost over a hundred dollars. Several of my cousins' families had passes; Brenda and I didn't. We wouldn't have been able to go every day anyway because we didn't have bus money or money for drinks and food. We were fortunate that Cathy's grandfather allowed her to have us at his pool whenever we couldn't or didn't go to the Burnham pool.

By the end of the day at the Burnham pool, we would be water-logged, our eyes would be pink from the chlorine, and our skin would be a little darker from the sun. We changed our clothes in the changing room near the diving boards, and waited outside the fence on the curb until Dad picked us up around three forty-five. I have many fond memories of those trips to the Burnham pool. The pool trips really were an oasis in my desert of depression during that time of my life. I was extremely glad it was summer, and eagerly looked forward to the next three months. Life was so much better when there was no school.

PART III
JULY 1966 – JUNE 1967
Time Line

July 1966 – NAACP rejects Black Power concepts; black uprisings in Omaha, Chicago, Brooklyn, Jacksonville, and Cleveland.
August 5, 1966 - 4,000 whites confront Martin Luther King marching with 600 in Chicago.
August 9, 1966 – Gemini 10 shoots pictures of world surfaces.
August 1966 – Another Beatles tour: Beatlemania occurs again; Black uprisings in Atlanta.
September 1966 – Linda begins 9th grade
September 11, 1966 – First elections in South Viet Nam.
November 5, 1966 – Walk for Peace and Love and Freedom in New York City.
November 8, 1966 – First Black elected in Senate (Massachusetts).
November 1966 – Lunar Orbiter II transmits photos of moon.
December 12, 1966 – Linda's 14th birthday.
December 1966 – 385,000 American troops in Viet Nam.
January 1967 – Toronto group starts to help draft resistors; Leary's LSD. "Celebration" arrives in San Francisco.
January 1967 – United States, USSR, United Kingdom sign treaty banning nuclear weapons in space.
January 27, 1967 – Apollo 1 blows up.
February 1967 – Beatles release "Strawberry Fields Forever."
April 8 – 10, 1967 - Black uprising in Nashville.
April 15, 1967 – 1965 draft card law held unconstitutional by US first Circuit Court of Appeals; 400,000 march from Central Park to United Nations against the Viet Nam war.
April 16, 1967 - Black uprising in Cleveland.
June 16 –18, 1967 – Monterrey Pop Fest.
June 30, 1967 – 448,800 US troops in Viet Nam.

Popular Songs

"Red Rubber Ball," The Cyrkle; "Wild Thing," The Troggs; "You Can't Hurry Love," The Supremes; "Reach Out I'll Be There," The Four Tops; "You Keep Me Hangin' On," The Supremes; "Devil With A Blue Dress On" & "Good Golly Miss Molly," Mitch Ryder & The Detroit Wheels; "I'm A Believer," The Monkees; "Georgy Girl," The Seekers; "Penny Lane," The Beatles; "Happy Together," The Turtles; "Groovin'," The Young Rascals; "Girl, You'll Be A Woman Soon," Neil Diamond

Chapter 16

One Saturday after breakfast, I went out to the old shed that was attached to our garage and got out my blue metal Radio Flyer wagon. Brenda and I both had gotten one a few years before for Christmas. I pulled the wagon around the corner of the shed and said to Dad as I continued out our gravel driveway, "I'm going to collect papers today."

"Okay," he answered. "Just be careful when you're along the road."

"I will," was my reply.

When Brenda and I were previously at Mrs. Leeper's store, she told us that if we wanted to earn some money, Mrs. Semple would pay us for old newspapers. Mrs. Semple was an elderly lady who owned a dog kennel at the edge of Mount Pleasant. She sold poodles, Pekingese, Pomeranians, boxers, terriers, and Chihuahuas. She also boarded dogs for people on vacation.

Mrs. Semple needed newspapers to line the dog cages. So for several months, Brenda and I periodically went around the neighborhood gathering old newspapers. Most people were glad to give us their old papers because then they wouldn't have to burn them. After we gathered a wagon full, we pulled the load down to Mrs. Semple's house. We would knock at the front door, and Mrs. Semple would come to the door and tell us to take the papers around to the side of her house. Then she would open the gate of the fence and lead us down to the little red building that was the kennel. There was also a smaller white building to the left side of the red building. That was usually where she kept the poodles. I liked to go down there because I got to see all the puppies. I loved animals, especially baby animals.

That day, Mrs. Semple had me pull the wagon into the middle of the large kennel. The building was twenty-by-thirty feet. It had a cement floor and wooden siding painted red. On the right side as you entered was one large cage about eight-by-ten with an eight-foot high wire door. Mrs. Semple kept the largest terriers in that cage. The remainder of the right side had various sizes of smaller cages layered up to the ceiling. That is where Mrs. Semple kept her small terriers, Pomeranians, and Pekingese. The cages on the bottom had wired runs to the outside. The left side of the building consisted of large cages with runs to the outside. There were six cages. Mrs. Semple kept the larger dogs there: boxers and any large dog she happened to be boarding. In the center of the building were several small wooden cages with wire doors for the puppies.

Mrs. Semple had me stack the wagonload of papers on top of the first cage in the middle of the kennel. While I was doing that, she asked, "Linda, how would you like a job here?" I looked up from my stacking and saw Mrs. Semple standing beside me in her blue floral-printed dress and white apron, with her hands on her hips, looking at me inquisitively. She had curly silver hair that was partially pulled back at the sides with bobby pins. Mrs. Semple was probably in her late sixties.

When I had digested her question, I answered, "I would like that."

"You see, I need someone to help me clean cages, scrub the floors, and clean the runs," she said as she motioned to different parts of the kennel. "Do you think you could handle that?"

"Yes," I responded as I envisioned having my own money. I thought that would be great.

"Well, you'll have to check with your parents and make sure it's all right. If it is, you give me a call, and we'll set up a time for you to start."

I had finished unloading the wagon while Mrs. Semple was talking. I straightened up and said, "Yes, I will. Thanks," I added as I followed her back out of the kennel, up the sidewalk, and out the gate. She paid me for the papers at the gate. We generally got a quarter; that day, she gave me thirty-five cents.

As I pulled my wagon along Route 322 on my way home, I was happy. My parents would be surprised that I had a job, I thought. I pulled my wagon down over the hill and into our alley. When I got to our house, I discovered Dad was still in the garage. I pulled the wagon to the entrance of the garage, dropped the handle to the ground, and went inside. "Dad, guess what?" I asked enthusiastically. Before he had a chance to respond, I blurted, "I got a job!"

"Really! Doing what?" he asked, as he turned away from the grinder, where he was grinding the end of a bolt, and looked at me.

"Changing the papers in the cages, scrubbing the floors, and cleaning out the dog runs for Mrs. Semple," I answered, trying to repeat everything she had told me. Then I continued, "But, she said I would have to make sure it was okay with you and Mom. Is it okay?" I asked.

Dad pause momentarily and then replied, "Well, I don't see anything wrong with that, but see what your mother thinks."

"All right," I answered as I hurried out of the garage and into the house. Mom was sitting on the couch in the living room folding clothes. "Mom, is it okay if I work for Mrs. Semple?" I asked excitedly as I stood by the couch beside her.

Mom looked up at me as she continued folding a basketful of towels, and asked, "What would you be doing?"

Again I repeated what Mrs. Semple had told me.

Mom sighed and said, "I suppose it would be all right."

"Good!" I exclaimed. "She said I should call her if it's okay," I said as I picked up the telephone book that was on the stand underneath the phone. I leafed through the Reedsville section until I had located Semples Kennels and called the number. Milroy and Reedsville were both listed under Reedsville in the United Telephone book. Mrs. Semple answered, "Hello."

"Hi, Mrs. Semple. This is Linda Bishop. My parents said it is okay with them for me to work for you," I hurriedly informed her.

"Oh good! Could you start this coming Saturday?" she asked.

"Yes," I answered as visions of personal independence danced through my head.

"I'll see you at nine-thirty then," Mrs. Semple said then added, "Good-bye."

"Good-bye," I responded.

When I hung up the telephone, I was in a state of euphoria. This was the best I had felt for quite some time. I had made it without crying for three days. Maybe things were getting better. Maybe my pills were working. That day was definitely a good day.

I then remembered that I forgot to ask how much I would be paid or how long I would have to work. It didn't matter, though, because I would find out on Saturday.

The following Saturday, I went to work for Mrs. Semple. I was to be there at nine- thirty a.m., but I got up early and made sure I was at work ten minutes early. Mrs. Semple opened the gate at the side of her house for me to enter, and I followed her to the dog kennel. When we reached the kennel, we entered and Mrs. Semple walked over to the first cage in the center of the building. She rolled up the papers inside that cage and removed them through the wire cage door. She then demonstrated how fresh papers should be spread on the cage floor. When she had finished, she asked, "Do you think you'll be able to handle that?"

"Sure," I answered.

"Well, you go ahead and get started on the cages along that wall," she instructed and motioned toward the cages on the right side of the kennel with her elbow. "You can throw the dirty papers in the trash can," she said as she threw away the papers she had in her hands from the cleaning demonstration.

"Okay," I said as I started cleaning my first cage.

Mrs. Semple watched for a few minutes; then she left the kennel and returned to her house. Her house had pink siding and was two stories high. It smelled like perm solution at the front door. Years later, I discovered that the shrubs she had in her front yard were what emitted that distinct odor. It's strange what things stick with you for decades.

As I finished the first cage, I lined the inside floor with fresh newspapers and closed the cage door. Mrs. Semple had put the dogs out in their runs on the right side of the building. Since there were three tiers of cages, she had to put two or three dogs in each run. They were the Pomeranian and Pekingese dogs.

I particularly remember a reddish-brown male Pekingese named Foxy. He had fathered quite a few puppies, and he was a cocky little dog. Another very pretty dog was Jettabelle, a black Pomeranian. Her fur was extremely shiny, and so black, she almost looked blue. Jettabelle was afraid of the other dogs, particularly Foxy, and she spent most of her time outside cowered in the corner against the kennel and beside the fence.

It was fun working at the kennel. Often there were puppies in the cages with their mothers, and I could play with them when I cleaned the cages. They would have to be moved from one cage to another until the cleaning was done. Of course, I would get to hold and cuddle them in between the transition.

Mrs. Semple came in and out several times as I was cleaning the kennel. When I was finished cleaning the cages, she showed me how to mop the floor with a large wooden handled mop and metal scrub bucket. When that was finished, she took me outside and explained how she wanted me to clean the dog runs.

I was given a large white plastic five-gallon bucket and a small wooden handled metal shovel. Mrs. Semple had closed the run doors, so the boxers were locked inside the kennel. In these large individual runs, there were number-two limestones on the ground. The runs for the small dogs on the other side of the kennel had grass inside the runs. The small dogs weren't nearly as destructive as the larger dogs who would tear up the grass. Mrs. Semple explained how to clean the runs: "Now you take the shovel and scoop up the poop and put it in the bucket. Try not to get too many of the stones. After you finish, take the bucket out to the far corner (she pointed to the corner she was referring to) and empty it. Then bring it over here to the side spigot there and rinse it out, and then clean the shovel. Do you have any questions?" she breathlessly asked me.

"No," I answered as I realized I was about to become a "pooper scooper." That part of the job I did not like. There were flies everywhere and it smelled horrible. If the poop had been there a while, I learned you could scoop it up and put it into the bucket whole. That helped to eliminate the odor. If it was fresh, however, forget it. It was messy, it stuck to the shovel, and was totally disgusting. When you cleaned the cages inside, you could wrap everything in the newspapers that lined the floor, and it wasn't nearly as messy.

There were six large runs that were four-feet-wide and twelve-feet-long. It seemed as though it took forever to clean those runs. I was always thankful when the bucket was empty, washed, and ready to store in the outside storage room that was attached to the back of the kennel.

When I finished with the runs that day, I returned to the house following the narrow cement sidewalk to the back door. Mrs. Semple had been in the kitchen and saw me coming. She opened the back door that was half window, leaned against the kitchen door, and asked in her shrill voice, "Are you finished?"

"Yes, I just finished the runs, emptied the bucket, and put it away." The entire day's work had taken about three and a half hours.

"Well, I believe that will be enough for today," she said. "Hold on, I'll be right back," she added and closed the door as she returned to the kitchen. A few minutes later, she again opened the door, leaned against it, and opened a small black leather change purse. She fished out two dollars and seventy-five cents and handed it to me. We had never discussed how much she would pay me. I had no idea what to expect. That seemed like a lot of money to me; I was thrilled.

"Thank you," I said as I pushed the money into my pants pocket.

Mrs. Semple asked, "Do you think your sister would like to help you clean the kennel?"

"I don't know," I responded. "I could ask her."

"Well, you ask her, and if she wants to help, just bring her along next week."

"I will," I said as I walked to the side gate and let myself out.

"Good bye, Linda," Mrs. Semple said.

"Good bye," I responded and started on my way back home.

When I got home, I entered the house through the front door. Brenda was on the couch watching television. "Look what I got," I said as I pulled the money I had just earned out of my pocket. "Mrs. Semple said that if you want to work there, too, you could go up with me next Saturday."

"What do you have to do?" she asked.

"Clean out the dog cages, change the papers, and clean the runs," I replied. "Cleaning the cages isn't too bad. It's fun to play with the dogs. The only part I don't like is cleaning the runs because it stinks and it's yucky."

"How much did you make?" Brenda asked as she picked up the bag of Snyder's pretzels that were on the coffee table. She reached in, rattling the bag, pulled out a handful of pretzels, and laid them on her lap.

As I said, "Two dollars and seventy-five cents," she chomped down on a fat pretzel and began chewing.

"Yeah I guess that would be all right," she said with a mouthful of pretzel.

Brenda and I fought often like most siblings, but we also looked out for each other and did things together with our friends. When we were younger, many people thought we were twins because we looked alike, and Mom often dressed us alike. I never understood why she did that.

"Okay," I responded. "You just need to go with me next Saturday."

Brenda and I worked for Mrs. Semple for the next two years, mostly on Saturdays. Eventually, I would be promoted to cleaning her house as her health declined. She had a large boxer named Ginger that I grew attached to. Brenda continued cleaning the kennels after I began cleaning Mrs. Semple's house. Occasionally, we still would collect papers in the neighborhood and take them to the kennel. Our experience working at Mrs. Semple's was one more thing Brenda and I had in common. Those experiences drew us closer, and we were already close. We would remain so throughout the years of our lives.

Chapter 19

My depression episodes had decreased throughout the summer, but they still had not ceased. I continued to take medication. My visits to Doctor McNabb had been reduced to once a month. On numerous occasions, Dad remarked that he was concerned that my progress was too slow.

Later that summer, Mom and Dad had heard about a doctor in McVeytown who was supposed to be good with treating depression although he was a general practitioner . His name was Dr. Schooley. Dad was still concerned because although my crying episodes were reduced, I still had them fairly often, and he wasn't sure Dr. McNabb was treating me correctly. Consequently, they decided to take me to see the new doctor. Dr. Schooley's office was in a big two-story yellow house in McVeytown, which was about twenty two miles from our house.

Dr. Schooley didn't schedule appointments. You would just go in and wait your turn. I remember being surprised on my first visit. The waiting room was very crowded. In fact, there was only one vacant chair, so Mom took the chair, and I sat on the floor beside her. Mom had a dress on, so she couldn't sit on the floor; I had shorts on.

The wait in Dr. Schooley's office seemed to take forever. It was more than an hour before they called us in. There was a sign-in sheet on a small table right inside the door, and each time the nurse came out, she would call out the next name on the list. Five or six people had been called since we arrived. Finally, the nurse came out and called, "Linda Bishop." Mom and I stood up. The nurse said, "This way please." We followed her into her office.

Inside, a familiar procedure was repeated. She weighed me, measured me, and checked my blood pressure. She then informed me, "You may have a seat there," as she pointed toward a chair near her desk. The nurse looked at Mom who was in another chair beside me and said, "I'll need to get a little case history from you." Mom nodded. The nurse then asked Mom numerous questions about my medical history.

When Mom told her I had been Dr. McNabb's patient, she asked about current medications. Mom produced the medication bottle. The nurse copied the information onto my record from the label. She then left her office and entered Dr. Schooley's office. When she came back out, she said, "You may go in now." I followed the nurse, and Mom followed me into the examination room.

Actually, Dr. Schooley's examination room and office was one large room. At one end, he had a desk with several bookcases filled with books. At the other end of the room was the examination table along with several small tables and a white metal cabinet. There was a screen divider between the two sections. As we entered that room, I saw Dr. Schooley for the first time. He was a small-framed man about five feet, nine inches tall. He had dark hair and wore large black rimmed glasses. He was wearing a white lab coat. He said, "Hello, Linda and Mrs. Bishop. Please come over and have a seat." Dr. Schooley was sitting behind his large wooden desk. There were three wooden chairs placed side-by-side in front of his desk, all turned toward his desk. Mom and I walked over and sat beside each other facing Dr. Schooley. He had my chart in front of him.

"How are you, Linda?" he asked.

"Okay, " I answered.

"I see you've been having some problems, and Dr. McNabb has you taking some medication."

I nodded my head, but didn't respond verbally.

"Why don't you tell me what the problem is?" Dr Schooley asked as he looked directly into my eyes.

"I…I really don't know," I answered as I looked down at my feet. I didn't like to look him in the eye. It made me nervous.

"Do you feel sick?" he continued, still looking at me.

"Sometimes I get headaches," I said. When they're real bad, my stomach hurts."

"Has the medicine you've been taking helped your headaches and stomach aches?" he inquired.

"Not really."

"Do you have any problems at school?" he asked as he scribbled something in his book.

"Not with classes…I just get upset sometimes."

Mom spoke up and added, "A lot of times she cries when it's time to go to school."

"Why don't you want to go to school?" he asked.

"I don't really know…" There were several moments of silence. "I just get sad at school."

"Can you tell me why you get sad?" Dr. Schooley asked.

"I don't know," I answered, looking down at my feet. I knew why, but I wasn't about to tell a stranger. How could I tell him how some of the kids were cruel? How could I tell him I hated it there? How could I tell him that I had no friends in my class? All my friends were in different sections. I couldn't tell him that; I couldn't tell anyone.

"All right, Linda, I want you to go over to the examining table and hop up there," he instructed. I jumped up and sat on the edge of the table, and Dr. Schooley checked my heart, looked into my eyes with his little light, and measured my blood pressure. He again wrote something on my chart. After Dr. Schooley had finished writing, he looked at my mother and said, "Mrs. Bishop, would you mind waiting with my nurse so I can talk with Linda alone?"

"No, that will be fine," Mom responded as she stood up and walked out of his office. I had the feeling she wasn't sure she should leave me there. That was strange; he was doing the opposite of what Dr. McNabb had done.

When the door had closed behind her, Dr. Schooley walked over to his desk and asked, "Why don't you come over here and have a seat?" He motioned to the chairs where Mom and I had initially been seated.

I followed him and sat down in the same chair I had taken when we first went in.

After I was settled and he had taken his seat behind the desk, Dr. Schooley looked directly at me and stated, "Sometimes it's easier to talk when our parents aren't listening. Do you agree?"

I wasn't sure what I thought. This was all so strange to me. "I guess," I answered.

"What is bothering you, Linda?" Dr. Schooley asked as he leaned toward me, folded his arms and placed them on his desk, attempting to establish eye contact.

"I don't know," I answered, refusing to look directly at him. I didn't like him asking me questions.

"Would you say you are sad now?"

"Yes."

"Why are you sad?"

"I don't know. I just feel sad," I said. I was getting frustrated with him asking me the same thing in different ways. I had my hands on my lap, and I began fidgeting and twisting my fingers.

"I want to ask you some questions that might confuse you. If you don't understand or want to ask me anything, please feel free to do so. Okay?"

"Yes," I said, wondering what the heck he was going to ask me.

"Sometimes people do things that we feel are wrong, but we don't know why. They may say something that doesn't seem right, or they might touch us where we don't think they should. This would confuse us and sometimes make us sad. Do you understand what I'm saying?" Dr. Schooley asked.

"I believe so," I answered, but I didn't really understand.

"Has anyone touched you in a way you feel was wrong?"

"No," I quickly answered.

"Has anyone done anything you feel was wrong?"

"No," I lied. I didn't realize until many years later that Dr. Schooley was trying to ascertain if I had been sexually abused. I certainly wasn't sexually abused; we had no physical contact of any kind in my family. What I was thinking about were the cruel things some kids said to me. Also, about when Dad punished me unjustly. I often wondered if he loved me; he never said he did.

"Linda, what's wrong?" Dr. Schooley was asking me when I jerked back to reality.

"Oh, I just was thinking about something," I answered.

"Is there anything else you would like to tell me?" he asked as he wrote something in my file and then looked back at me with concern.

"No," I said. I wasn't about to tell him what I had just been thinking.

"All right. If that ever changes, please feel free to tell me anything, no matter how small or big a problem you feel it may be. Will you promise me you'll do that?"

"Yes," I promised although I had no intention of telling him anything. What could he do anyway? He was here, and I would be there. I was convinced that my best protection would be my silence.

Dr. Schooley asked, "Will you please go out now and ask your mother to come back in here? You may wait with my nurse for a few minutes while I talk with your mother." I remember thinking that he was now doing the same thing that Dr. McNabb had done.

I jumped down from the table and left the examining room. "Mom, he wants to talk to you, " I told her as I entered his nurse's office. Mom went into the examining room, closing the door behind her, and I took a seat to wait for her to return. The nurse didn't say anything; she just looked at me and smiled.

Mom exited the examining room a few minutes later. I stood up as she paid the nurse, and we left the nurse's office, went out the front door, and walked down the street to where Dad had parked the car.

As Mom and I opened our doors and got into the car, Brenda began whining, "What took you so long? I didn't think you were ever coming back out."

Dad added, "It did seem like a long time. What time is it?" he asked.

Mom glanced at her watch and replied, "Almost eight o'clock. He had a whole waiting room full of people when we went in. Maybe that means he's a good doctor."

"Well, what did he say?" Dad asked Mom.

She replied, "He examined Linda, then sent me out of the room to talk to her alone; then I went back in to talk to him while she waited in the nurse's office. He thinks the medicine she is taking is too strong. He prescribed something milder for her."

"So what does he think is causing this?" Dad asked as if I were not there.

"Depression," Mom replied.

"What's causing the depression?" he asked in a somewhat agitated tone.

"I don't think he knows," Mom answered.

"What did he say to you?" Dad asked me, looking at my reflection in the rear view mirror.

Oh no, I thought as I answered, "He just asked me what the problem is."

"What did you say?" he pushed.

"I told him I don't know." I was silently hoping he wouldn't drill me on this because I didn't want to talk about it.

Dad didn't ask me anything else that night or during the remainder of our trip home. He and Mom talked quietly, but I just had again tuned them out. I often escaped that way mentally. Brenda didn't say anything either.

Chapter 18

That summer I found myself reading quite often. My cousin Kathleen had given me a box of books that included the Nancy Drew series, Annie Oakley books, and a number of others. I loved to sit on our back porch with my back leaning against the siding and withdraw from the world as I immersed myself in the mysteries within those books. After I had read the entire box of books, I read them again and again. We had a local library in Milroy, but my parents never took me there. I had been there several times while I was in elementary school. My class had walked over there to borrow books. Reading was one way to escape from the world around me. I spent many lazy summer afternoons on our back porch reading. I was still depressed, but the change in my medication helped some.

Another favorite pastime of mine was walking in the woods near our house. There were several popular paths I took. Generally, I would take Spot with me. I liked to retrace the trips Steve and I had taken two summers before. My time with Steve seemed magical, and I would remember those walks throughout my life. Steve and I had never written to one another after that summer. Once I wrote him a letter but didn't send it because I would have had to ask my parents for a stamp, and I was afraid they would learn why I wanted one. Perhaps that is why Steve had never written to me. Still, he had gotten my address, and I did often wonder why he hadn't written to me.

Sometimes on summer evenings, Dad, Brenda, and I, and both dogs would go on an excursion into the woods. One Saturday evening, Mom even went along, as she occasionally would. After going out Lingle Valley Road for approximately one mile, we turned back a dirt road that led to the Evergreen Lodge.

The lodge was a two-story wooden camp nestled in the forest against the mountain. It was quite beautiful there. A carpet of rich green moss surrounded the camp, and just a little sunlight was able to trickle through the thick forest canopy. The setting was even more beautiful in winter because snow would cling to the pine branches, and it would look like one of those winter scenes on Mom's calendar that hung on our kitchen wall.

Generally, no one was at the camp during the summer for they used it mainly as a hunting camp. There was a narrow wooden bridge that crossed the small mountain stream leading to Laurel Run, the larger stream that ran into the reservoir which we crossed on our way to the camp. The dogs ran across that bridge and went down a small grassy embankment on the right side of the stream to get a drink of water. Brenda and I also liked to drink from the stream, so we followed them down over the embankment. We made sure to go a little upstream from the dogs, though, to make sure our water was clean. We both cupped our hands and scooped up the ice-cold, fresh water. As we drank, the water leaked through our fingers and dripped down the front of our shirts. We were warm anyway, so it didn't bother us.

While we were drinking, Brownie and Spot had rushed past us and were in the woods a short distance from us, yelping. Brenda and I hurried over to see what was going on, when to our horror, we discovered yellow jackets swarming all around us. We stood there stomping and waving our arms as we screamed and swatted at the bees. They seemed to be all through my hair and I felt several stings. When my initial panic subsided a fraction of a degree, I heard Dad yelling, "Run! Get off the nest and run." I began to take off through the woods with no direction. I figured that Brenda was behind me, but I didn't stop to look. Eventually, my running took me back to the mountain stream, and in exhaustion, I collapsed in the water and washed my stings. Brenda came shortly behind me and followed my example.

When we caught our breaths, we realized that we were lost. I had no idea how long we had been running. We decided to walk in a direction we believed would take us back to the road. After we walked through the forest for about ten minutes, we heard something moving through the trees behind us. Brenda and I stood staring at where the noise was coming from when Spot broke through the thick mountain laurel and happily ran toward us. "Here girl," I called in relief as I realized we were rescued. Brownie, Dad and Mom weren't far behind.

As soon as Dad caught up to us, he began lecturing, "Never stay on a bees' nest. You two really stirred them up. What the heck were you thinking?"

"I didn't know it was a nest," I moaned as Brenda and I followed them out of the woods and returned to the road.

Mom said, "When we get home, you'll have to put some corn starch on those stings."

I counted four bee stings and Brenda had three. The dogs had several stings, too, but they already seemed to have recovered.

We began our journey home then since Brenda and I were wet. Throughout our walk home, Mom and Dad gave us a replay of how we had looked on the bees' nest and running. By the time we arrived at our house, it almost seemed funny. Almost! The bee story would be repeated many times after that painful experience.

The next day was Sunday, and we were going to Greenwood Furnace State Park, located in the mountains of northeastern Huntingdon. During the summer, Mom's family would meet on Sunday afternoons at different state parks for picnics. The most popular state parks we visited, in addition to Greenwood Furnace State Park, were Whipple Dam, Poe Valley, Reeds Gap and Alan Seeger. Brenda and I always preferred the parks with swimming areas. Greenwood Furnace was one such park.

The entrance was along Route 305, approximately a thirty-minute drive from our home. A six-acre lake and more than 400 acres of woods offered swimming, family camping, hunting, hiking, and picnicking. Our family generally chose a picnic site to the left of Route 305, located on the opposite side of the road from the dam because it was less crowded. It was farther to walk to the beach, however.

All of Mom's sisters and their families would go on these picnics, but her brothers never participated, though. I don't know why. Each family would pack casseroles and desserts to be shared by everyone. Jugs of Kool Aide and iced tea were always brought, too. Occasionally, they would cook hot dogs, hamburgers, or ham. Generally, three or four picnic tables would be placed end-to-end to provide enough seating space since Mom had seven sisters, and they all had two or three children.. The tables were located in a spruce and pine grove setting. Some pavilions were available, but usually, they were taken before we arrived.

After we arrived that Sunday and Dad parked the car, Brenda and I, along with a group of our cousins, crossed the road and went to the dressing house to change into our bathing suits. Then, we all moved to the beach area that consisted of a 300-foot sand beach that ran along the east side of the dam. The state provided lifeguards to patrol the swimmers, and there were ropes in the water that marked the parameters of the swimming area. We swam and lay on the beach until Uncle Jimmy came down to round us up for lunch.

The food was always wonderful. That day we had cold meat loaf, baked beans, potato salad with Grandma Eward's special dressing, macaroni salad, several different cakes, including chocolate with peanut butter icing, vine-ripened tomatoes, home-made pickles, and an assortment of drinks. We all ate until we were stuffed.

After lunch, my cousin Gary, who was three years older than me, led a group of us on a hike: Connie, Carol, Gloria, Bobbie, Denny, Rick, Stevie, Cathy, Darlene, Brenda, and me. There were many short hiking trails. That day we took the trail that led around the edge of the lake. We had been on it many times before, but it was still fun to do it again.

When we returned to the picnic area, we learned that some of the others had gone back to the lake to swim. Most of us still wore our bathing suits under our clothes, so off we went to join them at the lake. We continued swimming until seven o'clock that evening when the life guards went off duty. The park closed at dusk, so we returned to the dressing room to change into dry clothes, then went back to the tables to pack up everything before leaving for home. Of course, I made sure I grabbed a slice of chocolate cake before my Aunt Marie packed it away, for hiking and swimming sure could make me hungry.

As Dad drove home, Brenda and I talked about what fun we had. Dad always took the back way home; he would turn off Route 305 in Belleville and head to Barrville. There were a number of Amish and Mennonite farms on that route. Many of the young Amish men would be out in their buggies on Sunday evening returning home from courting their sweethearts. Brenda and I liked to look out the back window after Dad passed them and we would wave. They usually returned our waves, and we would giggle about it. Dad would tease us and ask if we wanted to marry one of those Dutch boys. He said they might even be our cousins since my great grandparents on Dad's side were Dutch. That always amused us.

Days like that Sunday almost made me forget my depression. As we turned off Route 322 into Lingle Valley Road, however, I felt a sadness overcome me. I really didn't know why. I wanted the day to last forever; I never wanted to return home. Upon pulling into the driveway, Dad instructed Brenda and me to help unload the car. As we did, my sadness increased. Tears started to form at the edges of my eyes, and I struggled to hold them back. Inside, Mom put everything away. Dad turned on television and lay down on the couch to watch *Bonanza*. I sat down on the other side of the sectional and watched with him.

About halfway through the program, during one of the commercials, I decided I was again getting hungry. When I entered the kitchen, I saw a black dish with a saucer covering the top setting on the kitchen table. Mom had sliced cucumbers and onions that Aunt Betty had given her from their garden and covered them with a vinegar dressing. After I had gotten a can of soda out of the refrigerator, I walked over to the table and removed the lid from the dish. I fished out a large slice of cucumber with my fingers and began chewing on it. I didn't care much for the onions. I hadn't realized that Dad had walked up behind me.

"You damn little hog!" he shrieked. He viciously picked up the cucumber and onion dish and turned it over on top of my head. He continued ranting, "I never want to see you do something like that again. Do you think anyone would want to eat those after you had your filthy fingers in them?" he asked.

I initially was in shock. When it subsided, I was terribly humiliated. Sure, eating with your fingers wasn't the best manners, but I never expected him to go ballistic. As I removed the dish from my head, I could smell the vinegar that had soaked into my T-shirt. Pieces of cucumber and onion were in my hair. My mother had now entered the kitchen and was wiping up the vinegar that had spilled onto the table as Dad continued his ranting.

"Werdna, don't you think that's enough?" she asked.

"No I don't. The little brat doesn't need to be so hoggish. Other people want to eat them, too," he continued as he left the kitchen and returned to the couch.

By that time, tears began to flow down my cheeks. After I combed the remaining pieces of vegetables from my hair with my fingers, I threw them into the waste basket in the corner, and left the kitchen. On my way upstairs, to change my clothes, I started to sob. *How could he be so cruel?* I thought. It wasn't like I did something horrible. I felt that he just didn't like me and used any excuse to punish me.

I changed into a nightgown and took my vinegar-soaked clothing down to the basement. In the bathroom, I towel-dried my hair. I didn't wash it because Dad was already in a bad mood and whenever someone drew water, the pump would kick on in the basement. He could hear it in the living room. I would always get in trouble for using too much water and making the pump kick off and on. He claimed I would make the motor burn up. If someone used more than half an inch of water in the tub, he would start yelling. I certainly wanted to avoid arousing his anger any more that night, so I just tolerated the strong smell of vinegar.

I went back upstairs and crawled into bed. I could still hear him downstairs complaining about my manners. I tried to silence my sobs so he wouldn't hear me. I didn't understand why he had to ruin such a nice day by treating me like that. The ironic part of the whole situation was that I had seen him use his fingers to do the same thing for which I was getting into trouble. I hated his double standards. I vowed to myself that someday I would run away, and he could never hurt me again.

That summer Dad purchased an old 1951 Harley Davidson three-wheeled servi-car motorcycle that had formerly belonged to Baron Yetter, a friend of his, who had purchased it from the local police department. It was considered economical and maneuverable at that time, and the 3-wheel platform made it stable in snow and ice. The back had a storage area with a lid that lifted. Dad removed that container and replaced it with a homemade wooden box that was about three-by-three and sixteen inches high. The motorcycle was bright red, and Dad painted the wooden box yellow.

On warm summer evenings, he would load the entire family into the box and drive us along the mountain roads near our home. Occasionally, he would take a main road to get where he was headed. Boy, did people stare at us as we whizzed past on that unique vehicle! Helmets were not required then, so we sat in the back holding onto the side of the box with our hair blowing everywhere. The mountain roads were not paved, and the rides were far from smooth. We would take pillows along to help cushion the shock from all the bumps.

One evening in late August, Dad said to Brenda and me, "Let's go find some huckleberries."

Brenda and I squealed with delight.

Dad instructed us, "Tell your mom to get some bags and come along."

I ran into the house and found Mom in the kitchen finishing the supper dishes. She hadn't worked that day, so she gave Brenda and me a break. "Come on, Mom," I said. "Dad wants to go pick huckleberries, and you're supposed to bring some bags."

As Mom gathered the bags that she stored under the sink, she instructed me to "grab the pillows."

I went into the living room and gathered the pillows from the couch, and threw them into the box on back of the motorcycle. Mom came out a few moments later with the bags. She tucked them underneath her left arm as she pulled the back door shut with her right hand and turned the knob, making sure it was locked.

Mom, Brenda, and I climbed up and took our places in the box as Dad got on the motorcycle and started the engine. He drove us out the alley and turned left onto Lingle Valley Road. We crossed the bridge, passed the Thomas' farmhouse and the archery range, and continued out the valley. Dad drove for approximately three miles until we reached the fork in the road. If we went right, we would be on Spruce Mountain Road and if we went left, we would be on Conklin Road. Dad turned left and we continued on Conklin Road about seven or eight miles until we came to Stone Creek Road. There, he took a left toward Alan Seeger State Park. He drove several miles farther and stopped at the park.

Alan Seeger State Park was named in honor of a young American poet who had fought and died in World War I. The park consisted of 150 acres of woods with hiking trails and a picnic area. We stopped on the other side of the bridge that ran though the park by the water pump to get a drink. Stone Creek ran through the park, and there were magnificent specimens of eastern hemlock and white pine. An abundance of thick rhododendron was also plentiful.

After we had all quenched our thirst with the cold mountain water, Dad continued driving through the park and on to Bear Meadows, a natural area that covered more than 300 acres. There were all kinds of trees and shrubs. The huckleberry bushes were also abundant there and the blossoms had turned to fruit since it was August.

Dad parked the motorcycle, and we got out near a patch of huckleberry bushes. We began picking them and putting them into our bags. We all picked and ate berries for about forty-five minutes. Dad then announced that it was time to head for home. Prior to getting into the motorcycle, Mom emptied all the small bags into the larger bag that she had brought along. She then placed the berries in the corner of the box on the motorcycle.

Dad said Brenda and I could each take a turn riding up front on the motorcycle on the gas tank in front. Brenda went first while Mom and I rode in the back. When Dad got back to Alan Seeger Park, he slowed down because there was some sort of commotion going on in the park. Four or five cars were parked near a pavilion, and a group of people were standing there watching something. As we got closer, we could see what they were looking at.

There was a black mother bear and two baby cubs eating something near the garbage can that stood beside a picnic table. Dad pulled over to the side of the road and turned the motor off. We sat there for about fifteen minutes watching the bears until the mother turned and led the cubs into the thick brush at the edge of the park. We had seen bears in the wild before at my Grandma Eward's house, but it hadn't been often enough to take away the fascination.

Dad said it was still Brenda's turn to ride upfront as we all prepared to leave the park. We again continued on Stone Creek Road and turned right onto Conklin Road . Shortly before we got to the fork in the road, Dad said it was my turn to ride up front. Just as I had positioned myself on the gas tank of the Harley, Mom yelled, "Oh no!" She discovered that she had accidentally sat on the bag of huckleberries as she held up the bag to show us.

That accident infuriated Dad. He shouted numerous choice words at Mom as he revved the motorcycle engine and proceeded to give me the most thrilling motorcycle ride of my life. Bugs were stinging my face as we flew through the valley toward our house. My rear was becoming numb from the vibration of the machine and all the bumps we were hitting. When we pulled into our driveway, I was relieved to get off the cycle. Dad was still angry about the huckleberries and continued to vent his hostilities on Mom well into the evening. He sure didn't think it was funny then, but a few days later, he saw the humor in it. Huckleberries always remind me of my wild motorcycle ride on that three wheeled Harley.

Chapter 19

My ninth grade school year started that September. Scenarios similar to the "hair cut day," as I thought of it, when I had been teased and taunted the previous year, occurred several times a week throughout ninth grade. The teachers never seemed to notice what was going on, or worse yet, if they did, they ignored it. It was hard being the class scapegoat. I grew to absolutely despise school. Each night I would continue to watch the clock and count the hours until I had to return. On weekends, I was beginning to do things with some of my friends, again. Sometimes I would go up to Cathy's house, and we would try on clothes, listen to records, or just talk.

On one such day, I went to visit Cathy at her house while her mother was at work. We had taken Cathy's record player into her mother's bedroom to dance since it was a much larger room than Cathy's. That day while we were listening to "You Can't Hurry Love," dancing, and generally just messing around, we discovered her mother's sun lamp on the small table beside her bed. As we discussed our new find, Cathy explained how her mother used the lamp. During the course of our discussion, Cathy exclaimed, "We should use this lamp to get a good tan! Wouldn't it be great to go to school tomorrow with a tan? "

"Yeah, good idea!" I exclaimed exuberantly. "Let's get a tan!"

Cathy turned on the sun lamp, and our tanning session began. We reasoned that if you could get a tan in five to ten minutes, you would really get a good tan in twenty minutes. However, we didn't bother reading the directions on the box beside the bed.

We both put our faces over the lamp, about eight inches from the bulb, and just stood there. After approximately twenty minutes had passed, we turned the light off. We were certain that the next day, we would each have a good tan, and we planned what we could wear to really set it off.

The next morning when I awoke, my face was stiff, and it hurt to open my eyes. I jumped out of bed and ran down to the bathroom to look at my face in the mirror. What I saw looking back at me really frightened me! I looked like a monster. My face was swollen. My eyelids were so puffy there was only a small slit where my eyes had been. My entire face and neck were bright red. *Oh no*, I thought as I continued to look in the mirror. I left the bathroom and went into the kitchen to ask Mom what I could use to relieve the pain.

"Mom," I said, and that was as far as I got.

"What happened to your face?" she shrieked.

"Cathy and I tried to get a tan with her mother's sun lamp. My face really hurts. What can I put on it?" I asked as I placed my palms on my cheeks and tried to absorb the heat.

Mom went into the bathroom, lecturing the whole time about our stupidity. When she returned, she had a tube of first aide cream. "Put that on all over your face," she commanded. "Make sure you don't get any in your eyes."

"I'll try not to," I said. "What about my eyelids? Should I put something on them?"

"No you better not," Mom replied. "Just hold a cool cloth on them for a while," she instructed.

The cool cloth did feel good, but my eyes began hurting again shortly after I removed it. "I can't go to school like this," I stated.

"Oh yes you can," Mom insisted. "That was a stupid, dangerous thing to do. Now you're not taking off of school because of it."

I realized that Mom was very angry with me, so I didn't argue. I got ready for school and reluctantly went up the hill to the bus stop. Elmer and Wayne were already there. I was running later than usual. They saw me and stared.

Eventually, Elmer asked, "What's wrong with your face?"

"I got burned," was my reply.

"You look awful," he continued

"Thank you," I said sarcastically.

Cathy wasn't on the bus. Her mother had allowed her to stay home. I thought life really was unfair. In homeroom, I did fine. Students looked at me strangely, but no one said anything. When the bell rang, I proceeded to math class. As soon as I entered the classroom, I knew trouble was about to begin. "What happened to you?" Tracy loudly asked as I took my seat. "Did you plug yourself into an outlet or something?" Several students near her snickered.

"No," I said without looking at her. "I got burned," I added.

"How'd you do that?" Tracy pried.

"With a friend's sun lamp," I reluctantly told her.

"How stupid!" Don't you know how to use one?" she asked. I didn't answer. Frankly, I was very tired of Tracy. My pill was still working, and she was having no affect on me. That bothered her more than anything. As a result, she badgered me more.

"Didn't anyone ever teach you anything?" she harassed.

"Apparently, they didn't teach me as much as they did you." I stated with sarcasm.

That shut her up some. Too bad I couldn't respond like that all the time. I cared too much usually and always tried to keep the peace. There comes a time, though, when everyone must take a stand. That day was my day.

"Well, you're stupid," she said as she turned and left the room. I felt elated. It felt great to stand up for myself. If I could only keep that feeling without the pills. It was much better than being depressed.

For the next few days, my face continued to hurt, and then it peeled for the next few weeks. Large flakes of skin came loose everywhere. I thought the tops and insides of my ears would never stop peeling. My eyelids flaked forever, too. I sure learned a lesson. I never wanted to see another sun lamp as long as I lived

Brenda and Cathy were in 8th grade that year. Occasionally, I would pass them in the hall when we switched classes. On Thursday afternoons, I had study halls with them in the cafeteria. Charlene Osborne, a friend of theirs, had study hall there on Thursdays, also. Charlene was quite an extrovert. I sat near her, and she would always be passing notes to someone. Some of the tenth grade students were in there, too. Ken Banks sat at the table next to mine. I thought he was really cute. Ken had straight black hair, and he was tall and thin. He was quite a character and had a tendency to get in trouble for talking. Charlene would pass him notes through me.

Through that process, Charlene became a friend of mine, also. Brenda, Cathy, and I began to run around with Charlene after school occasionally. She lived in Milroy, so it wasn't too far for us to go. When other transportation wasn't available, we would ride the green and white public bus to Milroy, using part of our lunch money to pay. At that time Charlene lived in the lower part of Milroy in a two-story house that her mother rented. Her mother and father were divorced. She had one older sister, Tina, and one younger sister, Teresa. We would just hang out and generally have Dad or Cathy's mother pick us up when it was time to go home. Charlene's mother didn't seem to mind us being there.

Charlene always liked talking about boys. During our conversations, I once told her that I thought Ken Banks was very cute. She agreed, but told me he liked Elsie Knepp. Elsie was pretty as well as wild, and I thought I would never have a chance against her.

During the next Thursday study hall after my confession, Charlene sent Ken a note telling him I thought he was cute. I was absolutely mortified! When the monitor wasn't looking our way, he slid his chair along the row of tables until he was across from me and loudly whispered, "So you think I'm cute?"

My face must have turned scarlet as I said, "I don't know." How stupid a response, I thought, as soon as I said it.

He just chuckled and slid back to his original position. Throughout the remainder of the study hall, I sneaked glances at Ken whenever I could. Once in a while he would be looking at me and our eyes would lock. Gee that guy was cute. I couldn't believe he would even look at me.

The following day was Friday, and my family went to town on Friday evenings to do our grocery shopping. On our way, Dad stopped at the Esso gas station in Milroy to fill up the car for the week. I was shocked when Ken came out to pump our gas. I think I surprised him, too, when he noticed me in the back seat. When we were leaving Ken waved. Dad turned around and asked me, "Do you know that kid?"

"He's in my study hall at school," I answered.

"Well, stay away from him," he commanded. "I talk to Harvey sometimes when I stop in there, and I heard that he's a wild one."

Harvey owned the gas station, and Dad sometimes hung out there after work. I wondered what Dad meant about Ken being wild, but I didn't ask him. Maybe I didn't really want to know. I was thrilled that Ken had waved to me. I couldn't wait until the following Thursday when I would again have a whole study hall with him. I continued to fantasize about Ken during the remainder of our trip to Lewistown.

The following Thursday, I was almost ecstatic as I entered the cafeteria and looked for Ken. He wasn't there yet. A few minutes later, he entered and went to his table. My eyes followed him the whole time. He looked up and smiled at me as he took his seat. That smile was enough to make my heart race. I smiled back, and then tried to act like I was studying. What a joke! Who could study?

When the study hall was about half over, Ken slipped up to my table and whispered, "Hey." I looked up at him, and he threw a note at me and then went to his original spot. It read: "Would you like to go on a hayride with me next Saturday? We'll leave from the Lutheran Church in Milroy. If you want to go, you could meet me there."

Would I ever like to go, I thought. I was thrilled. I couldn't believe Ken had asked me to go on the hayride with him. I tore a sheet of paper out of my notebook and wrote: "Yes, I would like to go," and folded it in half three times. After the bell rang, I handed the note to Ken as he walked past.

Charlene saw that exchange and asked, "What was the note for?" I excitedly told her what had happened. "You better be careful if you go with him," she told me. "He's wild and who knows what he'll try under the blanket."

"What do you mean?" I asked.

"I just mean he might try something because he hangs around with Elsie, and everyone knows she puts out. Besides, he's sixteen and you're only thirteen."

"I'll be fourteen soon," I stated.

"Still, you better be careful," she warned as we parted in the hall to go to our separate classes.

That night at the dinner table, I told Mom and Dad, " I've been invited on a hayride by Ken Banks"

"Well, you're not going," Dad replied.

"Why not?" I asked almost in a panic.

"You're not old enough to date," was his response.

"It's not a date. It's just a hayride and it's a church hayride." I reported.

"Absolutely not," Dad said. "Besides, I know about that Ken Banks, and he's wild. He drinks and runs about with a wild bunch of kids. You can't go."

"But I have to," I pleaded. "I already told him I would go."

"So, just tell him you're not," Dad said with no compassion.

Mom said, "You know you're not allowed to date until you're sixteen. You're just too young to go anywhere with a boy."

"No, I'm not," I tried in desperation, but I knew Dad had made up his mind, and I didn't have a chance. I wanted to go so badly I could hardly stand it; it just wasn't going to happen.

The following Thursday, I saw Ken in the hallway near the gymnasium. I walked up to him and said, "I won't be able to go on the hayride. My dad said I'm not allowed," I informed him.

"I know," Ken said. "Your dad stopped in for gas last night, and he told me you were too young to date. That's too bad. We could have had a good time."

"Thanks for the invitation anyway," I said as I turned and walked away, brokenhearted. Why did Dad want to ruin my life? Then to top it off, he had talked to Ken! Something finally seemed to be going right, and he had to ruin it.

When I ran into Charlene in the hallway, she said, "I heard you can't go on the hayride."

"No, I can't," I answered.

"It's probably for the best," she said. "He's bad, you know."

I found it hard to believe that Ken was bad. He seemed so sweet to me. My crush on him would continue throughout all of ninth grade. Later, I heard he had taken Elsie on the hayride. That information made me burn with jealousy. I wondered why I couldn't have any of the fun. Other kids my age were allowed to go on church hayrides with boys. Again I learned life was not fair.

My interest in boys was increasing. It seemed that I could go nowhere without thinking about the boys who seemed to be all around me. I guess it was just puberty. In December, I turned fourteen, but I still had two years to wait before I would be permitted to date.

Christmas that year seemed to be extra depressing for me. There was just something about the holidays that made me think more about Grandma. I would get sad when I remembered the big Christmas feasts she had helped to prepare. After Grandma's death, Dad again set the Christmas tree in its original spot where Grandma's bed had been. Somehow it didn't seem right to celebrate Jesus' birth in the spot that had almost been Grandma's dying place. Actually she had gone through the dying process in that space; she was removed just an hour before she drew her last breath.

Throughout the entire Christmas break, I had difficulty shaking the depression. It got dark early, and I would go into the kitchen and stare out the window at dusk, looking toward the mountain where Steve and I had held our picnic. Again I would watch the clock as dusk approached and dread the impending darkness that I knew would be there. It was at that time that life seemed the most difficult. I hated how darkness engulfed the valley. I began to understand why Jesus was referred to as the "light of the world," and Satan was associated with darkness.

Christmas was also a sad time because I had distanced myself from God. I searched for the joy that the world proclaimed at that time of the year more than at any other time. Joy seemed to elude me, however, no matter how hard I tried to find it. Whenever I heard Christmas carols sung, I yearned for God's love. Later, I learned it was there all along; I just refused to see it.

As the Christmas break neared its end, I again felt anxious about returning to school. Even though it was sad at home over the holidays, I believed school would be worse. No matter how closely I watched the clock, and I did watch it closely, time moved forward. Much too soon, I was back at school and again exposed to the pain I so desperately wanted to escape.

My crush on Ken continued throughout the school year. I still saw him in study hall, but he had lost interest in me. That added to my depression.

Occasionally, I would find some relief from the internal pain I experienced. Our church youth group provided some of that relief. That year in January, our church group, that usually met once a week, except in summer, took the teenagers to the Farm Show that was held in the Farm Show Building in Harrisburg. The leaders had arranged for a school bus to transport the kids. Charlene Osborne, Linda Jones, Brenda, and I went with the group. Charlene and Linda weren't members of our youth group, but we took them as our guests. Of course, we were not permitted to invite boys. We were going during school time, but it would be an excused absence. That made it even better, getting out of school.

The Farm Show was the largest indoor agricultural event in America. It began after New Year's Day and continued for one week. It was located along Cameron and Maclay Streets in Harrisburg. It was approximately 60 miles from Lewistown and took about an hour and a half to get there.

The day we left for the show, everyone was excited. I sat with Charlene on the bus. We each had taken along a few dollars. Admission was always free; however, we would have to buy our supper that evening. We took a bagged lunch. The doors opened at nine a.m. and would remain opened until nine p.m. We left Milroy at seven a.m., so we arrived at the complex shortly before it opened.

None of us had any real interest in farming issues or animals, but it was fun walking the circle around the arena. When we tired of that, we would go in to rest in the arena. Throughout the day, there were different events going on. We caught a couple of the livestock shows. Thousand of animals were on display which included, sheep, swine, horses, cattle, goats, and rabbits.

We had absolutely no interest in the farm equipment, so whenever events involved equipment, we walked around again. During our journeys that day, we met a group of boys from Mechanicsburg. There were four of them, too: Jeff, George, Gary, and Ed. We spent the remainder of the day and evening with them. All of us had a good time walking around together, taking in some of the shows, and enjoying all the junk food.

I got to sit beside Jeff. He told me he was fifteen. I had just turned fourteen in December. His family lived on a farm, so he had more interest in the animals and equipment than I did. He particularly enjoyed the youth rodeo, which included team roping, saddle and bareback riding, bull riding, steer wrestling, calf roping, breakaway roping, goat tying, pole bending and barrel racing. During our walks, we visited some of the 4-H Club and FFA (Future Farmers of America) exhibits. Jeff told me he was a member of the 4-H Club. To prove it, he recited the 4-H Club Pledge:

"I pledge
my HEAD to clearer thinking,
my HEART to greater loyalty,
my HANDS to larger service,
and my HEALTH to better living
for my club,
my community,
my country,
and my world."

He also informed me that he was a member of the FFA. He didn't seem like a farmer to me, though. Many of the boys in our high school were farmers, and some of the students teased them about smelling like cow manure. Jeff didn't smell, and he was cute.

Time passed much too quickly. Before any of us were ready to leave, we had to meet our youth group leaders to begin our trip back home. We had all been told to meet at the front entrance at eight-forty-five p.m. since the complex closed at nine. We said our good-byes to the boys, and rushed to the front entrance since we had only a few minutes to spare.

On the way home, I again sat with Charlene. We had a grand time reminiscing about the boys we had just met. I had never been to the Farm Show before that year, but after that trip, I looked forward to going the following year.

During the remainder of my ninth grade school year, I continued to experience bouts of depression from time to time that usually were brought on by feelings of isolation and rejection in school. After school, I was pulling myself together. I believe I had worked through the grieving process; however, the damage to my self-esteem that had resulted during Grandma's sickness and after her death would remain with me throughout my high school years. I managed to become a survivor through all of my experiences, and I eventually made it through the ninth grade. Soon winter passed and spring arrived. Then it was Memorial Day again.

Mom's family picnics began on Memorial Day when they opened the state parks. That year we went to Reeds Gap State Park for the first picnic of the season. It was the closest state park to our home.

Reeds Gap State Park is located in New Lancaster Valley, which is about seven miles from Milroy. The park was built by the Civilian Conservation Corps and dedicated to the public in 1938. In 1965, two swimming pools had been built in the park. Admission was free, so that park grew to be my favorite.

Dad had told Brenda and me that we were allowed to take Cathy and Betsy with us on our picnic that Memorial Day. During the past couple of years, they had gone on many of the family picnics with us. It was even more fun for us to take our friends with us. When we arrived, we went to the bathhouse and changed into our bathing suits and hit the pool. The deepest spot was five feet, so diving was not permitted. We still had a great time doing handstands in the water and swimming all afternoon.

While we were in the pool, numerous cousins joined us. We had contests to see who could stand on their hands the longest, who could hold their breath the longest, and who could swim the most laps without stopping. Many wonderful memories were made during those summer afternoons.

When it was time to eat, Uncle Hank came after us that day. Hot dogs and hamburgers were on the menu along with all the other goodies, such as baked beans, fried potatoes and onions, homemade cakes, watermelon, and drinks. We all ate until we were satisfied, then gradually the kids began to head toward the pool again. They didn't lock the gate on the pool until seven, and we made sure we remained in the pool until then.

Occasionally, a few of Mom's sisters and their husbands would swim, too; however, most of them sat around the picnic table talking. Sometimes, too, they would go on walks along the many trails in the park. The younger children spent a lot of time at the playgrounds in the park whenever an adult was not available to monitor them at the pool. There were lifeguards on duty, but younger children still needed to be supervised.

That night as we rode home, Cathy, Betsy, Brenda, and I talked about what we would do all summer. We had only two more days until school was out. We planned on going to the Burnham Pool the first Monday after school ended for the summer. Dad agreed to pick us up after work. We would ride the bus to Burnham and walk over to the pool from the red light where we had to get off the bus.

When that Monday arrived, we did exactly as we had planned. We made our trip to the Burnham pool. It was a great start to our summer vacation. We made several more trips to the pool that June, and the other nice summer days were spent at Cathy's grandfather's pool. Life was so much better when there was no school.

PART IV
JULY 1967 - JUNE 1968
Time Line

July 23 – 30, 1967 – Black uprising in Detroit; largest U. S. riot of the century.

July 27, 1967 - Black uprisings in Toledo, Ohio; Rochester, NY; Pontiac, Michigan; plus more than 100 other cities; National Guard called out for first time in a quarter century.

September 1967 – Linda starts 10th grade.

December 12, 1967 – Linda's 15th birthday.

December 1967 – Beatles release "Magical Mystery Tour."

December 1967 – 486,000 troops in Viet Nam; 15,000 had been killed and 60% of those in 1967.

January – May 1968 – 40,000 students participate in 221 major demonstrations at 101 campuses.

February 16, 1968 – Draft deferments for most grad students and all occupational deferments eliminated.

March 16, 1968 - Robert F. Kennedy declares candidacy.

April 4, 1968 – Martin Luther King shot and killed at Memphis motel.

April 4 – 11, 1968 – Black uprisings in Chicago, Baltimore, Washington, DC, Cincinnati, Boston, Detroit, Philadelphia, San Francisco, Toledo, Pittsburgh; more than 129 cities in 29 states total

April 11, 1968 – Major call-up of reserves for duty in Viet Nam.

May 2 – 17, 1968 – SCLC Poor People's March on Washington.

May 13, 1968 – United States and Vietnamese begin talks in Paris.

June 5, 1968 – Robert F. Kennedy shot at Ambassador Hotel in LA.

June 8, 1968 – James Earl Ray arrested and accused of Martin Luther King's murder.

Popular Songs

"Windy," The Association; "A Whiter Shade Of Pale," Procol Harum; "Ode To Billie Joe," Bobbie Gentry; "To Sir With Love," Lulu; "Expressway To Your Heart," The Soul Survivors; "I Heard It Through The Grapevine," Gladys Knight & The Pips; "Hello Goodbye," The Beatles; "Woman, Woman," The Union Gap; "Love Is Blue (L'Amour Est Bleu)," Paul Mauriat & His Orchestra; "Young Girl," The Union Gap; "Honey," Bobby Goldsboro; "Mrs. Robinson," Simon & Garfunkel

Chapter 20

Since Dad and Mom had purchased our house from Mrs. Muttersbaugh, Dad had completed many remodeling projects. In the summer of 1967, he decided the house needed a new roof, and he began his roofing project. Funds were very limited, so he had to complete all the work himself. Mom, Brenda, and I were his assistants. I didn't like to help with his projects. I usually ended up getting into some kind of trouble.

He began his project by first removing all the old shingles on the front half of the roof. Brenda and I helped to tear off the old shingles and throw them to the ground. Later, we would gather them up and throw them in Dad's trunk, so we could take them to the dump. Mom didn't think Brenda and I should be on the roof because it was dangerous, and she was afraid we would fall off. Dad insisted that we would be fine.

After we removed the old shingles from the front of the house, we began to tear off the black tar paper. The tar paper was very old and crumbled into little pieces as we removed it. Our roof was very steep once you were off the porch portion. The only place I was frightened was right at the edge. After the tar paper was removed, we had to spread tar onto the roof so that Dad could roll the tar paper onto it.

While Brenda and I were spreading the tar with putty knives, we got into an argument. Brenda said I had gotten tar on her hand on purpose, and she rubbed tar on my forearm with her putty knife. That made me angry, so I, in turn, rubbed my putty knife on her forearm.

It was about that time that Dad took notice of what we were doing, and he began yelling at me. Whenever Brenda and I fought, it seemed that he always took her part. Perhaps it was because she was younger and smaller than I, and often people try to protect the smallest person. Also, it may have been because he had been the youngest sibling in his family, and from what I had heard, he was not protected. Regardless, though, I felt that Dad didn't like me because he always protected Brenda, and I was the "bad" daughter.

He came over to where we were hunkered on the roof, grabbed hold of my right arm with his left hand, and jerked my putty knife out of my hand with his right hand. He then said, "You always have to cause trouble, you little brat. How do you like having tar all over you?" Then he filled the putty knife with tar and rubbed it down the length of my right arm. He was hurting my arm from squeezing so tight. I felt the tears sting my eyes as I fought not to release them. I had not done anything that Brenda had not done. I wondered why I always seemed to be punished, but she was not.

After he released me, I sat there feeling sorry for myself. I did not dare to say anything for I feared he might slap me. When he turned his head, I wiped my eyes and nose on my shirt because I knew I would not be permitted to leave the roof until the work was completed.

Throughout the remainder of the morning, as we continued to tar the roof, I thought about how nice it would be to escape from there. I wished my life could be like my friend Cathy's. She never had to help do yucky things like I did. She hardly ever saw her father.

Finally, lunchtime arrived, and we descended the ladder to go to the kitchen for some chicken noodle soup and peanut butter sandwiches. First, though, I had to remove the tar that had dried on my arm with gasoline. I hated the smell of gasoline. Whenever Dad repaired people's cars, Brenda and I had to clean his tools with gasoline. The smell of the gas and grease has remained with me throughout my life, and whenever I smell either, those memories are stirred.

When I entered the kitchen, Dad was telling Mom about me putting tar on Brenda's wrist. I truly do not recall him ever saying anything nice about me, but he criticized me often. I was convinced that he did not like me; I thought he might even hate me. That confused me, for I did not understand why. I also did not understand why he never touched me, and had never told me that he loved me. I don't believe he ever told Brenda that, either, but I could tell he liked her. He did say nice things about her, and occasionally he put his arm over her shoulder.

I slid behind the table and ate my soup and sandwich in silence. The remainder of the afternoon would be hot and tiring. I was not looking forward to it. Again, time had become my enemy.

Often Mom would defend me. I don't think she favored me over Brenda, I just think she saw the injustices and tried to stop them. She never said anything to me about it, however.

Sometimes when Brenda and I would get into arguments at night in our beds, Dad would yell at us. Their bedroom was right next to ours, so you could hear everything. If we didn't shut up, he would get out of bed and come over to punish us. Generally, Brenda would get one slap, but he would keep slapping me while he told me what a brat I was. Mom would usually get into the middle of these episodes by trying to make him stop hitting my head. I remember her often saying, "Werdna, not her head. Quit hitting her head," and she would try to pull him away from me. She also would instruct me to "Cover your head," so I would raise my arms to shield my head from the hits. She would point out to him that he always punished me more severely. They generally would get into an argument over that, and I would feel responsible.

That confirmed what I already knew; I was treated unfairly. It was not my imagination; Mom saw it, too. She was not very affectionate, either, but she had held me when I was younger, and I didn't feel that she hated me. She treated Brenda and me equally.

When lunch was over, we again went up on the roof to finish the roofing. Dad had already put the tar paper on, so he had to nail on the shingles. He had chosen white shingles because he said the house would stay cooler in the summer since they would not absorb the heat as much as dark shingles would. I didn't care if they absorbed heat or not; I just wanted to get finished so I could get off the roof. Brenda and I had to hand him the shingles and help him hold them in place.

We finished about six o'clock that evening, and Dad said that after we got cleaned up, he would take us to Frosty Freeze to get a blue-plate-special so Mom wouldn't have to cook. Frosty Freeze was an ice cream stand and grill two miles east down Route 322 on the outskirts of Milroy. There were a few seats inside, but I knew ours would be takeout. We never went inside restaurants to eat. I never knew why; I just accepted it, as that was the way it was. The blue-plate-special consisted of two hamburgers, French fries, and coleslaw. I was extremely tired and hungry by the time we got our food back to the house, and I recall that I couldn't remember food ever tasting better. Dad also had picked up a bag of Big Wheel ice cream sandwiches, so we all had one of them for dessert. Shortly after eating, I went to bed and instantly fell asleep when my head hit my pillow due to extreme exhaustion.

The following Saturday, we repeated the same procedure as we roofed the back side of the house. I didn't get any tar rubbed on me that week. It was still a long, hot, tiring day, and I looked forward in anticipation to another blue-plate-special that Dad had promised us when we finished.

Later that evening, while we were sitting at the kitchen table enjoying our blue-plate- specials, Dad surprised Brenda and me by handing us each a ten dollar bill. Now that was a lot of money to us. It also confused us as we sat looking at the money. Dad must have read our confusion because he said, "That's for helping with the roof. Get yourselves a new summer outfit or something."

"Thanks," both Brenda and I responded, hardly believing our good fortune. Dad could be very nice when he controlled his temper. Most of the time he did have it under control except when he worked on remodeling, and vehicle projects; they just seemed to set him off.

As the summer wore on, my friends and I were getting bored. One particular event especially stands out in my memory. Betsy, Cathy, Brenda, and I were sitting on Betsy's porch watching the traffic pass on Route 322 when we began cooking up our idea. "We should sleep out some night," Betsy stated. "That would be fun."

"I like that idea," Cathy added. "Why don't we do it tonight?"

"Yeah," I added. "Let's do it tonight."

"But, we don't have a tent, do we?" Brenda asked.

After we all thought for a moment, we agreed that we didn't have a tent. "Does anyone know someone we could borrow one from?" I inquired.

"Nope," Cathy answered.

"I don't know anyone," Betsy added.

"We don't either," Brenda responded for her and me.

"I know what we could do," I excitedly commented. "We could make one!"

"How?" all three of the others asked.

"If we could find some cardboard, maybe that would work," I speculated.

"Yeah, that might work," Cathy agreed.

"Where could we get cardboard?" Betsy asked.

"Does anyone have some old boxes?" Brenda asked. We agreed that no one did.

"We could get some at a store," I stated.

"Maybe Mrs. Leeper has some in her back room," Cathy said.

"Yeah, let's go check with Mrs. Leeper," Betsy suggested. She then stood up and jumped over the banister heading toward Mrs Leeper's store. The rest of us trailed behind her. We all crossed Route 322 and went into Mrs.

Leeper's store. When Mrs. Leeper came through the curtain from the backroom, Betsy asked, "Mrs. Leeper, do you have any old boxes we could have?"

"Why, no girls; Ralph just burned them all this morning." Ralph was Mrs. Leeper's son-in-law. "What do you want boxes for?" she asked. Mrs. Leeper was sort of a busybody.

"We want to tear them apart and make a tent out of them," Betsy told her.

"Do you know where we can get some big boxes?" Cathy asked.

"No…not really," Mrs. Leeper told us.

We all sighed our disappointment as we left the store. "Thanks anyway," Betsy said on her way out.

Outside, we all took a seat on Mrs. Leeper's front porch and thought of places where we might get some boxes. We began naming stores in Milroy since there were no other stores in Mount Pleasant besides Rothrock's Tropical Fish store next to Mrs. Leeper's, and we didn't think they would have any boxes. Cathy asked, "What about Barnett's?" Barnett's was an appliance store located on Main Street in Milroy.

"Yeah, they would have boxes…big boxes!" Betsy exclaimed.

"Let's call and see if they have any," I suggested. Everyone was in agreement that we should call, so back across Route 322 we went and followed Betsy into her house while she looked up the number and called.

"Hello," we heard her say. "We're trying to find some big boxes, like refrigerator boxes. Do you have any there that we could have?" she asked.

We couldn't hear the other side of the conversation, but Betsy inquired, "Could you keep them for us until we can pick them up? " There was a pause, then she said, "Sometime today." Another pause, and she said, "Thanks."

When Betsy got off the phone, she reported, "They have four or five boxes that we can have, but we have to get them today. Now, how are we going to get them?"

"We could just walk down and get them," I suggested.

"It's really not that far," Brenda added.

"Let's go," Cathy urged.

Everyone agreed, so we began our journey walking east along Route 322 for approximately a mile. When we reached the upper end of Milroy, we left Route 322 and walked down North Main Street and turned in at Barnett's warehouse. When we went inside, an elderly man walked up to us and asked, "May I help you?"

"We're here to pick up the refrigerator boxes, Betsy announced.

"Oh, I see. They're here in the back," he informed us as he led us to the back of the warehouse and showed us the boxes. "Help yourselves," he told us. We each chose a box and started out of the warehouse. The man chuckled while we wrestled with the boxes, trying to get them out the door. Finally, they were outside, and we were on our way back home. We each were responsible for one box. It would be the box we would sleep in.

It was a hot, humid July day, and as we half-carried and half-dragged the boxes along, we got extremely thirsty. No one had thought of bringing any money along. By the time we made it up the huge hill on Main Street, we were totally exhausted, even more sweaty, and very thirsty.

"I wish someone would come along and take us and our boxes home," I said.

"Me too," Betsy agreed.

We were then back at Route 322 and a lot of traffic was passing. "Why don't we hitchhike?" I excitedly suggested.

"Yeah, let's hitchhike," Brenda urged.

"Okay. What do you think, Betsy?" Cathy asked as she looked around the right edge of her General Electric refrigerator box at Betsy.

"Let's do it, but if our parents find out, we're really going to be in trouble," Betsy cautioned.

"Well, we'll only be able to go in a truck, and if anyone tries anything, we could escape. There's four of us anyway," I reasoned.

Everyone agreed. As we stuck out our thumbs, we began giggling. It seemed so strange to stand there along the road like that. None of us had ever hitchhiked. It was kind of scary, too, but still fun. We would only stick out our thumbs when a pickup truck was headed toward us.

After about twenty minutes, we got lucky and an old, dark green Chevy pickup pulled over to the side of the road about ten feet in front of us. Inside was an older gentleman with a woman we assumed to be his wife. "You girls need a ride?" he called out of his window.

We left our boxes, walked over to the side of his truck, and explained what we were doing. "That sounds like fun," he said. Then he instructed, "Just throw your boxes up on there, and hop up yourselves. How far do you want to go?" he asked.

"To Mount Pleasant, right across from Lingle Valley Road," I replied.

We all laughed and carried on as we awkwardly lifted our huge boxes onto the back of the truck and then hopped on ourselves. After all the boxes were in place and we were situated on the truck, the man put his old truck into gear, and we were off with a jerk. It was one of the most fun rides I had ever had. We were impressed with ourselves for finding a way to get those boxes home.

When we came to Lingle Valley Road, he pulled off and waited for us to unload. We thanked the man before he again pulled out onto Route 322 and disappeared toward the mountain. We only had to carry the boxes down over the hill from there. When we reached our house, we parked our boxes in the front yard, and Brenda and I led everyone into our house to get drinks. After our thirsts were satisfied, we again went outside, sat on the porch, and planned what we were going to do with the boxes.

Our plan was that we each would sleep in a box. After discussing the plan for several minutes, we carried our boxes to the patch of woods across from our house. Cathy suggested we should lay them on something so they wouldn't get damp by morning. I went over to the garage and found some sheets of plastic Dad had used when he painted; I returned to the woods with those.

We spread the plastic on the pine needle floor of the woods and then positioned our boxes where we wanted them. We laid them out in a T-formation. Betsy suggested that we fasten them together at their openings. Brenda went to the garage and came back with a spool of Dad's wire and wire cutters. We all proceeded to wire the boxes together. The box with its end facing our house was the one we decided should have the door. It was Brenda's box. We cut three sides of a square opening and folded it back.

Brenda pushed a piece of wire through the flap so that after we were all in our own boxes, she could wire the door shut so that we would be secure. Each of us cut a small window on the side of our box that could also be pulled shut with a piece of wire. In addition, we decided we better throw some of the plastic on top in case it rained. When that was done, our sleeping quarters were ready.

We crawled into the boxes, and faced forward so that everyone's head would be in the center. We discussed our plans for that evening while lying there in our homemade tent. It was decided that we would have a cookout consisting of hot dogs and potatoes. At that time, the margarine our parents bought came in small metal containers with plastic lids. We had discovered that these containers were perfect for cooking sliced potatoes on the hot coals of a camp fire. We would slice potatoes very thin and add butter, salt, and pepper, then cover the top with aluminum foil and lay it on top of the fire's coals. We would cook our hot dogs on sticks and eat on a picnic table Dad had put by our fire ring. My Uncle Jim had made the table for us.

When Dad and Mom came home that night, we proudly showed them our homemade tent and asked if we could sleep out. They both agreed that it was all right with them. Betsy and Cathy got permission to sleep out, also.

Later that night we carried out our plans. We had planned on having soda to drink which we did, but Betsy brought us an additional beverage we had not planned on. She had taken two cans of beer from her dad's supply for us to drink. On occasion, her parents had given her a sip of alcohol, but the rest of us had never drunk any. That was a big deal to everyone, and we knew we would be in big trouble if my parents caught us drinking beer.

Mom and Dad joined us in the woods, Dad built the fire, and we had our cookout. After the hot dogs and potatoes were gone, Mom produced a bag of marshmallows, and we all used our hot dog sticks to roast them. Dad and Betsy liked their marshmallows toasted to a golden brown. They were very careful not to get the marshmallow too close to the fire, and it seemed to take them forever. The rest of us liked to catch ours on fire and watch the outside burn before blowing out the flame and popping the black ash- coated melted marshmallow into our mouths. After everyone had their fill of marshmallows, Mom and Dad announced they were going to bed. We could hardly contain our excitement as we realized we would soon be able to enjoy our beer. When we were certain they were in the house for the evening, everyone crawled back into the boxes, and Betsy produced the two cans of beer from her bag. We decided Betsy and Cathy would share a beer, and Brenda and I would share one.

The beer had not been cold to begin with; then Betsy had placed it in her bag inside the boxes when she arrived. When I took my first sip, I was surprised at how horrible it tasted, as I'm now sure everyone else was. No one would admit that, though. We continued passing and sipping the beer until it was gone as we all told each other how great it tasted. I don't believe anyone got drunk on half a beer, but we had convinced ourselves that we had. We sang an assortment of songs well into the night before (we believed) we passed out from intoxication. I remember thinking what a good singer Betsy was as she sang all the popular songs of the time, and we all eventually drifted off to sleep.

The next morning, I couldn't wait to get out of that box. I believe that experience made me claustrophobic. I felt miserable. I was dirty from the cookout the night before and tired from being up half the night. Apparently, everyone else felt like I did, for shortly after we were all awake, Betsy and Cathy left for home while Brenda and I returned to our house to continue our sleeping.

It had been a fun experience that each of us would probably never forget due to its uniqueness. Throughout the years, I have told numerous people about our box adventure. We kept the boxes in the woods for about a week and then a thunderstorm was their downfall. After the storm was over, we discovered that the boxes were wet and a few days later after they had dried, we made a bonfire out of them. Those boxes were even fun during their destruction.

I had other adventures that summer. Dad decided it would be fun for the family to picnic along the Juniata River with the many families in the area that enjoyed that kind of recreation. The Juniata River is approximately 100 miles long and is the second largest tributary to the Susquehanna River. It was relatively shallow and gentle which made it attractive to many central Pennsylvania residents for a source of water recreation.

Dad purchased a used john-boat so that we could all go out on the river, and he also rented a river frontage lot from the Fishers in Granville. The Fishers owned a farm, and for extra money, they divided all of their river frontage land into lots and rented them out for the season.

Our lot was 50-feet wide and looked down over a four-foot bank that leveled off near the river. That recreational activity actually created a lot more work for our family because the lot had to be mowed, and where it was too steep for the lawn mower, the weeds had to be cut with a sickle. I don't think my mother ever liked it at the river, but aside from the weed cutting and additional work, Brenda and I had a good time.

Several weeks after we had rented the lot, Dad came home with another surprise. He brought us an eight-foot rubber raft. Brenda and I thoroughly enjoyed that raft. On numerous occasions, we took Betsy and Cathy with us when we went to the river, and we all would go out on the raft while Mom and Dad went on the boat. Dad fished a little, although he was never a fishing fanatic like some of the other men at the river. Mom didn't fish; she just rode along and watched Dad. Betsy, Cathy, Brenda, and I would find a deep hole in the river, throw out the anchor, and jump in for a swim. The bottom of the river was either muddy or stony, so we all wore old sneakers, for often we would need to walk on the river bottom in the shallow areas. We spent a lot of time at the river that summer.

Mom would usually pack a picnic lunch, and we would all return to our lot where we relaxed in the shade as we ate our lunch on a blanket. Generally, we would go to the river either on a Saturday or Sunday. Once in a while, we went both days on the same weekend. We always went home for the night.

Some of the other people would camp overnight, but Mom wanted no part of that.

One day while just Dad, Mom, Brenda, and I had gone up to the river, I pleaded with Dad to let me take his boat out on the river by myself. He kept telling me how it was much more difficult to row his boat than the raft, but I insisted I could do it. When I had finally worn him down, I proceeded to take the boat out. Before I realized what was happening, the swift current carried the boat out to the middle of the river, and even though I was rowing as fast and hard as I could, I continued to drift down the river. I panicked and yelled for Dad's help. He was already running along the river bank, attempting to throw me a rope so he could tow me in. Eventually, after many attempts, I caught the rope and held onto it as tightly as I could while Dad pulled me to safety. Of course, when I was safely tied to the tree along our lot, Dad lectured me about what he had told me. I didn't want to hear it, but I had no choice but to listen. I never asked to take the boat out by myself again.

Chapter 21

Dad decided he wanted to tear down our old wooden porch that summer and build a new block and cement one. That was another major undertaking Brenda and I had to assist with. Our porch had four white wooden posts that held up the roof. Dad jacked up the porch roof with two-by-fours and then removed the posts and wooden flooring from the porch. He then dug a six-inch footer around the perimeter of the porch, and mixed and poured in the bags of cement with sand that he had purchased from Claster's Building Supply in Lewistown. When the footer was ready, he purchased cement blocks, and began laying them on the footer he had built until they were three layers high.

Since our front porch ran the whole length of our house, there was a large area that needed to be filled in before the cement could be poured for the porch. Dad threw in large stones and anything else he could find for fill. When he had filled in most of the area, he ordered some small stones to complete the filling job. These number-2 stones were poured on top of the other fill and leveled off. Dad had built a wooden form around the edge of the blocks to make a three-inch lip that would extend out over the blocks. At that time, he decided that he would also build forms for a sidewalk that would begin at the edge of our porch and continue to the edge of the road, and a smaller one would branch from that sidewalk and continue around the side of the house to the basement door. Before that, flat stones had been laid down to make our sidewalk. These had gone into the porch for some of the fill.

After the forms were all completed and Dad was certain that everything was level, he called and ordered the cement. I remember the large cement truck making the delivery. Brenda and I watched as the cement quickly shot down the shoot onto the fill. After the porch was filled up, Dad had them pour cement into the sidewalk forms.

When the cement truck left, Dad and Mom frantically worked the cement on the porch to get it smooth and even. Since that was very time consuming, he gave me a trowel and quickly instructed me on how to smooth out the cement in the sidewalk forms. He had only poured concrete in every other one. I had no idea what I was doing, but I tried my best to do what I believed he wanted me to do. Brenda wasn't assigned a task; she just stood there and watched.

While that whole process was going on, our neighbor, Mrs. Lewis, came down to watch. I knew that irritated Dad because he often had said she was nosey, but he didn't say anything to her. She asked numerous questions as she watched. I just kept my head down and continued to attempt to smooth the cement.

After Dad and Mom had finished the porch, he came over to where I was working and stood over me, watching what I was doing. He began yelling at me and telling me that I was messing it up. He used some foul language, and I was embarrassed that Mrs. Lewis was hearing him talk to me like that. A few years before, I had helped her at Vacation Bible School, and she had gotten me to play the teacher on the Sunday School float in the Memorial Day parade.

Dad continued yelling and became more irate. He said I had taken too long and the cement was setting and was now messed up. When he got angry like that, it frightened me. I just kept my head down and tried to fix the cement. He began to kick me in the ribs as he followed me across the front lawn, kicking me farther each step of the way. I was mortified! How could I ever again face Mrs. Lewis? I was afraid to look up. Mom again came to my rescue. She diverted his attention long enough for me to stand up and scurry away. Tears were streaming down my cheeks as I finally looked up. I was greatly relieved to see that Mrs. Lewis was no longer there. My ribs hurt, but my pride was hurt most of all.

I wiped my face and hid behind the house until Dad had calmed down. I couldn't leave because I knew I would get into more trouble. When he had finished with the sidewalk, Brenda and I had to clean up the tools and put them away.

Later that night, Dad lectured me about how I never listened to anything he said. He went on to say that I had no common sense, and I would never amount to anything. I had to sit and listen, for I was not permitted to respond. My ribs ached where he had kicked me, and I kept thinking that someday I would run away, and he would never be able to hurt me again. Still I pondered why he seemed to hate me. I truly did not understand.

A few days later, Dad mixed his own cement for the remaining portions of the unfinished sidewalk. He poured the cement and correct proportion of sand into his wheelbarrow and then sprayed them with water from the hose until it reached the right consistency. Brenda and I liked to use the hoe to mix the cement. That was something we were able to do without getting into any trouble. Dad then poured the wheelbarrow full of cement into the sidewalk forms. I was glad he had time to smooth those sections so I didn't have to do it.

When my father wasn't angry, I believe he felt guilty for treating me badly as he often did. He never said that he was sorry, however. It seemed to me that he just couldn't talk to me. I wondered why he didn't like me and why some of the kids at school didn't like me, either. It only seemed logical that it must be me. How could I make them like me when I didn't understand why they didn't like me? That made me feel sad and very lonely. I tried to analyze what was different about me, but I could find nothing.

Since my sessions with the doctor for my depression, those feelings would often return, but I had learned to keep them to myself. I felt I had to hide my abnormalities. My depression upset my parents, and they would fight about how to deal with it. Dad would just become more angry with me and say I only wanted attention. I thought about that, and maybe I did want attention, but not that kind. It would just make me feel more stressed.

I believe a relationship with God would have helped me to cope with my pain and loneliness. I missed having a relationship with God, but I was afraid to again place my trust in Him. I believed it was better to ignore Him completely than to risk betrayal once more. Little did I know that just because I chose to ignore Him did not mean He chose to ignore me. Later, I would realize that He was there all along, patiently waiting, knowing the ending even before the beginning. He had placed His mark upon me; I was His; I just didn't know it.

Brenda and I continued to attend church, but it was meaningless to me. I saw all the people profess to love their neighbors, but I knew it wasn't real. They listened to everything that Jesus was supposed to have said, then did nothing. If they truly loved their neighbors, why didn't they help them? Oh, they helped a little here and a little there, just so they felt good about themselves and could say, "Look what we did," but why could they not see the pain right next to them? That all frustrated me. The way they looked at me as though I was an insignificant annoyance frustrated me, too. They made it clear that I was inferior to them, and I should feel honored to be permitted to worship with them. That attitude made me despise those so-called "Christians." They were hypocrites, and I wished I didn't have to be around them. I did like the feeling of holiness I sensed when I was in church, though, and I still believed in God even though I could not communicate with him.

Chapter 22

My first trip to the seashore took place during the summer of 1967. Cathy's mother graciously decided that she would take Cathy and a group of her friends to the beach. Cathy asked Brenda and me to go with her. She had also asked Betsy, but she was going to Rehobeth Beach in Delaware with her family. Cathy then asked Donna Switzer, a friend of hers and ours who was two years younger than me.

Faye was going to take us to Wildwood Beach in New Jersey. She talked to our parents to make sure it was all right with them. Mom and Dad said Brenda and I were allowed to go. Donna's parents also gave permission. Faye said all we needed was spending money and some money to help purchase the food. She would pay for the apartment she had rented. Mom and Dad made arrangements to pay Faye, and Brenda and I began saving money for our trip. In addition, our parents had to buy us things like beach towels, sun tan lotion, and new flip flops. Dad was as generous as he could afford to be. It really stretched their budget to give us money to go, but he did it. His mood swings really confused me, but I was glad he was allowing us to go.

Brenda and I could barely contain our excitement as the time to leave approached. Cathy had been to the ocean before, but we never had and neither had Donna. Finally, the day arrived to leave. Cathy sat up front with her mother, and the rest of us were in the back of Faye's Rambler. We left at six a.m. and chatted for the first several hours of our trip before Faye got us started singing songs. We sang our hearts out as we expressed our joy in music. I remember Faye singing some of the songs alone because we didn't know the words. The one that stands out in my mind was "The Church in the Wildwood," I guess because we were headed for Wildwood, New Jersey. It went like this:

The Church in the Wildwood

There's a church in the valley by the wildwood,
No lovelier place in the dale;
No spot is so dear to my childhood
As the little brown church in the vale.

Oh, come, come, come, come,
Oh, come to the church by the wildwood.
Oh, come to the church in the vale;
No spot is so dear to my childhood
As the little brown church in the vale.

Oh, come to the church in the wildwood,
To the trees where the wild flowers bloom;
Where the parting hymn will be singing,
We will weep by the side of the tomb.
Refrain

From the church in the valley
By the wildwood,
When day fades away into night,
I would fain from this spot of my childhood
Fly away to the mansions of light.
Refrain

By: William S. Pitts

    Faye sang the verses alone, but after the first chorus, we joined in. It was a pretty song, and it again reminded me of Grandma. I hoped that she flew away to the mansions of light.
    When we crossed the bay bridge, I was amazed at all the large ships. I also remember the distinct smell of the salt air. That smell I grew to love. When we arrived in Wildwood, we went directly to our apartment which was behind a larger house three blocks from the beach. We all unloaded our things from the car and sorted our clothes inside. Cathy and I put our belongings in the back right bedroom and Donna and Brenda put theirs in the one on the left. Since our bedroom was slightly larger, Faye also put her clothing in our

room, but she planned to sleep on the hide-a-bed in the larger kitchen-dining-living room area. When everyone was situated, we changed clothes and headed for the beach.

As we got close to the beach, I could hear the ocean before I saw it. After going up a rise at the edge of the sand, we stood on top and gazed upon the majesty of the Atlantic Ocean. Prior to seeing it, it was impossible to comprehend the awe I experienced. I never wanted to leave. I thought I had found paradise.

After we stood staring for several minutes, Faye urged us to go down on the beach to place our blankets and towels. The remainder of the afternoon, the four of us fought waves, looked for shells, and enjoyed the sun while Faye lay on her blanket getting a tan.

Later, when we returned to the apartment, and it was my turn to shower, I couldn't believe how much sand was in my bathing suit. As I showered, I thought about how much fun we'd had, and how I wished it could last forever. All the pressures of life that seemed to be back home had vanished there at the beach. I thought about how nice it would be to become a beach bum and never return to school. School still held much pain for me.

That first night, Faye made spaghetti and meatballs. It was fantastic! She said that since she did the cooking, we were responsible for doing the dishes. That seemed like a bargain to me. When we had finished the dishes, we were off to the boardwalk. Faye had a very bad sunburn on her back, so she allowed us to go without her. The end of the boardwalk was right where we had gone onto the beach that day. She instructed us to be back by ten o'clock.

When we got up on the boardwalk, I had another wonderful experience as we took in all the sights and sounds. It was great! There were several places that had in-ground trampolines where you could rent a turn for thirty minutes. We all tried that. I even attempted and completed a flip after receiving instructions on how to do it. I loved it!

Cathy and I were then both teenagers, and we didn't miss checking out all the guys on the boardwalk. Donna and Brenda were younger, and they didn't seem interested. We talked to several groups of boys, but that's as far as it went.

The boardwalk wouldn't be the boardwalk without taking in the amusement rides, and we had no intentions of missing those. We rode as much as we could afford to before we thought we better start back to the apartment. Before leaving the boardwalk, though, we made certain that we each got a snack. I remember I had french fries. They were wonderful!

On the walk back to the apartment, we talked about all the things we had done, and what we still planned on doing while at the beach. I realized I would have to curb my spending or my money would not last the entire time. When we got back to the apartment, Faye was still in her bathing suit, lying on her stomach as she watched TV. She had her bathing suit straps pulled down over her shoulders, and I could see how burned her back was. She asked Cathy to spray it with Solar Cane. We told Faye about everything we had done, and she said that it sounded like fun.

The four of us went into our back bedroom and talked well into the night until we finally retired in exhaustion. I recall that when I woke up the next morning, I initially couldn't remember where I was, but when my memory cleared, I was quite excited again.

After breakfast, we set off to explore the area. We discovered a little burger shack one block from our apartment. It was in the opposite direction from the beach. Music blared from the speakers attached to the outside of the building, and there were several picnic tables covered with yellow and white striped umbrellas on the left side for patrons. It was still early and we had all just eaten, but we ordered some ice cream and enjoyed the music while eating it. The song "Wendy" was popular, and it played over and over again. To this day, whenever I hear that song, I'm transported back to that burger shack at Wildwood. We returned there several times before the week was over.

As we walked back to the apartment, we encountered a middle-aged man sitting in the driveway in front of our apartment on a little wooden bench cleaning a bucketful of crabs. As he cleaned the crabs, he explained to us which parts were edible and which parts should be thrown away. I was fascinated. When we entered the apartment, we discovered that Faye was ready to go to the beach again. This time, she planned to rent an umbrella and just allow her legs to be sunned.

While on the beach, I applied my sun tan lotion, and each time I came out of the water, I applied more. I expressed my concern that my lotion would not last all week. Faye told me if I ran out, I could use hers. That made me feel better since I didn't want to spend any of my remaining money on sun tan lotion when there were so many more fun things to spend it on

Faye wouldn't permit us to go to the boardwalk every night. She said there were other fun things to do in the evenings. Every evening we spent some time walking on the beach after the crowds had cleared. We would search for shells, and see how far we could wade into the ocean without the waves getting our shorts wet. Each of us saved the shells we found to take home with us. For years, they would serve as reminders for us of the fun we shared that week.

It rained only once that week, and it was quite a thunderstorm. We weren't allowed out in the rain, but after it stopped, we walked to the beach. On the way, we waded through several inches of water that accumulated along the sides of the streets. When we got to the beach it was high tide, and I was struck by the threatening force of the waves. The ocean no longer looked inviting; it was frightening. As our gang stood and watched it, we talked about what we would do if we saw a tidal wave coming toward us. Now that was really scary. *I sure wouldn't want to drown*, I thought. It made me think of death again, and I wondered how many people had lost their lives in that huge mass of water.

Our week of fun ended much too soon. It was sad packing our belongings for our return trip home. I missed my parents, but I still wasn't ready to leave. At home I was often lonely when Mom and Dad were working; there was no loneliness that entire week. Also, I was depressed quite often at home for different reasons. I had not been depressed at all that week. Being the naïve, young girl I was, I believed that if I stayed there in Wildwood, I would never again experience those feelings. Of course, I would never find that out because we had to leave.

We took one more walk back to the beach that Saturday morning before we left Wildwood. As we walked down to the water's edge and stood gazing at the ocean, in my mind I said, *good-bye ocean; someday I'll see you again*. Later in my life I would make many trips to the ocean, but none would be as magical as my first trip to the beach that summer. It would remain one of my fondest childhood memories.

Chapter 23

It was August, and soon summer would be over and we would be returning to school. I still often thought of Grandma's death even though it occurred two years previously Throughout that period, Grandma remained the only person I knew who had died. That August, that fact was about to change, for I would again encounter death; only this time, it would be the death of a peer.

Often on summer evenings after my family had eaten our evening meal, Dad would drive us through the mountains on the numerous dirt roads in the area. It was hot in our house late in the afternoons, and it became even hotter from using the stove to cook supper. We didn't have air conditioning, only two fans.

After we had eaten our dinner the evening of Monday, August 15th, 1967, Dad said to all of us while we were still at the dinner table, "Let's go for a ride out Treaster Valley." That was where we had lived prior to moving to Shreader, which was where we had lived prior to moving to Mount Pleasant. Mom and Dad had rented a large farm house in the valley. Not far from the house, the paved road turned to dirt and you were in the mountains. Many people in the area and others from nearby cities had built cabins in the mountains on state-owned lands. The state would allow people to lease the land for ninety-nine years. I knew some of the people who owned cabins.

On our way to Treaster Valley, we passed through the village of Milroy and then took Back Mountain Road that led to other roads that would take us to the mountain. As we traveled along that road, we took a big right turn that led us past Joyce Goss' two-story farmhouse that stood close to the road. As we drove by, I saw her mother standing inside the doorway looking out the screened door. I knew where Joyce lived because on one of our other rides, I saw her sitting on the porch with her family. Joyce was an elementary school chum of mine.

After driving another half mile or so, we turned onto Cross Road, a township route between Back Mountain Road and Middle Road about two and a half miles north of Milroy. It was then that we came upon some sort of accident. There were two cars stopped in front of us, so we weren't able to make out what had happened. Dad told us to stay in the car, and he walked up the road to see what was going on. He was only gone a few minutes before we heard sirens and the Milroy ambulance and fire truck came speeding down the road past us. Mom said, "There must have been a wreck" as all three of us tried to see what was happening.

Before long, several other vehicles came up behind us, went around us, and stopped ahead. Mom, Brenda, and I were speculating about what might have happened when we saw Dad walking back toward the car along the side of the road. When he reached the car, he got inside and announced, "A tractor upset and a girl was killed." The word "killed" jolted me, and I could feel my heart beating faster within my chest. I clearly remember Dad hesitating before he turned around and looked at me. Then he said to me, "It's a girl you know…Joyce Goss."

Joyce had attended the same elementary school as I had, Armaugh Elementary School. Often we had played jump rope and hopscotch together on the playground. When we left elementary school and moved to the high school, we no longer had any classes together. I still would occasionally see her in the halls, though, and in the cafeteria. Joyce generally was sitting with Charlene Hammon, a Mennonite girl who was in the same section as she was. There were quite a few Mennonites who attended our school.

Dad was saying, "Dr. Walters pronounced her dead. They believe she died instantly upon impact. For some unknown reason, the tractor ran up a high embankment on the right side of the road and overturned on top of her. They believe she must have been driving too fast. Her father was there, but her mother doesn't even know yet."

I thought of seeing her mother standing at the door, not realizing that her daughter lay on the road, not far away, dead. I wondered if she somehow sensed something was wrong and that was why she was standing there. I thought about how sad it would be to have to be the person who would tell her that Joyce was dead. I speculated that it would be Joyce's father. The image of her two parents standing there grieving the loss of their daughter moved me beyond words. Joyce also had four sisters and a brother; I wondered how they would deal with the death of their sister.

Joyce's death seemed worse to me than Grandma's because she was so much younger. Grandma had at least had an opportunity to grow up, get married, and have a family. Joyce would never be able to do that. Again I wondered why God would allow death, especially the death of one so young.

I remembered once hearing an analogy to explain why people of all ages were permitted to die. The story said that God allowed people of all ages to die for they were all his flowers in heaven, and when you picked a bouquet of flowers, you wouldn't want all fully opened flowers in your bouquet. For that reason, God sometimes allowed babies to die for they were like the buds in his bouquet; he allowed youth to die for they were the partially opened flowers in his bouquet; and the adults and elderly were the fully opened flowers in his bouquet. By choosing people of all ages to die, God had a beautiful bouquet in heaven. When I had first heard that analogy, and I don't even remember when that was, I thought it made sense; but after directly confronting the death of a loved one, Grandma, and a friend, Joyce, I had great difficulty thinking of them as flowers in heaven in some sort of bouquet.

Dad had gotten into the car upon his return from the accident scene, turned our car around, and took an alternate route as he continued toward the mountain. As he reached the mountain and drove on the dirt road past all the mountain laurel and assorted evergreens, the cool breeze came through my window and brushed across my face while I contemplated where Joyce was right then. I knew her physical body was most likely on its way to a funeral home, but where was the essence of the person I knew? No matter how hard I tried to grasp the concept of death, it eluded me.

Since Grandma's death, I had thought about death many times, but it was just too abstract; I couldn't perceive something so far outside of anything I had ever experienced. The unknown frightened me.

I half heard Mom and Dad in the front seat discussing the accident and Joyce's death, yet I was in a world of my own. I realized that just like when Grandma had died, everything would continue as if nothing had happened. That bothered me more than anything. I guess I wanted the world to stop for at least a moment to acknowledge Joyce's death, celebrate the life she had lived, and say, "We'll miss you." Years later, it hit me that was what funerals were for.

After we completed our ride through the mountain, we returned home, and it seemed strange to me that in a way, I felt as if nothing significant had happened. Yet in another way, I felt as if nothing would ever be the same. I knew Joyce was gone forever just as everyone who died before her. Again I struggled with trying to understand where she was. I wanted to cry, but the tears would not come. Joyce had been my friend, but not a close friend. In a way, I felt as if I was betraying her because I was not appropriately mourning her passing.

The next day, there was an article on the front page of the *Lewistown Sentinel* reporting Joyce's accident. I hungrily read it. The article told that she was the fifth young person to be killed in a Mifflin County highway accident that year. It said that her parents were Cloyd J. and Mary Ann Lingle Goss. It also reported that Joyce's middle name was Ann. I marveled that I had known her, but never knew her middle name. The article continued, saying that she was found in the middle of the 14-foot wide dirt road, face down and with the seat of the tractor resting on her body. In my mind, I saw the road and could feel the summer evening as I pictured Joyce lying there with that tractor on top of her. She had been born on September 22, 1951, in Armagh Township, and it was Armagh Township where she had died that summer evening of 1967.

That Thursday, I thought about what was going on at Joyce's funeral. The services were being held at the Bohn Funeral Home in Reedsville at two p.m. Her body was to be laid to rest in the Salem Cemetery on the outskirts of Milroy. I had been to that cemetery once, and I pictured what Joyce's grave must look like.

Joyce would have been going into tenth grade the following month. Later at school, I would see her former classmates and wonder if they remembered and missed Joyce. Of course, I would never express that to them.

I never did shed any tears for Joyce, but over the following few years I thought of her often and still occasionally do. The reality of how quickly a person's life can end never lost its enthrallment. Throughout the years, each time I heard of a child dying, I would again think of Joyce. Her death reminded me again that we are all mortal.

Chapter 24

Just as happened after Grandma's passing, life went on as usual after Joyce's death. The following weeks of summer continued in an uneventful fashion. Before we realized it, school was starting again. That year I was a sophomore. Mrs. Reigle was my homeroom teacher. Things were a little better, but I still didn't like school. Once you're labeled as strange, it's very difficult to change your status with high school students.

One evening a few weeks after school started, I rode my bicycle to Leeper's Store. I had some lunch money left over because I didn't eat every day. Some days I wouldn't go through the lunch line and saved my money. When I arrived at Mrs. Leeper's store, I parked my bike along her front porch and went inside. As I looked at the potato chip rack and lunch cake shelf, Mrs. Leeper came out of the back room. "How are you today?" she asked.

"Okay," I said as I tried to make up my mind about what I should purchase.

Mrs. Leeper asked, "Would you be interested in babysitting for one of the construction workers?"

"I don't know," I replied. "Who is it?"

"Jim and Judy Newsome," Mrs. Leeper answered. "Jim works for the Wright Construction Company from Columbia, Georgia. They're here to build the new road. He and his wife are staying down beside the Lewises in that camp. They have two children. When Jim was in here the other day, he asked me if I knew of anyone who would want to baby sit. I thought of you. If you're interested, you should go down and see them."

"All right, I'll do that," I replied as I picked out a pink snowball cake and laid it on the counter while I counted out my change to pay for it.

I took my cake out on the porch, sat down with my legs dangling over the edge, and devoured it. I sat there a few minutes longer and watched the traffic go by before I decided to hop back on my bike, cross Route 322 and returned home.

When I arrived at home, I went into the house and saw my parents were in the kitchen. They were "figuring out the bills" as they put it. I said, "Mrs. Leeper said some construction worker asked her about a babysitter, and she gave them my name. They live beside the Lewises in that camp. Do you think I should go see them?" I asked.

Dad said, "Well that's up to you. It would give you some extra spending money."

Mom asked, "How old are the children?"

"I don't know," I replied.

"You never did any babysitting, Linda. Do you think you could handle that?" Mom asked.

"Sure I could," I replied. I was fourteen years old, soon to be fifteen, and I thought I could handle almost anything. Anything that is except school. I said, "I'm going up to talk to them," and I decided to walk instead of ride my bike.

The camp was up past Sammy Fleck's house. I had to cross Lingle Valley Road and go up the alley. I passed Sammy's house. Next I passed the camp owned by the Bishops; they lived in Florida and spent their summers in Pennsylvania. They had the same last name, but were no relation to me. The Lewises' red-brick house was next. The camp the family lived in was beside the Lewises' on the left side of the alley. There was only one home past that camp; it was Mrs. Fry's house. She was a physical education teacher at Chief Logan High School. A lot of mountain laurel grew in the woods surrounding the camp, and there was a small stream that ran through the wooded area and eventually ran into Lingle Run on the other side of Sammy Fleck's house.

Cathy, Betsy, Brenda, and I spent many hours walking on the trails through the mountain laurel and playing in the water. In the spring, we would gather frog eggs and keep them in a large gallon jar and watch them hatch into tadpoles. The alley itself was a dead end dirt road. That particular day, the dirt was damp from an earlier shower, so it stuck to my feet and made a gritting noise like someone rubbing sandpaper as I made my way toward the camp. On the right, several yards from the camp, there was a wild hickory nut tree from which Betsy, Cathy, Brenda, and I had gathered nuts the previous fall. Then we had taken them to the bridge and broken them open with stones so we could retrieve the nut meats inside.

When I arrived at the camp, I went to the front door and knocked. A short, young woman answered the door. "Hello," she said in her heavy southern drawl. I would learn she was from Georgia; that was where the construction company her husband worked for was located.

"Hi," I replied. "I'm Linda Bishop. Mrs. Leeper told me I should see you about a babysitting job."

"Sure, come on in," the woman said as she opened the screen door.

"My name is Judy Newsome and my husband Jim and I have two children. James is three years old," she said as she motioned to a little boy who was sitting on the floor playing with blocks. "Dixie's the baby. She's four months old. She's upstairs sleeping."

The camp was constructed with gray cinder blocks. The first floor consisted of one large room that served as a living room and kitchen-dining room. The stove, refrigerator, and kitchen table were on the right side of the room. The couch and several chairs were on the left. To the far right at the front of the room was an open stairway that led to the bedrooms, I assumed. I later learned there were two bedrooms upstairs.

Judy asked me, "Have you ever done any babysitting?"

"No," I replied. "But I really like kids. I worked at Semple's Kennels and cleaned Mrs. Semple's house," I added.

"How old are you?" she asked.

"Fourteen. I'll be fifteen in December." I added. Judy was only nineteen, and Jim was twenty-one I would learn.

"Well, Jim and I might go out tonight. He's not here now. How could we get in touch with you?" she asked.

"I live in the second house on the left across Lingle Valley Road," I answered." Our house is white with dark green trim.

Judy said, "We don't have a phone, so we'll just have to stop in."

"That'll be okay," I responded.

As I walked back to my house, I wondered how I was going to take care of a baby. I didn't think the three-year-old would be a problem, but the baby had me a little worried. I thought I could always walk home with the children and ask my mother what to do if I had a problem. When I arrived home, I related what had happened. Dad didn't say much of anything about it, but Mom questioned me. "How old are the baby and little boy?" she asked.

"Four months and three years," I answered.

"I don't know about you taking care of an infant. There's a lot involved with that. It's not as simple as caring for an older child. You have to change diapers, burp them, and be very careful with their heads," she lectured.

"I know. I thought of that. If I really have a problem, I could bring the children here and get you to help," I said.

"Oh…really. Well I guess that's true, but you'll have to be very careful," she added.

"I know, and I will."

Later that day at about four-thirty, an old 1956 blue Ford pulled into our driveway, and a young man got out and came up our sidewalk. When he reached our front door, he knocked loudly. I answered the door. "Are you Linda?" he asked in a heavy southern accent which told me immediately he must be Jim Newsome.

"Yes," I replied.

"Hi, I'm Jim Newsome. I came to take you to our house if you still want to baby sit for us tonight."

"Sure I do," I said, and told Dad, "I'm going with him to baby sit." Dad nodded, and I followed Jim out to his car; we went back up the alley to the camp. When we got inside the house, Judy was holding Dixie, and James was eating chicken noodle soup and a peanut butter and jelly sandwich.

"Hi," she said. "I'm just giving James his supper, and I fed Dixie. She should be good until later this evening. I have a bottle of formula in the refrigerator, and there's a supply of diapers there in the diaper bag." She pointed to a pink and white vinyl bag setting in the corner by the sink. "There are also clean clothes in there," she added. "Do you have any questions?"

"What time should I put them to bed?" I asked. I really wasn't sure what else I might need to know.

"Just let James play until he gets tired; then he'll lay down and sleep. Let him sleep down here on the couch. If he wakes up upstairs alone, he'll be frightened," Judy stated.

"Okay," I responded as I examined the couch she was referring to.

Judy continued her instructions. "When Dixie goes to sleep, lay her on her stomach on the couch and put a pillow beside her so she doesn't roll off." She handed Dixie to me to hold as she finished talking.

"Okay," I again responded. I hoped I was holding Dixie correctly.

"Do you have any other questions?" Judy asked me as she picked up her jacket from the clothes rack in the corner and grabbed her purse from beside the couch.

"No. I can't think of anything else," I said, shifting Dixie from my left to my right hip.

"There are snacks on top of the refrigerator if you get hungry, and there is soda inside. James usually likes a snack before bedtime," Jim added.

I acknowledged by shaking my head.

"See you later," Judy said as she went out the door.

Jim held the door and said, "We will probably be back around one or two. That isn't too late, is it?"

"No, that's all right," I answered.

Jim left and closed the door behind him.

It then struck me that I was on my own with two small children. They didn't have a phone, and they didn't have a TV. *I must be crazy*, I thought as I stood there in the middle of that large room holding Dixie. It was still daylight when they left, but I worried about nightfall approaching.

Dixie was probably going to be a blond like Judy. She had thin white fuzz all over her head. She smelled somewhat sour. I assumed she must have spit up on her jumpsuit. She seemed content as I stood there holding her.

About that time, James realized his parents had left, and he stood up from playing with his toy trucks, and said, "Where'd Mommy and Daddy go?"

"Oh, they had to go away for a little while," I tried to answer reassuringly. "They'll be back soon," I said, and I was beginning to think the sooner the better. James was a cute little boy. He had light brown hair like his father, and he was very pleasant.

"Will you play with me?" he asked.

"Sure," I said, and I sat down on the floor, faced Dixie forward and sat her between my legs, then picked up one of the trucks James was playing with. It was going to be a long evening. Eventually, Dixie got bored with sitting there, so I picked her up, stood up, and carried her around the room. After about twenty minutes of her fussing, it occurred to me that she might be wet.

I was about to have my first diaper changing experience. I got the diaper bag out of the corner, pulled out a cloth diaper (it was before Pampers,) and a pair of plastic pants. I felt Dixie's clothing. Her outfit wasn't wet, so she wouldn't need a clean one. I carried her over to the couch, laid her on the blanket, and proceeded to change her diaper. Luckily, she was only wet. After I figured out how to fold the cloth diaper, I removed the wet one, laid it on the floor, and pinned on the dry cloth diaper. The plastic pants went back over the diaper. All those years of playing with dolls finally paid off.

Now I had a dilemma because I didn't know where to put the wet diaper and plastic pants: inside or outside. It hadn't occurred to me to ask, and evidently Judy didn't think of it, either. I fastened Dixie's jumpsuit, picked her up again, and wandered around the room trying to decide what to do with the soiled items. I saw a plastic bag on the corner of the counter. I decided to put the soiled diaper in the bag and lay the bag near the steps.

By then, James had tired of playing with the trucks. He asked, "Will you read me a story?"

"Do you have any story books?" I asked.

"Uh-huh," he replied as he hurried over to a scarred wooden magazine rack beside the end of the couch and picked up two children's books. He had *The Three Little Pigs* and *Little Red Riding Hood.*

"Which one would you like me to read?" I asked him.

"This one," he replied as he held up *The Three Little Pigs*. As I sat there reading to James, I noticed it had gotten dark outside. The camp was pretty much isolated, and I was a little frightened. That was the first time I had ever been alone after dark without a peer or an adult. Now I was in charge. It was an odd feeling. Even though I was frightened, I felt I must be brave for the children. After I finished the story, I made sure both doors were locked, and pulled the curtains shut.

I then returned to the couch and sat beside James and continued holding Dixie. Again, time had become my enemy and the minutes inched by. I read *Little Red Riding Hood* to James next. The big bad wolf was frightening me. Dixie had fallen asleep, and I had her lying on the couch on her stomach as Judy had instructed me to do. After the second story was finished, I got the chocolate chip cookies down from the top of the refrigerator and gave several cookies to James. I then opened the refrigerator and found the milk bottle. I poured James a glass of milk to drink with his cookies. When he finished, we returned to the other end of the couch. I told James stories I remembered from other books I had read, and he finally fell asleep around midnight.

Shortly after James went to sleep, Dixie woke up and was fussing. I got her bottle out of the refrigerator, set it in a pan of hot water and changed her diaper while we waited for the milk to get warm. After the bottle had warmed, I tested it on my left arm like I had seen people do on TV, and I fed Dixie and put her over my shoulder to burp her. I gently patted her back until she burped. I continued to rock her back and forth in my arms until she again went to sleep; then I sat on the couch and held her.

Around one-thirty, I was awakened when Jim and Judy got home. I was still holding Dixie. James was still sleeping on the other end of the couch. There was another couple with Jim and Judy. "Hey," Jim said. It appeared he had been drinking although I really had little to compare it with. My parents didn't drink, and I believe the only person I ever saw intoxicated was our alcoholic neighbor, Dot Fisher. Once on a hot day, I had encountered Dot in a drunken state lying in Lingle Run in her bathing suit singing "Beautiful Dreamer."

Jim introduced the other woman as Sarah and the man as "The Fugitive." I later learned that Sarah was Judy's cousin, and "The Fugitive" was her boyfriend; he also was a construction worker. Jim told me the Fugitive would take me home. He paid me, and I followed "The Fugitive" to his car. His car was a blue GTO that had "Fugitive" painted on each side. I was uneasy about going with a strange man. I semi-reluctantly got into his car, and we sped toward my house. As I got out, he handed me a five dollar bill and said, "Here kid; buy yourself something."

"Thanks," I said as I scurried into the house. Mom was sleeping on the couch waiting for me to get home. As I entered the house, she woke up. "Look how much I got!" I exclaimed. "This guy called The Fugitive brought me home and gave me five dollars for nothing."

"I don't know about this," Mom said. "I don't like you out this late, and I don't like some strange man bringing you home. Why is he called "The Fugitive?"

"Oh Mom, it's fine," I stated. "I guess he just likes that name." I wasn't about to tell her they were drinking, or my job would be over.

"How did the kids behave?" she asked.

"Okay...I read James a couple of stories, gave him a snack, and he went to sleep. I had to change Dixie's diaper twice, but she was just wet. She got hungry, and I gave her a bottle, too," I excitedly reported.

"It sounds like it went okay. You better get to bed now so you can get up for church," Mom instructed me.

I was happy as I climbed the stairs to my bedroom. In addition, I was proud that I had managed to survive the evening without any problems, and I had been in charge of two small children.

Throughout that year, I continued to have babysitting jobs for Judy and Jim. On numerous occasions, Cathy, Betsy, and Brenda would join me at the camp while I was working. They seemed to be fascinated with The Fugitive, and as I learned more about him, Sarah, Judy, and Jim, I realized they were not above breaking the law. That became very apparent one Sunday afternoon when Betsy and I agreed to take them to see the Amish in the area.

Sunday was a good day to see the Amish because they would be out in their buggies going to and from church functions. The back road to Barrville was especially traveled by that sect since there was less traffic. That was where Betsy and I chose to take them that day since they had asked us to show them where the Amish lived. Brenda and Cathy stayed behind to watch James and Dixie.

Betsy and I rode in the back seat of The Fugitive's car with Judy. The Fugitive was driving, Sarah was in the middle beside him, and Jim was up front on the passenger's side. When we encountered our first buggy full of Amish, the southerners began whooping and yelling out the windows at them as we followed them for a short distance and then passed them. Each new buggy we passed brought additional shouts of enthusiasm from the group. Sarah and Judy yelled, "Hey, you cute little Dutch boys." Jim jokingly asked several of the Amish boys, "Will you give us a ride in your buggy?" They never waited for a reply, but drove away laughing. Betsy and I later discussed how strange their behavior was.

While driving on a straight stretch of road with no buggies, we came upon a flock of white ducks near a farmer's pond. That is when The Fugitive asked, "Who wants roast duck for dinner?" Sarah, Judy and Jim began shouting, "I do," and the chase began. The Fugitive pulled over to the side of the road, and he and Jim jumped out of the car, found several stones beside the road, and began throwing the stones at the ducks. The flock went wild, and scattered everywhere. Judy and Sarah thought the whole escapade was hilarious, but Betsy and I did not.

Betsy and I got out of the car and attempted to chase the ducks farther away. Ducks evidently have small brains because some of them ran straight toward danger that happened to be The Fugitive and Jim. Those two continued throwing more stones as a few of the ducks ran close to them. It was at that time we saw a beige sedan coming down the road, and Jim yelled, "Here comes someone," as he picked up a dead duck he had struck with one of his stones. The Fugitive and Jim ran to the car, Jim threw the duck on the floor in the back, and Betsy and I hid in a small patch of woods on the other side of the road. The Fugitive yelled out the window to us, "Stay there. We'll be back for you."

Betsy and I were terrified as we watched them drive away and the beige sedan slowly drove by where we were hiding. A few minutes later, we saw The Fugitive's blue car speeding from the opposite direction toward us. It swerved to the side of the road near the patch of woods, and the back door flew open as we heard Judy call, "Hurry up and get in the car."

We did as she commanded, and as the door closed behind us, Betsy began screaming, "Get it out of here. I mean it; get it out of here," and she threw her legs up over me. I then saw the dead duck on the floor.

The southerners thought Betsy's behavior was quite amusing. Judy moved the duck to her side of the floor, when she saw tears in Betsy's eyes and realized she was serious. The remainder of the way home, the four of them instructed us not to tell anyone about what had happened. We both promised that we would not. Did they think we were crazy? We didn't want to get into any trouble, either.

Betsy and I could not wait to tell Cathy and Brenda what had happened. It was just so bizarre. We told and retold that story whenever we reminisced about those construction workers while sitting on Betsy's front porch. They definitely brought some excitement into our lives.

They were not the only construction workers we knew. Since many of them were working on the road that ran directly in front of Betsy's front porch, we came to recognize most of them. We didn't know all of them by name, so we made up names for them. Often they would stop and go into Leeper's Store. That had given us the idea to sell food to them.

During the fall, Dad had bought peaches and apples by the bushel, so Brenda and I would contribute some of that produce to our sale table. Betsy and Cathy would contribute whatever they could find in their homes. Usually, we would make some lemonade or iced tea. When the workers stopped at Leeper's, we would convince them to purchase something from us. We didn't make a whole lot of money doing that, but we had a good deal of fun.

One Saturday near the end of October, when I went up to Jim's and Judy's house, I learned that Sarah was preparing to go back to Georgia. I was shocked to learn that she was married. She and her husband had separated, so she came to Pennsylvania to visit her cousin Judy and get away for a while. I wondered what The Fugitive would think about her leaving. I also wondered if he knew she was married.

Jim and Judy were taking Sarah to the Harrisburg International Airport. Sarah seemed to be very happy as she waltzed around the camp singing the chorus to "I Heard It Through The Grapevine."

That was the last time I saw Sarah. Occasionally, I would see The Fugitive's car pass by Betsy's porch, but I never again rode in his car. I continued babysitting for Jim and Judy, but it was never as exciting.

Chapter 25

The tenth graders were scheduled to have their eyes examined at school that year. Since I was then in tenth grade, that included me. Eye exams, like any other exam, made me nervous. It was silly to fear having an eye exam, but somehow I felt it was bad to fail. For that reason, every time I had to read the eye charts, I cheated. We had to hold a card over our one eye, and read the chart with the other eye. I had known for quite a while that I was not seeing correctly out of my left eye. I tried to keep that a secret because I didn't want to fail, and I didn't want to wear glasses. Even when I was young, I realized something was wrong when I looked through my toy binoculars and could only see out of the one side if I closed my other eye.

When it was my turn to have my eyes examined this time, I attempted to cheat as before, but it didn't work. We had to look through a machine, and my secret was revealed. It was obvious I had some sort of vision problem. The nurse gave me a card that informed by parents I needed glasses. I was not happy about that.

Mom scheduled an appointment with Tri-State Optical since Dad's insurance would pay for glasses from there. It turned out that I had numerous vision problems. My left eye was what they referred to as a "lazy eye." In addition, I had astigmatism and was nearsighted. They had me pick out the frames I wanted and said my glasses would be in the following week.

When I got my glasses, I hated them. The left lens was very thick, and I thought they made me look retarded. My parents made me wear them, so at home I kept them on. At school, I did not. I didn't wear them when I went out with my friends, either. When I had my school pictures taken, I had to wear them, and that disgusted me. Later in my life, I would have severe vision problems, and I wondered if I could have prevented them.

The same month I got my glasses, Dad bought an ATV (all terrain vehicle) called a Scrambler. It had six wheels, three on each side, and it also could float in water. The top was red, and the bottom was white. There were two seats. We had great fun with that vehicle.

Dad would take the whole family for rides in it out Lingle Valley. We would go down the road to the reservoir, take the path through the woods to the log, and drive across the water. We could feel the vehicle floating when the tires could no longer touch the bottom of the creek. It worked great in the snow, too.

After the first snow had fallen that year, Dad took us out Lingle Valley to the fork in the road, and turned around. We really had to bundle up because the cold air blowing on our faces could be severe. It was a tight squeeze when everyone was in the vehicle, but we still enjoyed it. Brenda and I said that people would think Dad was Santa Claus in his little red and white Scrambler.

Once, after the novelty of the vehicle wore off, Dad permitted me to drive it without him being along. It had a pull cord to start it, so he started it for me, and gave me a mini-lesson on how to drive the thing. When my lesson was finished, I took Brenda with me and we headed out Lingle Valley. I decided to go down to the reservoir. When I got to the bottom of the hill, I turned, and put it into neutral so that I could wipe the steam from my glasses. It was then that the engine stalled.

I jumped out and made numerous attempts to start the engine, but I evidently could not pull the cord hard enough or fast enough to get it started. I was getting extremely frustrated, and finally in desperation, I instructed Brenda to go get Dad. I hated to do that because I knew I would be in trouble, but I had no other choice.

After Brenda left, I sat there for about thirty minutes dreading Dad's arrival. I attempted to start the engine again a few times, but had no better luck. Before long, I saw Dad and Brenda round the corner of the reservoir road in his 1959 Chevy. He had traded his 1956 Ford for the Chevy. Dad exited the car and began to lecture me about what he had told me; "Be careful not to stall it." *Here we go again*, I thought.

It took Dad no time at all to get the Scrambler started, and then I had to drive it back to the house because he had to drive the car. He wouldn't allow me to drive the Scrambler after that. That was okay with me because I didn't want to be stranded again.

It seemed that if I wasn't getting into trouble at home, I was being harassed at school. My new glasses gave Tracy still another reason to tease me. She began calling me "four eyes." That was one of the reasons I refused to wear the glasses at school. I vowed to myself that someday Tracy would pay for all the pain she had caused me. I had no idea how, but I still wanted to believe there would be justice in the end.

During my tenth grade year of school, there was much racial turbulence going on in our country. We had recently experienced black uprisings all across our nation. The National Guard was even called upon to restore order in our cities. In addition to all of the racial unrest, there were many student demonstrations on college campuses protesting the Viet Nam war. More and more American soldiers were dying in the war effort, and many Americans were asking why.

That December I turned fifteen. It remained an awkward time for me. I still didn't care for school, but I no longer was severely depressed. Gradually, I had emerged from the black hole I felt I had been in and inched my way back toward what I considered a normal existence. It had been a long, long struggle and I hadn't quite made it to the top.

Tracy remained a constant irritation at school. She never seemed to tire of harassing me. My gym bag was even a source of amusement for her. I was embarrassed about my gym bag because it was different from all the other girls' bags. They all had cute little train cases with mirrors on the lids and locks on the outside. My gym bag looked like a miniature version of the boys'. It was a red and beige vinyl bag with a zipper on top. Mom and Dad, being as practical as they were, thought that was a much better bargain and would serve the same purpose. Little did they know how much grief that bag would cause me.

Perhaps Tracy sensed my embarrassment about the bag, and that is why she chose to make fun of it. It began in gym class as we were changing into our gym suits. Our suits were one piece maroon jumpsuits. We had our names embroidered over the pockets of the suits. As I was pulling my gym suit up and slipping my arms into the sleeves, I heard Tracy, on the other side of the locker, saying, "Can you believe anyone would buy such a stupid gym bag? Just look at it; it's for little boys, not girls." I knew instantly she was talking about my gym bag.

I always tried to hurry up and get my things out of the bag and put it on top of the locker before anyone noticed what kind of bag I had. Mom and Dad didn't know how I felt about the bag. I didn't want to hurt their feelings. Most likely they wouldn't have bought me another bag anyway because they would have viewed that as a waste. I continued dressing as quickly as possible so I could escape into the gym, away from Tracy.

In the gym, I took my place in the lineup, and waited for our teacher, Mrs. Sherlock, to start the class. I saw Tracy leaving the locker room and pretended that I did not. When she got close enough for me to hear, she sarcastically called, "Linda, is that your cute little boys' gym bag on top of the locker?" I was mortified. *How should I answer?* I thought. Everyone was looking at me.

"I suppose it is," I answered. "Since you like it so much, I'd be glad to let you use it if you wish," I continued in the sweetest voice I could muster. Now everyone began to howl. I believe Tracy was in shock. She never expected that response. It was during the laughter that Mrs. Sherlock made her entrance and began clapping her hands to quiet the class so she could begin roll call.

Hallelujah! I guess I shut her up. Not too long after that episode, they began selling cloth gym bags with the school name Kishacoquillas on them at the school store, and I was one of their first customers

On April 4th of that same year, Dr. Martin Luther King, Jr. was shot and killed at the Lorraine Motel in Memphis, Tennessee while standing on the balcony. He had been there in support of striking sanitation workers. When we discussed that in our history class the following day, Tracy participated in the discussion and expressed concern for the blacks. I recalled how I had heard her refer to people as "nigger lovers" in the past, and I knew it was just a show.

As I had watched the news reports on television, I felt extremely sad for Dr. King's family. His death was such an injustice. It made we wonder how I would feel if someone killed my father. Again I thought about Grandma and her racial hatred. I believed it was my generation's responsibility to end that hatred or at least try.

Tracy continued her harassment throughout the remainder of the school year. In May, the Student Council sponsored a clash day and a dress-up day. On clash day, we all dressed in plaids, stripes, and paisleys all mixed together. I wore a plaid skirt and a paisley blouse. As I walked into science class, Tracy walked up behind me and said, "Linda, don't you know that today is clash day? I thought you would wear matching clothes since you clash the rest of the year."

How do you respond to a rude comment like that? Tracy just wore me down because she never seemed to tire of humiliating me. That day, I wasn't in the mood to deal with her, so I just didn't respond at all. She sure made my life miserable, though, and I couldn't wait until there would be no more Tracy. Clash day was no longer any fun. It is really sad that one person was able to have such a negative effect on another's life and get away with it.

I wasn't at all sad when June arrived, and several days later, school was out for the summer. I felt such a sense of freedom knowing I wouldn't see Tracy for several months. During the summer, I was pretty much back to normal. I didn't cry nearly as much because I wasn't sad as often. I began spending more time with my friends that year. Sometimes I even felt as though I would make it to graduation. The previous year, I could not have made that claim.

Chapter 26

While at work during the summer of 1968, Dad heard about a real good deal on a tent. It was a large, twelve-by-twelve, light yellow tent with a floor attached. He decided to purchase the tent for Brenda and me because after the refrigerator box episode he knew we enjoyed sleeping out. Before that, we had slept on our porch several times, too. Dad didn't tell us about the tent; he surprised us. On June 6th, he brought it home from work with him.

Brenda and I were riding our bikes down the alley returning from Cathy's trailer when we saw Dad in the driveway unloading something from the trunk. As we both rode into the driveway and parked our bikes, I got off and walked over to the back of the car to see what Dad was doing. He was lifting the tent from the trunk. "What's that?" I asked.

"A big tent," he replied as he carried it up the sidewalk and laid it on the front porch.

"Who's it for? I asked, tagging behind him as he returned to the trunk and took out a canvas bag. Brenda had also meandered over.

"Yeah, who's it for?" Brenda asked, leaning over the side of the car to get a better view of the trunk.

"Well…I suppose it's for two girls I know," Dad teased as he looked at us.

"For us? " I questioned. I was totally surprised.

"Really!" Brenda exclaimed.

As Dad closed the lid of the trunk and carried the canvas bag to the porch, he said, "I thought you kids might like to camp out in the woods with a tent. I always liked to camp out when I was a kid," he added.

"Sure we would. It was great when we slept out in those boxes," I said while I examined the contents of the canvas bad. The stakes to the tent were in the bag, along with different lengths of rope to tie them to the tent.

"When can we put it up?" Brenda asked, as she too checked out the contents of the bag.

Dad was counting the stakes. When he finished, he replied, "Maybe tonight after supper." He then gathered the stakes and rope and put everything back into the canvas bag and laid it on top of the tent.

Brenda and I couldn't believe our good fortune. We hadn't even asked for a tent, but we had one. As Dad, Brenda, and I prepared supper that evening, Dad told us stories about camping out when he was a kid. He and his brothers didn't have a store-bought tent. They usually just slept out under the stars with a blanket. That idea didn't appeal to me. I wanted to sleep out, but I was glad the tent had a floor to keep out unwanted creatures.

After supper that evening, Brenda and I hurried to finish the dishes so we could help Dad setup the tent. He had chosen a clearing in the center of our woods that was level and had no weeds growing due to the thick layer of pine needles. First he spread out the bottom of the tent with the door facing toward our house. He then instructed Brenda and me, "Get the stakes out of the bag and lay one beside each canvas loop." There were four canvas loops on each side of the tent, sixteen stakes in all. As Brenda and I laid out the stakes, Dad said, "You'll need to put one of those pieces of rope with each loop on the sides of the tent." There were four loops on the two sides of the tent; the front and back had none.

As Dad hammered in the stakes around the perimeter of the tent, Brenda and I attached one of the eight lengths of rope to each side loop. Dad then took the metal poles out of the bag. After he had put several of the pieces together, he said to me, "Hold this while I go to the back." Dad then proceeded to put several more lengths of pipe together in the back. "Slide the top of the pole through the loops on the top of the tent," he instructed me. He put his pole through the back top and then fastened it to mine in the center. "Push the pole straight up," he instructed. I did as he told me, and he did the same in the back. It was then beginning to look like a tent .

"Hold this," Dad instructed Brenda. She held onto the back pole while I held the front one. Dad wrapped the end of the first length of rope on the side around a stake, securely tied the other end to the canvas loop, and pulled it up and out. When he had stretched it tight, he pounded the stake into the ground. He repeated that procedure seven more times until both sides were four-feet high and the center of the tent stood eight feet high. It was finished, and it looked great.

Brenda and I helped Dad put everything away; then we rushed inside to call Cathy. She wasn't home, so we would have to wait. We next called Betsy, but she wasn't home, either. Since no one was home, Brenda and I returned to the tent to enjoy it ourselves. We lay inside for a couple of hours planning our first sleepover in the tent, and then we returned to the house.

The next night, Cathy, Brenda, and I slept out. Betsy had made plans, so she couldn't be with us.. First we had a cookout, making our butter-dish potatoes and hot dogs. They sure tasted good being made on the open wood fire. We then sat around the campfire for a while just talking, until the fire started to die down. Then it was time to move the party inside. We played cards by flashlight and talked for hours.

Not long after the flashlight was turned off, we heard a noise outside the tent; we all squealed. After calming down, I said, "That's probably just Mom and Dad trying to scare us, to be funny." The remainder of the evening, we heard nothing else.

The following night, we didn't sleep out. In the morning, I awoke to some sort of commotion going on downstairs. I blinked away my drossiness, and focused on Dad's words. I heard him say, "It's gone; someone has stolen the tent!"

That got my attention; I sprang out of bed and hurried downstairs. I looked out through the screen door toward the spot in the woods where the tent had been. Dad was right. The tent was gone! I saw the cat picture we'd had hanging inside the tent and a pile of blankets on the ground. That was strange. I wondered why they hadn't taken those.

Dad came back from his trip to where the tent had been in the woods, and told Mom, "Call the police and make a report. I have to get to work or I'll be late."

Mom was highly excitable, and that all seemed to overwhelm her. "What should I tell them?" she asked.

"Just tell them what happened," Dad instructed, and he left so he would make it to work on time.

Mom was flustered and fumbled with the telephone book until she finally located the State Police phone number. There was no local police in Mount Pleasant. After making her report, she hung up and informed me, "They're sending an officer over to talk to us. I don't know when he'll be coming, so you better get dressed."

"Okay," I said as I ran back upstairs to dress. I was sad the tent was stolen, but it was really exciting. "Brenda," I called as I was on my way to the bedroom. "Guess what happened?"

"What are you yelling about?" Brenda grumpily asked as she rolled over in bed and looked at me.

"Someone has stolen our tent," I said as I pulled my nightgown over my head and searched in my dresser draw for clothes. "The police are on their way to make a report."

"You're kidding," she said, not knowing whether she should believe me. After all, nothing had ever been stolen around there.

"No, I'm not! Mom said we should get dressed. The policeman will probably want to ask us questions," I informed her.

"Why? We don't know anything about it."

"I know, but he'll probably ask us questions about the tent," I said as I started down the stairs.

Mom was still flustered. "I'm calling Cathy," I said. "He may want to talk to her, too." Really, I just thought Cathy wouldn't want to miss all the excitement.

When I got her on the phone, I related all that had happened that morning, and she said, "I'll be down as soon as I get dressed."

Cathy, Brenda, and I hung around the house all morning in anticipation of the police officer arriving. Finally at 1:10, we saw a patrol car come around the corner and pull into our alley. We were instantly both excited and nervous; Mom was, too.

The patrolman parked in our driveway and came to the door. Mom greeted him there and told him to come in. He introduced himself as Officer Chatman. Mom offered him a seat in the living room. He sat down, opened his notebook, and began to ask questions. She filled him in as best she could; then he began questioning the rest of us. "How often do you girls sleep out?" he asked.

"We only slept out once in the tent," I volunteered. "That was the night before last, and we heard someone outside the tent, but we thought it was Mom or Dad trying to scare us."

"Have you slept out before that?" he asked.

Mom then told him all about our refrigerator box sleepover. We filled in some of the details that she had forgotten. Office Chatman noticed a piece of rawhide tied around Cathy's ankle and asked, "What's that rawhide for?"

"Oh, it's just a fad," Cathy explained. For some reason, that summer, a lot of kids started tying a strand of rawhide around their ankles or wrists.

"It doesn't mean anything then?" he continued.

"No," she answered. "It's just groovey." Brenda and I giggled when Cathy said this. Office Chatman didn't seem to think it was funny.

Officer Chatman didn't respond, but he wrote something in his notebook. He explained to Mom the police procedure in matters like those. Most likely the tent would never be recovered, he told her. Dad wouldn't be happy about that, and neither were we. Officer Chatman said that if they heard anything, they would be in touch with us, and he left.

That was the most excitement we had had all summer. We discussed the theft of the tent for the next several days speculating on who the thief or thieves might have been. It was kind of spooky when we realized that we could have been inside the tent when the thieves were there. It was the summer of 1968, and we weren't yet frightened of serial killers or any kind of killers. For the most part, our little community was quiet and very peaceful.

The following week, a good citizen found our tent at the dump and turned it in to the police. They had remembered hearing about it being stolen on the radio. The day Officer Chatman brought it to our house; Mom, Brenda, and I were there. Mom had the day off. Officer Chatman informed us how the good citizen had gotten the tent, but he had no clues about who had stolen it. He also suggested that we mark the tent somehow so it could be easily identified if it were ever stolen again.

When Dad returned home from work that night, Mom, Brenda, and I filled him in on everything that Officer Chatman had told us. We discussed different ways we could mark the tent. Brenda and I suggested that we paint designs on it. Dad said that was all right with him if that's what we wanted to do.

After supper that night, Dad, Brenda, and I again set the tent up in the woods on the same spot where it was positioned before. During the entire process, we all speculated about who the thief might be. It was a mystery that would probably never be solved. The next day Brenda and I accumulated the assorted leftover paints that Dad had in the garage and carried them over to the picnic table by the tent. Earlier, we had called Cathy and asked her to come down and help us paint the tent. As Brenda and I sat at the picnic table discussing what designs we wanted to paint on the tent and where, Cathy came walking through the woods. She immediately joined in our discussion.

In the end, we painted "B I S H O P" in large red letters on the right top panel of the tent; then we painted an assortment of different colored flowers and peace signs over the remaining canvas. Cathy painted "Flower Power" on the back. When the tent was finished, it sort of resembled one of those psychedelic hippie vans that were so popular during the sixties.

We sat back and admired our work as we made plans to attend the upcoming Youth Park dance on the following Tuesday. Cathy said, "I saw Marilyn in town yesterday, and she said she would like to go with us sometime." Marilyn Barr was a friend of ours from school who lived between Reedsville and Belleville in a mobile home. Her father's occupation fascinated us; he artificially inseminated cows.

"Let's ask her to go with us and then come here for a sleepover," I suggested. We all agreed that was what we would do. The next day, Cathy called Marilyn and the plans were made.

Tuesday evening, the day of the Youth Park dance, Faye transported Cathy, Brenda and me to Reedsville. As was prearranged, Marilyn met us there; her brother had dropped her off. She stashed her overnight bag in the corner of the Youth Park Building. That evening they were having a battle of the bands, and there were seven local bands present. All of the bands would have a turn to play, then one would be eliminated. This process would be repeated until only one band remained. The remaining band would be the winner. Our group danced all evening.

After the one band had finished and the next one was preparing to start, we were standing and chatting with a group of boys we knew from Milroy. The topic of our sleepover came up, and a plan began to form. I'm still not certain who initiated it, but we planned to meet the boys along Route 322 around twelve thirty and go to Red's Diner for a late snack. Red's Diner was a truck stop in Lewistown that was opened twenty-four hours a day. Dave Grant, a friend of ours and one of the group, would drive since he had a car and a driver's license. Our parents would never approve of that, so it had to be after they had gone to sleep.

At eleven o'clock, Dad picked up Cathy, Marilyn, Brenda, and me at the Youth Park, and we returned home. Upon arriving home, we got out of Dad's car and went over into the woods and entered the tent. Cathy, Brenda, and I already had taken our necessities over earlier, so only Marilyn had to transport her overnight bag to the tent. We were anxious and excited as we sat inside talking and waiting for the lights to go out at my house.

Finally, the lights went out. I switched on the flashlight, and Marilyn checked her watch; it was 11:45. I said, "Mom and Dad should be sound asleep by 12:15. It shouldn't take us any longer than that to make it to the top of the hill. We'll have to go the long way, though: out through the woods, along the creek past Sammy Fleck's house, and then up over the hill by Jane Carson's house. If we don't go that way, our dogs will bark, and Mom always hears the dogs barking. We'll have to be very quiet, too," I reminded everyone.

"Can we use flashlights?" Marilyn asked.

"Not until we get out of the woods and up by Sammy's house," I replied. "We don't want anyone to see us."

"We'll have to make sure we circle around my place, too," Cathy added.

"Everybody just has to make sure to be very quiet," Brenda cautioned. "What time is it now?" she asked several minutes later.

Again I switched on the flashlight and Marilyn reported, "It's 12:05."

"Ten more minutes," Cathy excitedly announced.

I periodically lifted up the door flap and checked our house to make sure there were no lights on. When I was satisfied that all was well, I instructed, "It's time to go. Everyone follow me. I'll take the flashlight, but I won't turn it on until we just can't see anything. Remember, be very quiet. If the dogs bark, we'll be caught," I further cautioned.

One by one we left the tent and quickly followed the path along the creek. At the edge of the woods, we all paused before dashing across Lingle Valley Road. We continued following the creek to Sammy Fleck's house, then took a right, crossing over his alley. I shined the flashlight ahead of me to see where we were going, then held it behind me so the rest of the group could see, too. When we were back on the gravel of the alley, I turned the light off, and we all rushed up the hill, trying to be as quiet as possible. By then, my heart was pounding so hard from the combination of fear and physical exertion, I thought all the neighbors should be able to hear it. Finally, we were along Route 322, and we made our way back down to the entrance to Lingle Valley road where we were to meet the boys.

As we approached, I could see Dave's car parked along Lingle Valley Road facing toward Route 322. We picked up speed heading toward the car since we were then on flat ground. They saw us coming and opened the back passenger door facing us. We squeezed in, managed to pull the door shut, and were off. We talked and giggled as we told of our adventure through the dark. As we approached Milroy, Dave suggested, "Let's go on a tour of Milroy before we head for Red's." Everyone was in agreement. He glanced down at his gas gauge and said, "I sure hope I have enough gas."

Pat Rogers, one of the boys in the car, worked at the local Esso gas station. He said, "Sometimes there's some gas left in the hoses after the pumps are turned off. We could stop and see if we're able to drain any out."

"Okay," Dave said as he continued on Route 322. We passed several cars before he reached the Esso Station and pulled in beside the pumps. Pat and Dave got out of the car. Dave watched as Pat got a can from behind the garage and tried the first pump to see if any gas remained in the hose. They repeated that process with all four pumps. When they had finished, there was very little gas in the can; not enough to even bother with. Pat was returning to the car after replacing the can behind the garage when a state police car pulled into the Esso station.

It was Officer Chatman. "Get down, girls," I instructed in a panic. All four of us quickly ducked down while the boys remained sitting up.

We heard Officer Chatman ask Pat, "What are you boys doing out this late?"

"We're just going home from the dance at the Youth Park, and I had to take a leak," Pat answered.

"Okay, but you better get home," Officer Chatman told him; then he pulled back out onto Route 322 and headed west.

"That was Chatman, the cop who investigated our tent theft," I informed the boys and Marilyn. Cathy and Brenda already knew.

"Boy, that was close," Cathy said.

"I'm sure glad he didn't see us," Brenda added.

Dave had started the engine and pulled back out onto Route 322. He then took a left into Milroy so we could take our tour before heading for Red's Diner.

Unbeknown to us, while all of that was transpiring, Officer Chatman had decided to do his duty and take a trip down Lingle Valley to check on our tent to make sure no one had decided to steal it again. At least that is what he later said. When he saw that the tent was there, he decided to make sure we were okay. He never revealed how he knew we were sleeping out, though. When he walked over to the tent, he discovered that we were gone. That evidently confirmed his suspicions that we were up to something, so he went into our house, awoke my parents, and asked if we were sleeping out. Mom informed him that we were. It was then that he told her we were not in the tent, and he thought we were with a group of kids he had seen earlier in Milroy. He had seen their car earlier in Mount Pleasant.

It is my understanding that my mother became hysterical, and Officer Chatman calmed her by telling her he didn't think anything bad had happened to us; he thought we had just sneaked out somewhere. By that time, Dad had joined them. Officer Chatman learned from them what we had done that evening and who all was with us. He said that he would patrol the area looking for us.

After Officer Chatman had gone, Dad decided he, too, would go looking for us. He and Mom both got into his car and headed down Route 322. As we sat at the Stop sign at the Intersection of Electric Avenue and Route 332, waiting for an oncoming car to pass before pulling back out onto Route 322,

Dad and Mom passed us. Brenda and I both recognized his blue 1959 Chevy and went into a state of panic. "That's Dad!" Brenda exclaimed.

"Go the other way," I instructed in a horror stricken voice.

Dad had seen us, also; he swerved off the road and quickly turned around and began to follow us.

"Out drive him!" I pleaded. Honoring my request, Dave attempted to out drive Dad.

Dad was speeding toward us and gaining on us as we continued west on Route 322. Shortly into the chase, we realized we were had and told Dave to pull over. He did, and Cathy, Marilyn, Brenda, and I began climbing out of the backseat. Dad had pulled off the road directly in front of Dave's car. Mom opened our door as we approached. Dad commanded, "Get in the car!" Our night of fun had turned into a nightmare.

As soon as the door was closed, Dad sped toward home, lecturing all four of us at the top of his lungs. He went through the whole gamete of scenarios of what could have happened. Mom was just sort of moaning.

I must admit, it didn't look good, and if I would have been in their shoes, I might have reacted the same way. However, it was all completely innocent. None of us had any romantic attachments to any of the boys; we were simply a bunch of kids looking for some fun. We had gotten more than we bargained for.

When we got home, Dad ushered us all into the house and had Mom call Cathy's and Marilyn's mothers. She briefly explained what had happened and requested that they come to get their daughters. I remember thinking how lucky they were because they got to leave. Until their parents arrived, Dad continued questioning all of us. When they had gone, Dad continued to lecture Brenda and me. He finished by telling us we were grounded until we were twenty-one and commanded us to "Get to bed!"

Shortly after we had all settled into our beds, I heard Dad say to Mom, "I heard a car go down the hill. I'm going to go check on the tent." He came through our room and descended the stairs. A few moments later, I heard the back door screech as he quietly opened and closed it.

It seemed that less than five minutes had passed before I heard him burst through the back door and yell up the stairs, "Lucy, get up and call the cops. That damn thief was over there again. I chased him and almost caught him, but he got away and ran up over the hill. I have his car keys, though. If I get my hands on him, he'll wish he never came near this place."

About that time, Mom charged through our room and down the stairs pleading, "Werdna, you better leave him alone. Leave that up to the cops."

"Don't worry about it, Lucy. Just call the police," he insisted.

I wondered whom he had just chased as I listened to Mom's and Dad's voices rise and fall downstairs while they waited for the police to arrive. "Brenda, are you awake?" I whispered.

"How could I sleep through that?" she whispered in reply.

"Who do you think he chased?" I asked.

"I have no idea," she said. Neither of us had any desire to go downstairs. We had gotten into enough trouble for one night.

We both were still awake when someone knocked on the front door. I heard Mom answer the door and her voice drifted upstairs. I couldn't believe it; Officer Chatman was downstairs again. Wouldn't that guy ever go away? Dad explained what had transpired with the intruder that evening. While that was going on, a license check was done on the vehicle that was parked by Inez's alley; the one Dad had taken the keys from. "The car is registered to a Benny Morris from Milroy," Officer Chatman informed my parents. He then asked, "Do you know Benny Morris?"

"I know who he is," Dad answered. He then explained how he knew who Benny Morris was. Brenda and I knew Benny Morris, too. He went to our school. He was one year older than I. His sister Janet had been in my class until she had gotten pregnant by one of the Miller brothers and quit school that spring. In fact, we had seen Benny at the dance the previous night. Now I wondered what he was doing in our woods.

As Dad and Mom continued talking to Office Chatman, our phone rang. That was about three a.m. Mom answered the phone and said, "It's the guy who was in the woods. He wants his keys."

Officer Chatman instructed, "Give me the phone." As he took the phone from Mom, he lifted the receiver to his ear and said, "This is Officer Chatman with the Pennsylvania State Police. We checked your license plate and we know that the car is registered to Benny Morris. That tent you visited tonight was stolen last month, and as of right now, you are the prime suspect. I suggest that you come up here right now to discuss this problem with me." We couldn't hear the other side of the conversation, but Officer Chatman asked, "Where are you calling from?" Another pause, then: "I'll see you within the next ten minutes." He hung up the phone.

Officer Chatman said to my parents, "That was Benny Morris. He claims he had nothing to do with stealing the tent; he was only checking to see if the girls were over there because he had been told by the other boys that the girls were going to meet them, and he couldn't find them. He's on his way up here now to talk to me and get his car keys back."

"How can you believe him?" Dad asked Officer Chatman.

"I don't know if I do," he replied. "I need to question him when he gets here."

"Where did he call from?" Dad asked.

"From the Dew Bud Inn," Office Chatman answered. The Dew Bud Inn was at the far end of Mount Pleasant, right before you started over the Seven Mountains toward State College. There was a pay phone outside. "He walked there and called his brother," the officer continued.

As he finished talking, we heard a car outside our house. Officer Chatman said, "That's him. I'll go talk to him." To my dad, he said, "Mr. Bishop, I would like you to stay in here so there isn't any trouble."

"All right," Dad reluctantly agreed.

When Officer Chatman came back inside, about ten minutes later, he said, "I believe his story. Should I release him, or do you want to press charges?"

"If he isn't the thief, I don't want to press charges, but why was he out there?" Dad asked.

"He claims he was left behind by the other boys and was just trying to locate everyone. Like I said, I believe he's telling the truth. You scared the heck out of him when you chased him."

"Well, then just let him go," Dad said. "He better not be up here anymore, though," he added.

"I don't believe he will be," Officer Chatman replied as he went back outside and told Benny it was all right to leave. He then returned to our living room and said, "Well, I'll let you people get some sleep. I'm sure you're quite tired. If we get any information about who took your tent, I'll be in touch with you. Good evening." As Officer Chatman departed, I heard Mom and Dad thanking him for his help.

I was beginning to get angry at Officer Chatman. He seemed to enjoy getting my friends and me into trouble, but he defended all the boys, even Benny Morris who was caught at the crime scene. It was a rip-off. I was experiencing firsthand the double standards for males and females that I would struggle with for many more years.

At that time I was fifteen years old. Dad said I was grounded until I was twenty-one. I sure hoped he didn't make that stick. Fortunately, he did not; two weeks later, Brenda and I were again allowed to go the Youth Park dances, but our days of sleeping out and sneaking out were over. We eventually were allowed to sleep out, but we would be afraid to leave the tent.

Part V
JULY 1968 – JUNE 1969
Time Line

July 1968 – Yellow Submarine Movie.
July 23 - 24 Cleveland Black Uprising.
July 1968 – U. S. troops in Viet Nam increased by 19,000 to 535,000.
September 1968 – Linda begins 11th grade.
November 31, 1968 – Lyden Baines Johnson orders halt to all bombing in Viet Nam.
December 12, 1968 – Linda's 16th birthday.
December 21 – 27, 1968 – Apollo 8 with three astronauts circles moon on December 24.
April 4 –6, 1969 – Demonstrations on the anniversary of Martin Luther King's death and anti-war demonstrations.
April 24, 1969 – United States launches biggest attack on North Viet Nam; war demonstrations in 40 cities in US.
April 30, 1969 – 543,000 US soldiers in Viet Nam.

Popular Songs

"This Guy's In Love With You," Herb Alpert; "People Got To Be Free," The Rascals; "Born To Be Wild," Steppenwolf; "Hey Jude, / Revolution," The Beatles; "Love Child," Diana Ross; "Worst That Could Happen," The Brooklyn Bridge; "Abraham, Martin And John," Dion; "I'm Gonna Make You Love Me," Diana Ross & The Supremes; "Build Me Up, Buttercup," The Foundations; "Traces," The Classics IV; "It's Your Thing," The Isley Brothers; "Get Back," The Beatles; "Good Morning Starshine," Oliver.

Chapter 27

In August 1968, Brenda and I were still going to Mrs. Semple's to clean. Several months earlier, I had been promoted to cleaning Mrs. Semple's house. Brenda cleaned the kennels. Thursday, August 22nd, we again went to Mrs. Semple's. On that day, however, when we rang the doorbell, Mr. Semple answered. "Hello girls," he said as he greeted us at the door. "Come on in. I'm afraid I have some bad news," he continued as we entered the living room and closed the door behind us. "Last night Mrs. Semple had a heart attack and passed away," he informed us and began crying quietly. Several minutes passed as Brenda and I just stood there. We didn't know what to say or do. Mr. Semple stopped trembling and went on, "Ginger (Mrs. Semple's pet boxer) was with her when she died. I wasn't home. Ginger was so upset, I didn't think she was going to let me into the house. Mildred was lying on the kitchen floor. By the time the ambulance got here, it was too late."

Brenda and I were both fighting back tears. Still neither of us said anything. Mr. Semple continued talking. "I really appreciate all the help you girls gave my wife. I want you to choose any dog you want to take home with you. You each may have one if you like."

Brenda and I looked at each other. We didn't know if we would be allowed to have a dog, but we were certain we wouldn't be allowed to have two dogs. Finally, I spoke up and said, "I don't think we'll be allowed to have two dogs."

"Well, then take any one you'd like," Mr. Semple said. As Brenda and I thought about that, he started talking about the dogs. He said, "My wife always kind of favored Foxy. He's a friendly dog. I shouldn't have any trouble having someone take him." He continued predicting a number of other dogs' futures. Then he came to Jettabelle. "Jettebelle is a problem though. I'm afraid no one is going to want her. She's not beyond biting, and she isn't friendly at all. I'll probably have to have her put to sleep." He went on talking, but I believe Brenda and I both no longer heard anything. We looked at each other and nodded our heads. Yes, Jettabelle would be the dog we would choose.

"Mr. Semple," I said when he had finished talking.

"Yes?" he answered as if his thoughts were far away.

"We would like Jettabelle," I said.

"Are you sure? She's not a friendly dog," he informed us.

"Yes," I said.

Brenda added, "We don't want her to be put to sleep."

"Oh...I see." Mr. Semple said. "Well, if you want her, she's yours. Do you think it will be okay with your parents?" he asked.

"Sure it will," I said, not at all sure.

"Dad always wanted a house dog," Brenda informed Mr. Semple.

"All right then. Let's go get her," he told us as we followed him outside and down the sidewalk to the kennel. After we entered the kennel, he took a leash from those hanging beside the door, and he walked back to Jettabelle's cage, opened the door, and took her out. He then fastened the leash to the small black leather collar around her neck. "You may keep the leash. I sure hope things work out," he said, handing Jettabelle to me.

As he walked us to the door, I said, "Thank you...I'm really sorry about Mrs. Semple."

"Me too," Brenda added with feeling.

"I know you are, and you're quite welcome. I'm glad you girls are giving Jettabelle a good home. Mildred would be pleased. Take care now," he said as he closed the kennel door behind us.

I was experiencing many emotions as I carried Jettabelle down Lingle Valley Road to our house. It was just beginning to register with me that Mrs. Semple had died. I had difficulty accepting that. I recalled that I had felt the same way when I first learned of Grandma's death. Much later, I learned that was referred to as denial. I had to adjust the way I thought. One minute everything was one way and the next, it was entirely different. Sort of like everything was turned upside-down. I felt sad about Mrs. Semple's death. I had never thought about her dying as I had thought about Grandma's death when she was sick. It was all so sudden. Poor Mr. Semple seemed lost. I wondered why he was selling or giving away all the dogs. Maybe it was just too painful for him since the kennel had been Mrs. Semple's business.

I thought about Mrs. Semple lying on her kitchen floor with Ginger running wild around in the house. What if that had happened a day later? Brenda and I might have found her. I was sure glad that hadn't happened. Brenda interrupted my thoughts and asked, "What do you think they're going to say about Jettabelle?"

"I don't know…I think Dad will like her, but you know Mom doesn't want a dog in the house."

"Yeah, I know," Brenda said as she walked beside me down the hill, reaching over occasionally to pet Jettabelle. "I hope they don't make us give her back," she added. Jettabelle seemed terrified and didn't move.

"Me too," I said. "It would be real sad if they put her to sleep."

We had reached the back porch, went up the stairs, and entered the house through the back door. Both Dad and Mom were sitting in the living room. They looked up as we entered.

"Guess what we have?" I said as I carried Jettabelle into the living room and sat down on the sectional between Dad and Mom.

"What's this?" Dad asked.

Brenda and I both began explaining about Mrs. Semple's death and how Mr. Semple had given us our choice of the dogs. Then we went into detail about why we had chosen Jettabelle, to save her life. We thought that would help win Mom over to our side.

Dad said, "I thought I heard an ambulance last night, but I wasn't certain. Mr. Semple must have called them when he got home and found her."

Mom compassionately said, "That sure is a shame. She really didn't look like she was seventy years old."

I thought Mrs. Semple looked ancient, so I couldn't imagine why Mom was saying she didn't look that old.

"Wonder what Mr. Semple will do with the kennel now?" Dad speculated out loud.

"He told us he's selling or giving away all of the dogs," I reported.

"Did he say what she died from?" Mom asked.

"He said she had a heart attack," I answered. "I know she wasn't feeling well for a few months; that's why she promoted me to cleaning her house."

All of a sudden, I felt extremely exhausted even though I hadn't worked. I was saddened by Mrs. Semple's death. I walked out into Grandma's old room and sat on the couch with Jettabelle. I heard Brenda in the living room asking, "It's okay if we keep Jettabelle, isn't it?"

Dad said, "I think so; don't you, Lucy?"

Mom hesitated a moment and then said, "We wouldn't want them to put her to sleep. I suppose it's all right."

I felt very relieved when I heard her answer. There had been enough death. I couldn't imagine killing a perfectly healthy, pretty dog simply because she was a bit mean. It would be murder as far as I was concerned. I was glad we were able to stop such a senseless death.

Jettabelle just cowered in the corner of the couch with a terrified look on her face. Her whole world was about to change. I felt certain it would be for the best. I knew Mrs. Semple would be happy we had her. She never would have wanted any of her dogs put to sleep.

I was sad each time I realized I would never see Mrs. Semple again. Her death made me think of my former prayer for Grandma. I still couldn't pray. I felt God's existence; I just found it impossible to believe He cared for me. If He truly loved me, how could He have taken Grandma away and ignored my prayers? I wondered if Mr. Semple would stop praying--if he did pray. It was confusing and difficult to understand where Grandma, Joyce, and Mrs. Semple had gone. I wanted to believe they still existed somewhere; it was more frightening to think otherwise.

During the last part of August that year, Cathy and I met two boys who were friends, Steve Weber and Bill Griffith. We met them at a Youth Park dance, and later began going on double dates with them. Steve had an old green Plymouth Belvedere; Bill had no car. I wasn't allowed to date until I was sixteen, so I couldn't tell my parents I was seeing Bill. We generally just met at the dances that summer, and occasionally, we would go for rides on the surrounding mountain roads.

The Laurel Reservoir was being built at that time, and that resulted in the need to reroute Route 322 out around the construction area. A tunnel was built for vehicles to temporarily pass through the construction area until the work was completed. The tunnel would eventually end up partially under water when the reservoir was completed. Betsy, Cathy, Brenda, and I had painted pictures inside the tunnel one previous afternoon that summer. We had speculated about how hundreds of years from then, archaeologists would find the pictures and try to analyze the people who lived during that period of history.

During one of our summer rides, Cathy and I told Steve and Bill about our paintings in the tunnel, and they decided they would like to go see them. Steve drove to the tunnel and parked near the entrance. We then walked through the tunnel. It was dark inside, but there was still enough light to see without a flashlight. They said they thought our paintings were neat. It was then Steve suggested that they should add to our paintings. So we all got back into his car, and he drove us to Brindle's Hardware Store in Reedsville where he purchased a spray can of hot-pink paint. We returned to the tunnel with that paint. It turned out that Steve and Bill weren't interested in painting pictures;

they wanted to spray-paint the word "Budweiser" on the wall of the tunnel. It was Steve's opinion that Budweiser was the best beer on earth. He was under the legal drinking age, but was still able to obtain beer. Generally, I believe he took it from his father's stash.

Cathy and I didn't think it was a good idea to paint the name of a beer on the tunnel wall, but we watched as they painted the word "Budweiser" in several locations. The largest display consisted of two-foot letters that extended approximately ten-feet in length. Steve and Bill laughed as they added to our speculation about archaeologists finding those paintings and learning that the best beer of our time had been Budweiser. Of course, they could only paint when no one was coming through the tunnel. Since drivers had to turn their automobile lights on prior to entering the tunnel, it was easy for us to see them coming, hide the paint can, and just walk along the side of the tunnel wall.

Cathy and I continued to see Steve and Bill throughout the remainder of the summer. We had many fun times going on picnics, swimming, and just messing around. I liked Bill, but I never had deep romantic feelings for him. I certainly wasn't in love with him. One summer night, they came over to our tent. We no longer would leave because we had learned our lesson. Steve drove out Lingle Valley Road to the corner and parked at the archery range; then they walked back the dirt road, crossed the wooden bridge over Lingle Run, and slipped into the woods on the other side. That wooded area was owned by Dad. Steve and Bill stumbled along the path through the woods until they found our tent.

Cathy and I were only fifteen, and neither of us were ready to become sexually active, but it became evident shortly after Steve and Bill arrived that they had other plans. We were naïve; it had not occurred to us that inviting them to our tent suggested to them that we wanted to have sex with them. Bill was sixteen and Steve was seventeen, and I guess their hormones were raging as were ours, but sex at that point for us was out of the question. We only wanted to neck, which in the end was all we did. When the boys left, they were still sexually frustrated but well aware that Cathy and I drew the line long before intercourse. We decided we would no longer invite them to our tent; it was just too easy for things to get out of control.

Summer ended much too soon, and it was almost Labor Day before we knew it. Dad had us help him pack the tent away for storage over the winter. We didn't know it then, but the following year, it wouldn't go up. Our lives would move on, and we no longer would want to sleep out in the woods across from our house; however, the memories we had shared inside that tent and with events related to our sleep-outs would stay with us forever.

Chapter 28

School started again the day after Labor Day, September 3rd, 1968. I was in eleventh grade. My homeroom was Room #206; Mrs. Reigle was my homeroom teacher. I wasn't as apprehensive about starting school as I had been in earlier years, but I still didn't like school. Somehow, I felt as though I were an outsider, and I never truly believed I belonged. There still was Tracy and her flunkies who enjoyed making my life miserable. Throughout the years, I learned there would always be people like Tracy, but as I got older, I learned how to better deal with them. For the most part, the times I spent in school were unhappy times. I still had no classes with my good friends, and I was always glad when it was time to go home.

I enjoyed spending time with my friends on the weekends and sometimes during the evenings of school nights. Because I didn't like school, I had no desire to participate in extracurricular activities. I did over the years, however, join the Math Club, Pep Club, Gym Club, Future Secretaries Club, and I played basketball one season simply so there would be something written in my yearbook. I worried about things like that. I worried far in advance about whom I would sit with on class trips, who would be my dance partner when we had square dancing in gym, and what I would say when called upon in my classes. I felt ugly and found it difficult to believe that any boy would desire to be with me even though I was seeing Bill, and the upcoming prom that year weighed heavily on my mind. I guess I really wasn't ugly; I just felt that way. I was tall and very skinny and had shoulder-length light-brown hair that I straightened as much as possible. I hated my glasses and refused to wear them most of the time.

I still did not like the feeling I got when I returned home to an empty house in the evening. Mom still worked at Hanover Cannery, and she was not home when we returned from school. That made me feel isolated and lonely even though Brenda was there. Brenda and I had been what later was referred to as "latchkey children" since the summer of 1965, after Grandma had passed away. When Mom did return home from work, she generally was exhausted, and often fell asleep on the couch while Brenda and I washed and dried the dishes.

Mom had been experiencing episodes of pain at different times throughout 1968. She visited Dr. Schooley on numerous occasions while he attempted to evaluate the symptoms and make a diagnosis. Eventually, he scheduled tests to be completed at Black's Hospital in Lewistown because he suspected the problem was Mom's gallbladder. It was there they discovered that my mom had a diseased gallbladder. Dr. Schooley referred her to Dr. Speece, a surgeon, at the hospital, and surgery was scheduled so that he could remove her gallbladder. The surgery took place in September, a week after school had started.

The day of the surgery, Dad made Brenda and me attend school. He took off work to be at the hospital during the surgery. I was worried because it seemed similar in my mind to Grandma going to the hospital. Even though I wouldn't even admit it to myself, in the back of my mind, I feared I would lose Mom, too.

The surgery was completed without any complications. The evening following the surgery, Dad took Brenda and me to the hospital to visit Mom. That made me feel better because I was able to see for myself that she was all right. She was required to stay in the hospital for one week. During school that week, my thoughts were often about Mom. When I returned to the empty house in the evening, I was even more aware of how much I missed her.

Brenda and I had begun to "run around" with Carol Barger, a girl in the neighborhood who lived "up back" as we called it. That meant behind Leeper's store. She was older than us and had her driver's license. She had a red Corvair that we would go cruising in. One of our favorite cruising spots was Lewistown. Many of our peers would meet along Market Street. Usually, the boys would all line their cars along the street, and the girls would drive down Market Street and check out what boys were out that evening.

We had met many of the boys at the Youth Park and YMCA dances. There were dances at both the Lewistown and the Burnham YMCA. The dances in Lewistown were held on Friday nights and had a live band; the dances in Burnham were held on Saturday nights with a DJ and records.

On Friday nights Carol would take us through the alley by the Lewistown YMCA, and we would beep the horn at the boys on the porch and sidewalk. She would pretend her automatic car had a stick shift, and would put it into neutral, rev the engine in front of the boys, then jerk it into gear to take off.

That, no doubt, did nothing to improve the functioning of her transmission. Carol, Brenda, and I never attended the Lewistown dances because we didn't feel comfortable around many of those kids; we always went to the Burnham dances. We also attended the dances at the Youth Park on Tuesday evenings during the summer and various school dances throughout the year.

The Friday night before Mom was discharged from the hospital, Dad allowed us to go with Carol. I believe he was trying to help us relax and forget our concerns about Mom for a few hours. It worked because we had a great time with Carol that night. We stopped at the Red Barn, one of the few fast food restaurants in the area, and had burgers and fries before driving through town. Sometimes we would go to a football game, wrestling match, or basketball game, but that night we did not. We just rode around and had a good time calling out to our friends as we drove by.

The next morning, Dad brought Mom home from the hospital. She wasn't to do any lifting for several weeks, so Dad, Brenda, and I had to temporarily pick up her duties until she recovered. During the day, Mom was home alone except for Jettabelle. Jettabelle was still a very frightened dog, even though she had been with us for over a month. She would lay in her dog bed in the corner of our living room and rarely leave, except to eat, drink, and go outside. Brenda and I would pick her up sometimes and hold her, but you could tell she was afraid.

Mom had to take six weeks' sick leave. During that time, Jettabelle bonded with her. Mom babied her throughout those weeks, and she began to follow Mom around the house. Before long, she began warming up to Dad and Brenda, too. With me things were different.

Jettabelle had decided I was her enemy. That was a new experience for me because generally, animals liked me. I guess they could sense that I was a true animal lover. I speculated many times about why Jettabelle didn't like me, and I came to believe that she remembered me taking her puppies from her when I cleaned her cage. I loved to hold them and pet them because they were tiny black fur balls and so adorable. Sometimes Dad would allow Jettabelle to lie on the sectional beside him. Whenever I would be sitting on the other end and stood up to walk into the kitchen or sitting room, she would race down the couch and attempt to bite me in the rear. I became conditioned to fear standing up. Jettabelle did others things to me also. She would chew my belongings, but no one else's. She particularly liked to chew my curlers. That was the age before blow dryers and curling irons. I actually slept in huge three-inch diameter curlers. To keep them from falling out of my hair, I would pull a bandana around my head and tie it into a knot in the front. That made sleeping very uncomfortable, but I thought it was preferable to frizzy hair.

I had been cursed with just enough curl in my hair to make it frizz. Sometimes Cathy and I would buy hair straightener and apply it to our hair. It smelled horrible. The box instructed us to use the extremely big-toothed comb that came with the solution to comb it through our hair. That procedure actually did straighten our hair, but it also stripped some of the color. Other times we would iron our hair to remove the curl. No price was too high to pay for straight hair; curls were definitely out. Years later, I would get a chuckle out of that when I would pay to get a perm.

The cry of the times was for individuality, when in reality, we all still felt the need to conform with our peers. It was okay to be different from society as a whole as long as you were different as a group. Our generation coined the term "free love" which actually meant free sex. Unfortunately, many learned that it was far from free for various reasons such as, pregnancy, sexually-transmitted diseases, and loss of innocence and morality. We attired ourselves in bell-bottom jeans, strands of beads and chains, and often discarded our bras as we listened to the music of our times.

In the fall of 1968, sometimes Steve and Bill would pick Cathy and me up after school. I remember once they were parked outside along the grass across from the semi- circle where all the buses parked. Cathy met me outside my homeroom to tell me she saw Steve's car outside during her last period class. We didn't want to go outside in front of all the kids in the buses because often Steve's transmission wasn't working right, and he would have to drive in reverse and jerk the gearshift into drive so the car would go forward. Fearing that would happen, we hid out in the girls' washroom until after the buses had gone. Only people staying for after-school activities remained when Cathy and I went out to meet the boys. Cathy was a majorette and was supposed to stay for practice, but she skipped practice that afternoon.

When Cathy hopped into the front seat with Steve, and I got in the backseat with Bill, Steve attempted to take off. The car would not go into drive, so he drove in reverse in circles where the buses had been parked until he was finally able to get the transmission to go into drive. Cathy and I were mortified. We kept hoping no one saw us, and we were very glad when we finally drove away.

The next day, I discovered that none other than Tracy had witnessed the entire scene with Steve and Bill. When I walked into English class and took my seat, Tracy turned to Nancy Taylor and asked, "Did you see Linda and her boyfriend yesterday?"

"No," Nancy answered.

"He must be a real jerk," Tracy said. "He was with some guy who has an ugly green car, and evidently he doesn't know how to drive because he drove around the circle backwards several times before they finally left, " she stated with a smirk on her face.

"No kidding," Nancy responded. "Who is your boyfriend?" she asked me.

"Bill," I answered. "His friend was having transmission problems. That's why he had to drive in reverse," I defended Steve.

"I'm sure," Tracy said sarcastically. "It wouldn't be that he's just retarded, would it?"

"No, it wouldn't," I replied in a tone that clearly indicated the conversation was over as far as I was concerned.

Tracy snickered and whispered something to Nancy. Oh, how I hated Tracy. I wished I could slap her across the face; she certainly deserved it. Tracy wouldn't stop, though. She continued harassing me: "I'll bet you'll even go to the prom with him, and maybe his friend will let him use that beautiful green car so you can make your grand entrance."

"Why don't you just mind your own business?" I asked her.

Her only reply was another chuckle. At that time, Mrs. Wilson returned to the classroom from the hall, so the harassment stop.

On December 12th, I celebrated another birthday. That birthday was special, though, for I turned sixteen. Sixteen was a milestone because I could obtain my driver's license. I had been required to take a driver's education course the previous year, so as soon as I reached age sixteen, I scheduled a physical with Dr. Schooley, completed an eye examination, and obtained my driver's permit. I still was not using my "lazy eye," and I was required to wear glasses whenever I drove.

Dad took me out to practice driving in his 1960 yellow Corvair. It was similar to Carol Barger's car: an automatic with a lever on the dash to switch gears. It was a fairly small, boxy looking car. Ralph Nader eventually declared them unsafe. When I first started driving, I felt as though I could not see out over the hood well enough, so Dad had me sit on a cushion. He kept telling me to look far out ahead of me while driving, but at first I had a tendency to look down at the road directly in front of my vehicle.

I also had enrolled in the driver's education driving course at school, so Mr. Weber took me out in the driver's ed. car. The first time he took me out for a lesson, he had me drive to downtown Lewistown and park in front of Wolf's Furniture Store so he could run in to make a payment. I was terrified because the driver's ed. car was a Plymouth, much larger than the Corvair. In addition, I felt anxious driving with Mr. Weber because authority figures always made me nervous, and there were other students in the car, which only added to my anxiety. I survived the trip, however, and numerous others that followed.

I had a tendency to try to maneuver turns without moving my hands on the steering wheel, which made it much more difficult. Once while I was practicing turns in Rose Ann, a housing development near Milroy, Mr. Weber struggled with trying to get me to understand that I had to make turns by crossing my hands and turning hand-over-hand as he called it. Once he touched my right hand and told me he was going to bite me there if I tried to turn again without moving my hands. He was kidding, of course, and his comment made me giggle, which in turn helped me to relax.

After several months of practice driving with both Dad and Mr. Weber, Mr. Weber scheduled the driving test at the testing center for me and Cindy Metzger, another girl in my class. At that time, the testing center was located at the Highland Park Firehouse. The examination consisted of two parts: an oral test and the driving test.

I knew approximately a week in advance when my exam was scheduled. Throughout that period, Dad kept telling me that I wasn't going to pass the driving test. He said I just didn't have the natural ability for things, such as driving, like Brenda did. That only made me more anxious about the upcoming test. I don't believe Dad realized what affect his belittling had on me. I had always felt that he didn't like me as much as Brenda. I never actually expressed those views, but I feel they contributed to my anxieties around authority figures.

The day of the exam, Cindy and I got into the driver's education car, and Mr. Weber drove us to the testing center. We went inside, and I was called upon first to go with the officer who asked the questions. I passed my oral test, and then followed the other officer to the car to take the driving part. He had me drive toward Chief Logan High School. We turned left off of Highland Avenue onto Sixth Street that was parallel to the left side of the high school. That street was on the far edge of Pleasant Acres, another housing development in the Lewistown area. It was there that the officer told me to make a three-point-turn. I completed the turn without any mistakes that I was aware of and then drove back to the fire department. The officer told me to pull in and park in front of the firehouse. I did that and sat there while he continued writing in his notebook. When he finally looked up at me, he handed me my permit and said, "Take this in and get it stamped. You passed."

I was ecstatic! "Okay," I answered as I got out of the car and went inside the firehouse.

I passed Cindy on her way out to take her driving part of the test. She asked, "How did you do?"

"I passed!" I exclaimed.

"Good," she said. "I passed my questions."

"Good luck," I called as she continued outside and I went over to the desk to have my permit stamped.

Mr. Weber said, "Congratulations; I see you passed."

"Thanks. Yeah I did," I said.

About twenty minutes later, the officer who had taken Cindy out driving came back into the firehouse and said something to Mr. Weber. He looked over at me and motioned for me to go outside. I went outside and got into the driver's ed. car. Cindy was sitting in the back seat crying. I didn't ask her how she did on her test because it was obvious. I had to contain my happiness about passing my exam until later.

When I got home from school that evening, I could hardly wait until Dad and Mom arrived so I could tell them I passed my driving test. Dad got there first, so I announced it to him. I was so glad his prediction was not accurate. I truly believe he was surprised. He said I could take the Corvair that night because I wanted to go out with my friends to celebrate. Later, Mom arrived home from work, and I told her the good news.

I called Cathy and Betsy to see if they could go out that night. They said they could, so Brenda, Cathy, Betsy, and I went out in the Corvair that evening. We stopped at Red's Diner to eat; then, since it was Mother's Day on the following Sunday, we purchased flowers for our mothers and put them on the back floor. As the evening progressed, Cathy's neck began to swell. We thought she was getting the mumps, but she said she didn't want to go home. The odor of the hyacinths we purchased was overwhelming inside the car. Hyacinths were one of Mom's favorite flowers.

After purchasing our flowers, we made several trips through town. It was a Friday night so there were many kids hanging out in town. We had a lot of fun as we beeped and waved to our friends. Time passed quickly and far too soon, we knew we had to call it an evening because I had to have the car home by midnight since I had a junior license.

Cathy looked terrible; you couldn't even tell she had a neck by that time. It had disappeared because her neck was swollen so badly. As we started home, she said, "I think I have a fever."

"You really don't look good, Cathy," I informed her. "You probably should see a doctor," I advised.

"I know. I wonder what's wrong. I didn't think you could get the mumps when you're this old," she said. No one replied to that comment, but I think everyone was contemplating Cathy's statement.

I took Betsy home first since she lived along Route 322. She got out of the Corvair, lifted her white hyacinth out of the back seat, and went into her house. Someone had switched the porch light on for her. "See ya," she called to us on her way inside her back porch. She had a screened-in porch and had to go through a door to get on the porch.

Cathy came next. I took a right onto Lingle Valley Road as I proceeded toward home from Betsy's. I then turned right into Cathy's alley from Lingle Valley Road. I was able to drive directly to the back door because that's where the two parking spaces were located. She too got out of the car, lifted her pink hyacinth out of the back, and pushed the door shut with her butt.

"See you later," I called out the window as I backed up and completed a three-point-turn in reverse.

When Brenda and I reached our house, I parked the Corvair in its usual spot in the woods, turned out the lights, and lifted the remaining purple hyacinth out of the back. We were headed toward the front porch when the porch light and pole light came on. The Mother's Day flower would be no surprise for Mom because I was certain she was the one who turned the lights on.

The next day, I didn't hear from Cathy or Betsy, so the following day I walked to Cathy's house. When I got there, I discovered that no one was home. From there I walked up the hill between her grandparent's house and the Carsons' house. Cathy's grandfather was outside, so I asked, "Mr. Havice, do you know where Cathy is today?"

"Oh my! Haven't you heard?" he asked.

"Heard what?" I replied.

"Last night she got very sick, and Faye had to take her to the hospital. They said she was dehydrated, and after they ran some tests, they discovered that she has mono. She has to stay in the hospital for a few days," Bud told me.

"Is she allowed to have visitors?" I asked.

"I'm afraid not. Mononucleosis is contagious. She won't be able to return to school until she is completely recovered, and we're not sure how long that will be right now," he continued.

"What hospital is she in?" I asked. There were two hospitals in the area: the Lewistown Hospital, and Black's Hospital. Both were located in Lewistown a few miles apart.

"She's in Black's Hospital," Bud replied.

"I'll send her a card," I said; then I turned to leave.

"I'm sure she'd appreciate that," Bud said.

I could hardly believe that Cathy was in the hospital. I had never known anyone my own age who had been admitted to the hospital other than for tonsillectomies. She had mono, too, and I was certain she had gotten it from Steve because she had not kissed anyone else lately, and it was called the "kissing disease." Steve didn't have mono, but I heard you could be a carrier and not get the disease. I sure hoped I wouldn't catch it. I remembered Cathy telling me her hair was falling out a few weeks earlier because she wasn't eating enough protein, according to her doctor. I thought perhaps she had gotten mono because her system was already run down, and she had no resistance.

I returned home and reported the news. Dad agreed to allow me to have the car later that evening so Brenda and I could go to Black's Hospital to see if we could visit Cathy from a distance.

Around six that evening, I drove Brenda and myself to Black's Hospital. It was a small, dark red brick hospital located on top of a hill on Buena Vista Circle in the lower end of Lewistown. It was the same hospital where Mom had her gallbladder surgery. The parking lot was directly in front of the hospital, and there were fifty steps leading to the front door. I'm certain the builders didn't think about handicap access when that building was completed. There was a road that left the parking lot and circled around to the back of the hospital. I parked in the lot and Brenda and I got out of the car, walked up the steps, and entered the front door.

Directly inside the door, a receptionist asked if she could help us. We explained that we were there to see our friend, Cathy. She checked her chart and told us that she was not permitted to have visitors. I asked what room she was in so we could send her a card. I could tell by the room number approximately where Cathy's room was located because there was an arrow pointing to the left corridor, indicating what group of rooms were located in that wing, and I remembered where the rooms were from visiting Mom. Cathy's room was one of the ones I remembered: Room 103.

As Brenda and I exited the building, I said, "I think we should drive around back and see if we can find Cathy's room. What do you think?"

"Yeah. Let's do it." Brenda answered.

So we got into the Corvair, exited the parking lot, and drove up the hill behind the building. The architecture of the building included a three-inch offset approximately two feet high all around the perimeter of the building. Fortunately, Cathy was located on the first floor. I would have hated to have attempted the fire escape. I parked the Corvair along the bushes in the back, and Brenda and I got out. We had narrowed our search down to three windows. By our calculations, one of those windows should have been the window of Cathy's room. We hesitated for a moment until we decided to try the middle window. It was decided that I would try first. I reached up over my head and held onto the brick window sill as Brenda boosted me, and I pulled myself onto the three-inch ledge. It was difficult to hold onto the ledge because it was brick. I slowly raised myself toward the window and peaked in. I saw an elderly woman lying in a bed, and I sure hoped she had not seen me. I quickly let go of the ledge and jumped down, fearing I would be caught.

Brenda was next. I boosted her up as she chose the next window--the one to the left of the window I had just checked. She slyly raised her head and looked into the window. "Bingo!" she exclaimed. I knew she had found Cathy. She tapped on the window and waved. Holding onto the ledge with one hand, though, made her lose her balance, and she jumped back down to the pavement. "She's in there, and she saw me," Brenda informed me. At that time, Cathy was at the window looking out and waving to us.

"How do you feel?" I yelled.

"Not too good," I heard her reply.

"When will you get out of there?" Brenda asked.

"They said I might be able to leave tomorrow," Cathy told us. She then added, "The doctor said I probably won't be able to return to school this year."

"That's too bad," I said, wondering if she would have to repeat her sophomore year of school. I sure hoped she wouldn't.

"We better leave before we get caught," Brenda cautioned.

"We have to leave," I informed Cathy. "We'll come see you when you go home," I added.

"See you soon," Brenda said as we turned and headed for the car.

Cathy nodded and waved.

As we drove away, Brenda and I discussed how pale Cathy looked, and we speculated about whether she would pass after missing so much school. We missed our friend and hated leaving her there.

We decided that since we were already in Lewistown, we might as well drive down Market Street to see who was out that night. That was a mistake. Bill was standing along the street with a gang of guys. As soon as he saw us, he jumped into a Mustang and followed us. I knew the car belonged to a friend of his because he had once driven it for one of our dates. He didn't have a car of his own.

It was strange, but since I was sixteen and allowed to date Bill, I didn't want to. He just wouldn't leave me alone, though. He was very pushy, and he wanted a commitment that I was not able to give him. I just didn't love him.

He proceeded to chase us around several streets until I got the idea to go to my cousin's gas station on Walnut Street. I knew Dad was there visiting because I heard him tell Mom earlier that he would drop her off at Grandma Eward's to visit, and he would go see Johnnie. I pulled into the parking lot at the gas station, jumped out of the car, and went inside. Brenda was right behind me. I mistakenly thought Bill would just leave. He didn't. He followed us inside. When he realized Dad was there, he simply said, "Linda, I need to talk to you."

I followed him outside, and he asked, "Why are you trying to get away from me?"

"I'm not really," I lied.

"Ever since you got your driver's license, you don't want anything to do with me. Don't you want to see me anymore?" he asked.

"Bill, we're not going together and never were. I'm just too young to get serious about anyone. You're a very nice guy, but I don't want to go steady with anyone. I hope you understand," I said gently even though I was disturbed with his behavior.

"Okay, I get the message," he snapped as he turned to leave and then jumped into the Mustang and squealed out of the parking lot.

I went back inside and told Brenda I was leaving.

Dad said, "That guy's really pushy. I don't think you should see him anymore."

I had only dated him a few times since I had turned sixteen.

"I'm not," I said as Brenda and I left.

Brenda giggled as we drove away. "I can't believe his nerve just coming inside there like he did. He's a real pest."

"He's a nice guy," I said, defending him. "I just don't want to go with him."

"Good," Brenda said, and we returned to Market Street to see what was happening.

Chapter 29

During the latter part of the 1960s the Civil Rights issues were still raging. In fact, we were right in the middle of the Civil Rights era during the sixties. Malcolm X was killed on February 21, 1965; Martin Luther King was organizing freedom rides and demonstrations across the south, and there were black uprisings all over the United States throughout the sixties. We, as a country, were also in the middle of the Viet Nam conflict. The United States began bombing North Viet Nam in February of 1965; by the end of 1967, more than 486,000 U.S. troops would be in Viet Nam and 15,000 would already be dead. There were draft card burnings and anti-war demonstrations on many campuses. Out of all that racial unrest, objections to the Viet Nam war, and the flower-power mentality of the times, many social protest songs were created, such as : "Where Have All The Flowers Gone?" "Eve of Destruction," "With God on Our Side," "Universal Soldier," and "Society's Child."

In my eleventh grade United States history class, we discussed in depth one protest song in particular: "Society's Child" by Janis Ian.

On Tuesday afternoon, November 5th, 1968, we all went into class and took our seats. Mr. Solt, our teacher, came in shortly afterwards and said, "Today I have a record I would like you to listen to." He then prepared the record player that set in the left-hand corner in the front of the room. He informed us while he was preparing the equipment, "I'll be putting the words on the over-head projector." After he said so, these were the words we saw:

Come to my door, baby
Face is clean and shining black as night
My mama went to answer
You know that you looked so fine
Now I could understand the tears and the shame
She called you "boy" instead of your name
When she wouldn't let you inside

When she turned and said
'But honey, he's not our kind'

She said I can't see you any more, baby
Can't see you any more

Walk me down to school, baby
Everybody's acting deaf and blind
Until they turn and say
'Why don't you stick to your own kind'
My teachers all laugh, their smirking stares
  cutting deep down in our affairs
Preachers of equality
Think they believe it
Then why won't they just let us be

They say I can't see you any more, baby
Can't see you any more

One of these days I'm gonna stop my listening
Gonna raise my head up high
One of these days I'm gonna raise up
  my glistening wings and fly
But that day will have to wait for a while
Baby, I'm only society's child
When we're older, things may change
But for now, this is the way they must remain

I say I can't see you any more, baby
Can't see you any more
No, I don't want to see you any more, baby"

"Society's Child (Baby I've Been Thinking)"
Written by Janis Ian
©1966 TAOSONGS TWO (BMI)/Administered by BUG
All Rights Reserved. Used by Permission.

Mr. Solt then played the record. The classroom was silent as we listened and followed along with the words on the screen. All you could hear was the moving, emotional voice of Janis Ian echoing throughout the room, along with the electrifying background music.

My emotions reached a new height as the meaning of the words registered in my mind. I was outraged that anyone would turn someone away because of their skin color, yet I knew it was true. Living in rural Pennsylvania my entire life to that point, I rarely witnessed racial prejudice on that level. Although my grandmother had been a part of that form of prejudice, I still didn't understand it, and I did not like it.

As we discussed the social ramifications of the song, Mr. Solt pointed out the following: "You know, at the beginning of the song, the mother was saying the girl could not see this young man because he was black. Later, the teachers and peers were saying she couldn't see him anymore. Then at the end of the song, the girl herself was saying she couldn't see him anymore, and finally, she said she didn't want to see him anymore. In essence, this song shows the transference and progression of racial prejudice." He continued, "More often than not, we adopt the values of our parents. Other authority figures also help to program us, too." I thought about that in my own family. My grandmother's parents definitely contributed to her belief that blacks were inferior. Then living in Alabama, she was surrounded by many bigots. In the end, she became one herself. Sadly, she never realized how wrong and messed up her thought processes were.

I, too, could easily have followed in her footsteps if left in the same environment. I believe there were several major events that changed my destiny. One was when my grandfather moved his family from Alabama to Pennsylvania. That move resulted in my father being surrounded with more individuals who believed in racial equality. Also, his father was not as prejudiced as Grandma's was.

I still missed my grandmother greatly, but as I matured, I was better able to see her flaws as a human being. There was still racial prejudice all around me, but I felt I had taken a step up from where my grandmother had been. As these thoughts were going through my mind, I heard some commotion behind me.

I turned around and saw Tracy whispering to Sue. I couldn't hear everything she was saying, but I did make out, "She's a nigger lover." It took me a while to realize that she was referring to me. Now that was the most ridiculous thing Tracy had ever come up with. To begin with, I had known fewer than five black people my entire life. I tried to ignore her, but it was obvious she wanted me to hear. While Mr. Solt was returning the record player to its original spot in the corner of the room, Tracy could stand it no more. She tapped me on the back and asked, "You're a nigger lover, aren't you?"

I had no idea how to respond to that, so I simply said, "No."

"Yes you are," she insisted. "Cindy Rager saw you dancing with one at the Y on Saturday night." Then I knew what she was referring to. Every Saturday night while school was in session, there were dances at the Burnham YMCA for high school kids. My friends and I often went.

"Are you denying that?" she asked smartly.

"No, I'm not denying anything," I stated. There were a group of boys who came from Huntingdon, a town about twenty miles west of Burnham, to attend the dances. On several occasions, I had danced with one of the black boys. I had thought nothing of it. Obviously, though, Tracy did. I didn't even know his name.

"So, you are a nigger lover," she proudly proclaimed.

Mr. Solt turned around abruptly and asked, "What was that, Tracy?"

"Nothing," Tracy said.

Mr. Solt continued, "I don't know about that. I thought I heard you call someone a nigger lover. Did I hear correctly?" he asked.

"No," Tracy stated emphatically. She was such a liar. I didn't think Mr. Solt liked her. She had even made fun of him before. Right after he got his contact lenses, he blinked almost continually. Tracy saw another victim and started laughing at him behind his back and encouraging others to do the same. He didn't care for that kind of behavior. I felt certain he sometimes heard her.

"Well, I certainly hope not," he continued. "You know this song is about that very kind of prejudice. Can anyone tell me why society wouldn't want a white girl to date a black boy?" Mr. Solt asked.

Jane Warner at the back of the room raised her hand.

"Jane," he called.

Maybe they were afraid they would have children, and the children would have problems because of an interracial marriage," Jane answered.

"That could be," Mr. Solt said. "Does anyone else have any ideas?"

I had ideas, but I didn't like to talk in class. It made me nervous, and everything I said Tracy would attack. That didn't mean I didn't have any ideas, though. I had plenty of them.

Bonnie Metz contributed, "Her mother probably doesn't want her friends to make fun of her daughter."

Troy Donovan added, "Her mother doesn't want to be embarrassed about her daughter's relationship."

"Why would she be embarrassed?" Mr. Solt asked.

"Because a lot of people see interracial couples as being bad," Jason Snook remarked.

"That's true, Jason. They do; but why?" Mr. Solt prodded.

"It's different. People don't like change. It has for the most part been whites with whites and blacks with blacks in this country," Dave Cavanough added.

"Is change wrong?" Mr. Solt asked Dave.

"No, change is not wrong…People just don't like it," he answered.

"So, people don't like change. Does everyone agree with that?" Mr. Solt asked the class. Everyone in the class agreed and nodded their heads or stated yes.

"So, are you saying that people don't like white girls to date black boys because it is a form of change?"

"Yes," the class responded pretty much in unison.

"Could it be also that blacks are viewed as inferior because most of them initially were slaves in this country?" Mr. Solt asked.

Again most of the class responded, "Yes."

"But because they are viewed this way, does this make it true?"

Nancy Foster raised her hand.

"Nancy," Mr. Solt called.

"No, it doesn't," she said.

"Then how can we change views without anyone being hurt?" Mr. Solt asked as he walked around the room. "Anyone?"

Jeff Prestley who was seated in the third row answered, "We can't."

"That's right, we can't. For example, in order to change people's attitudes about blacks and whites dating, someone will have to do it. The pioneers of change will always suffer the consequences. So we need to ask ourselves: 'Are we going to be pioneers to change what we feel is wrong, or are we going to resist change?'"

I didn't contribute to the conversation, but I felt all the emotion. It was great because in a way, Mr. Solt was slamming Tracy and her attitudes. Someone sure needed to, for she had gotten totally out of control. For once, I felt a teacher was on my side. I realized that I had already decided to be a pioneer of change. That is why I resisted my grandmother's beliefs which I felt were wrong. In a way, that was what the sixties were all about: change.

Often the people were divided into two groups: Those who felt an injustice was occurring and trying to change it, and those who tried to keep the status quo by resisting change.

The Viet Nam war was a good example of the split into two groups. One group resisted the war through actions such as demonstrations, protest songs, and draft dodging, while the other group marched into battle and supported the war effort, at least on the surface. The same split occurred with racial issues: those who supported segregation and those who did not. Now there were some who were more radical than others in promoting their views within each group, but basically, members of that group wanted the same end.

While we continued discussing these issues, the bell rang. I felt that was one of the best classes I'd had in high school. It addressed what was happening all around us, and it seemed more relevant to our lives. Some of our other classes seemed so removed from reality that they could be nothing but boring

As we all stood up and made our way into the hall, Tracy came up behind me and said, "You're still a nigger lover." Then she laughed as she and Sue went out around me, and they continued down the hall toward the stairwell. Some things probably would never change no matter how many pioneers of change existed.

Later that night at home and at the supper table, I related what had happened in our U.S. history class that day. I left out the part about me being a "nigger lover," however. I sure didn't tell my parents everything. When I finished reporting what had transpired, Dad asked, "So are you saying that you believe it's okay for interracial dating?"

"I don't see anything wrong with it," I replied.

"What do you think?" Dad asked Brenda.

"I don't know. Who cares anyway?" she responded.

"Well, everyone should care about what is happening around them," Dad lectured.

Mom added, "People should just quit trying to cause trouble."

"But, Mom," I said, "how is that causing trouble? They aren't hurting anyone; they're just dating each other."

"What if they would want to get married?" she asked me.

"What would be wrong with that?" I asked.

"Even if it didn't matter to them, they should think about what would happen to their children," Mom stated with great emotion.

I couldn't believe it. Mom was resisting change just like we had talked about in school. I said, "Nothing would happen to their children if we didn't make a big deal about it."

"Maybe you wouldn't, Linda, and maybe I wouldn't, but some people would. Then the children would suffer for the actions of their parents. Can't you see that?"

"No, I can't. If the children suffer, it's not because their parents fell in love and got married; it's because other people are prejudiced."

"That may be so, but you can't change people," Mom stated.

"Yes you can!" I exclaimed. "It's just like we talked about in class. People have to be pioneers of change or things will never change. When something is wrong, we should try to change it, not just accept it because that's the way it has always been. We have to question why."

"It sounds like they really got you stirred up in that class. Things aren't that simple. You'll learn that as you get older," Dad informed me in his tone that made me feel like a moron.

Here we go again, I thought. I understood quite well. Racial prejudice was wrong; there was no justification for it. Just because someone had white skin did not mean they were superior in any way. It amazed me that anyone could believe that. My parents didn't believe whites were superior to blacks, but they were promoting racial prejudice by allowing it to happen and not fighting it. Their message to me was that interracial dating was all right as long as someone else did it, but they didn't think it was wise because if marriage and children resulted, the children would suffer. I could understand their point of view; I just didn't agree with it. Just because it had always been that way didn't mean it had to always stay that way.

Chapter 30

The Viet Nam protests had continued to escalate during the early part of 1968. Between January and May, there were 40 thousand students participating in 221 major demonstrations on 101 campuses. February 16, 1968, draft deferments for most graduate students and all occupational deferments were eliminated. Politicians were split on the issue. On March 2, 1968, Robert F. Kennedy gave his speech to Congress about Viet Nam, and on March 16th, he declared his candidacy for president. By the end of March, on the 31st, President Johnson announced his decision not to run for president again.

The racial climate was also in much turmoil. On April 4, 1968, Martin Luther King was shot and killed at a motel in Memphis, Tennessee. His death instigated black uprisings in 125 cities in 29 states. Major cities involved were Pittsburgh, Toledo, San Francisco, Philadelphia, Detroit, Boston, Cincinnati, Washington D.C., Baltimore, and Chicago.

Every evening on the six o'clock news there were numerous reports on the Viet Nam War and all the current racial issues. We also were provided with videos of many of the happenings around the country. That made everything seem more real, and there were probably few homes in which there were not evening discussions regarding the latest reports. Everyone was touched in one way or another by those events.

Some of the students in my school had brothers who were in the service and stationed in Viet Nam. They were touched more directly, but everyone knew someone who was in Viet Nam or knew someone who had a family member in Viet Nam. Several families in our area lost young men in that war. That was very sad. There wasn't a day that went by that these stories were not discussed at every public gathering.

Even though I had experienced the death of a loved one, death was still mysterious and something that frightened me. I still thought about how grandma just ceased to exist. Each time I heard of someone else's death, I again thought of Grandma. Perhaps I always would, because her death was the first death that had greatly impacted my life. It seemed even worse to me when someone young died, like Joyce. I feel that a stronger religious foundation would have helped me to cope with these issues. I just didn't have it.

My family claimed to believe in God. We prayed before meals, and my parents had me baptized; however, other than that, we never prayed together as a family unit. Open prayer, like other emotional displays, was discouraged. Dad felt these were private issues, and we rarely discussed God. Dad required that Brenda and I to go to church, but he never went with us. I didn't understand why until many years later. Mom had taken us when we were young, but once we moved out of Burnham, and she could no longer attend her family church, she stopped accompanying us. So although I was exposed to religion, I didn't really understand it.

During our early elementary school years, Brenda and I attended Vacation Bible School each summer at a small church in Shreader. There were less than twenty houses in that village, and we lived close enough to walk to church. Mom had never gotten a driver's license, and Dad worked during the day, so we would have had no other means of transportation. Mom had to rely on others to transport her to work. I remember learning about Jesus in that small church, but after Grandma's death, I lost the blind faith I had as a child.

Prior to Grandma's death, I had prayed several times a day. After her death, even though I attended church, I no longer prayed. I was still very much distanced from God. I still felt betrayed that he hadn't healed my grandma. I wanted to be close to Him and needed to be close to Him, but I couldn't. Maybe if I would have had someone I could have discussed religion with, it would have been different. I don't know; I just know that I often felt lost and lonely.

Things were better than they had been. I no longer took nerve medication, although perhaps I should have. The crying spells were a lot less frequent. Actually, for the most part, outside of school, I was happy. I still didn't like school.

High school made me sad because I felt like I didn't fit in. I didn't have that problem in elementary school. It seemed as if I was left behind and could never catch up after my severe depression. Students were somewhat afraid of me. I had been different. I guess it was hard for them to see me any other way. It was a self-fulfilling prophesy, too. Because they viewed me as different, I felt different, and in turn acted different. I had become very introverted.

The isolation I had built around myself was similar to a prison cell. I was very lonely and desperately wanted friends to pal around with in school, but I literally felt locked inside. It was too scary to reach out, due to fear of being rejected by my peers. That rejection would be more devastating than loneliness.

Everything I did was done to avoid rejection. I wanted to make myself disappear as much as possible. I rarely contributed to any classroom discussions unless I was directly asked a question by the teacher. Then I would fear that my answer would be stupid, and the students would laugh at me.

I learned that teenagers could be very cruel. I rarely got new clothes. My cousins gave me their hand-me-downs which was okay. Brenda and I always looked forward to receiving those boxes of clothing. I knew Dad just didn't have the money to buy us all new clothes like many of the students had. The part I didn't like was how Tracy and her clique would make fun of my clothing. In my early years of high school, my sense of style was not the best, and often my clothes would not match. Tracy would harass me about how stupid I looked. Also, if the clothing didn't fit quite right, it gave her something else to laugh about.

The combination of everything made me feel as though I was always on guard. I screened everything I said, worried constantly about how I looked, and continually feared some kind of ridicule. Any kind of negative reaction from an authority figure would devastate me for a period of time much longer than what one would consider normal. An episode like that occurred in my English class.

Mrs. Armstrong passed out worksheets to the entire class that particular morning after we were all seated. She said, "Everyone is to complete this worksheet and turn it in at the end of class today--or tomorrow, if you do not get it completed today." She then instructed, "For now, everyone get out your textbooks, and we'll review your homework for today." We all did as she instructed. As different students were answering the homework questions, I was looking ahead in the chapter we were studying and completing my worksheet. I noticed other students were doing likewise.

When Mrs. Armstrong had finished reviewing the homework questions, she returned to her desk, and said, "You may use the remaining class time to complete your worksheets for tomorrow. If you get them completed, turn them in before leaving." I was almost done and happy that I wouldn't have any homework. I finished the two remaining questions I had on my worksheet and took it up front to Mrs. Armstrong's desk. As I was about to lay the paper on the right corner of her desk where we usually put our completed papers, she snatched it out of my hand and vehemently asked, "Did you do this while we were reviewing the homework assignment?"

"Yes," I meekly answered, for she was embarrassing me in front of the entire class.

"I thought so," she loudly declared as she shredded my worksheet in front of me. I was mortified. I didn't know what to do. Mrs. Armstrong continued, "Since you weren't paying attention and completed the worksheet when you weren't supposed to, you'll get a zero for the assignment. In addition, you will write one hundred times, 'I will pay attention in class.' This will be due tomorrow."

I could hear giggles behind me. It wasn't necessary for me to look to see who it was. I was certain one of the gigglers was Tracy. Mrs. Armstrong said nothing about them laughing. I returned to my seat and stared at my book. I could feel the burning of my tears, but I fought desperately to keep them from escaping from my eyes. Prior to that day, Mrs. Armstrong had been one of my favorite teachers. She had lost that status forever. I would always remember her as a cruel, heartless person. That night as I wrote each sentence, "I will pay attention in class," it was burned into my memory how much I didn't like Mrs. Armstrong; in fact, I felt like I hated her.

It was spring, and the students were thinking and talking about the upcoming prom. I was no exception. As I heard the discussions that were going on all around me, I worried about what I was going to do. In a way, I wanted to go to the prom, yet I couldn't see myself dancing beside people like Tracy.

In biology class, Pam Petton was telling Nancy Taylor that she was going to the prom with Neil Amic. Nancy said she would be going with her boyfriend, George. I wrote in my notebook and tried to act like I didn't hear them. I was no longer dating Bill, and I wasn't dating anyone else on a regular basis. I dated occasionally, but usually boys from other high schools.

As their conversation continued, Nancy eventually looked over at me and asked, "Linda, are you going to the prom?"

There it was: the question I had been dreading. I couldn't very easily ignore it. *How should I answer?* I thought as I said, "I don't know yet."

Nancy continued, "Did anyone ask you?"

"Not from this school," I stated, hoping to give the impression that someone did from another school.

"Were you invited to someone else's prom?" Pam asked.

Now I was in a real fix. What could I say? I decided I would lie for it was too painful to admit that no one had asked me. "Yes, I was invited to the Chief Logan prom," I said. I then continued the lie, "But, I don't know if I'm going to go."

"Oh, I wouldn't want to go to another prom and miss ours," Pam whined.

"Me neither," Nancy added. "Who asked you?" she asked me.

More lies were needed. "My ex-boyfriend," I answered.

"Do you mean Bill Griffith?" Nancy asked.

"Yes," I said. My anxiety level increased because I knew Nancy's boyfriend attended the same school Bill did. In reality, I hadn't even spoken to Bill since that evening at my cousin's gas station. I hoped they wouldn't discover my lies.

Their discussion then turned to what their prom gowns looked like. I was very uneasy. I couldn't wait until class ended. I so wanted to be a part of everything, but felt I was definitely out of the loop. It hurt to be isolated and sad when so many students were happy and excited about the upcoming prom. In a way, I felt like an alien. My world seemed to be so different from theirs.

At that time, I believed I was the only one feeling like I did. Years later, I would realize there were many young people with similar feelings. The school system at that time didn't address the problems of students like myself. They didn't seem to notice that all the school festivities only created pain for some.

I recall that Mr. Freeman, a math teacher, expressed concern during a study hall that Christie Felmley had said she wasn't going to go to the prom. Christie's father was a prominent physician in Lewistown. Mr. Freeman spent the hour trying to convince Christie that she should attend the prom. He stressed how important it was to participate in school activities. He named numerous boys who would be pleased to escort her. I could hardly believe my ears when he even offered to buy her gown if she would go.

I don't know why Christie didn't want to go, but Mr. Freeman eventually convinced her that she should attend. I remember thinking that he sure didn't care that I wouldn't be attending the prom. He didn't try to fix me up with any boys, and he sure didn't offer to buy me a gown.

That kind of behavior angered me. The unspoken message was loud and clear. Christie and people like her were important, but I, and people like me, were not. It seemed as though Mr. Freeman did not see me sitting just one table away. Why did her life matter and mine apparently did not? Wasn't I a human being, too?

The outrage I felt when I experienced prejudice of any form would later develop into a personal need to help others. I hated to see anyone mistreated for any reason. I hated to see blacks discriminated against. I hated to see handicapped people made fun of. I hated poor individuals to be given less opportunities. I hated domestic violence of any kind.

Later that month, the prom came and went. I didn't attend, but I did survive. Many students had good memories to store away with their other high school memories. I only had one more unhappy memory to add to mine.

Fortunately, not all my memories were bad. That Memorial Day, I celebrated along with many of the area youths. A number of the kids we knew celebrated by going to the all-night Burnham drive-in, which was located on Mill Hill on the outskirts of Burnham. Brenda and I were planning to attend with Robin Powell, Linda Jones, and Charlene Osborne. I had met Robin and Linda at the Y dances. Linda was a year behind me in school, and Robin was two years behind me. Robin's brother, Ed, agreed to take us since I wasn't allowed to drive Dad's car because I had a junior license. We were quite excited because the all-night drive-in was actually a big party.

When we arrived at the drive-in, we all got out of Ed's car since he wanted to be alone with his date. It didn't take us long to find a group of boys who attended our school. Dan Dahl had backed his pickup truck in beside the speaker so his friends could sit in the back of the truck and watch the movie. We joined them. It was fun watching people we knew drive by as they searched for a parking space. There were many waves and shouts of greetings exchanged.

Before long, the movie started. Not too many people were watching it. Word had spread that Beef Bigalow, a well-known football player from Chief Logan school, had arrived with lots of beer. The boys slipped away and headed for Beef's van. When they returned, they were concealing cans of beer under their jackets.

As the evening progressed, the group became more rowdy. Girls and guys began to pair off. I found myself holding hands with Dan. I had gone out with him once or twice. I thought he was cute. Before the evening ended, I found myself in the cab of his truck necking. Occasionally, someone would stop by the window and pass on some tidbit of information.

Information filtered down that "Amazon Annie" was near the front of the drive-in, in the back of a van providing sex to anyone who wanted to participate. She had gotten her name by getting drunk one night and wandering around in a cornfield in the nude. Rumor had it that there was a long line of guys at the van. Now that totally disgusted me. These boys were sickening. In fact, Dan angered me by talking about that with Mark so I got out of the truck and went in search of a more civilized group of individuals. Dan attempted to follow me because he couldn't understand what was wrong. What a jerk!

I encountered Robin again as I walked around. She had been drinking. I warned her that was not a good idea. It was too late because she was blitzed. I had to lead her back to her brother's car. Ed was making out with Joyce in the front seat. I opened the back door and pushed Robin inside. Ed sat up and turned around to see what was happening. I told him Robin had been drinking, and she was out of control. Ed instructed Robin to stay inside the car and be quiet. I didn't want to stay there because that wouldn't be any fun, so I left again.

I was looking for Brenda or Linda. I found Brenda with the group of girls and guys from Burnham. Some were drinking beer, but Brenda was not. I was relieved because I didn't want another drunk on my hands. I decided to hang-out with that group. We had a good time until Bill Griffith showed up. He had been drinking and had just gotten back from the van with "Amazon Annie." He was bragging about his conquest when he realized I was there. He came over to me and attempted to initiate a conversation. I told him to get lost. He made me sick, and I certainly wanted nothing to do with him. I couldn't believe how some guys acted. They really thought their sexual exploits made them men. How stupid!

I also couldn't believe how "Amazon Annie" acted either. Where was her head? I had seen her at school before. She was average height with huge breasts, and had bleached her brown hair blond. Annie was somewhat attractive, but dressed weirdly and usually had a cigarette hanging out of her mouth when off the school grounds She had become somewhat of a legend. Everyone knew who she was, but I wouldn't want notoriety at that price. The girls didn't like her because she was a slut, and the boys made fun of her even if they had sex with her. Double standards again; oh, how I hated double standards.

The last movie ended as the horizon became light right before sunrise. It was time to go home. Brenda and I headed back to Ed's car. When we arrived, Bob informed us that Robin had thrown up. She was now sleeping in the back seat. Linda was not there, and we had to look for her. By that time, many of the cars were leaving. Brenda and I walked back and forth through the rows in an attempt to locate Linda. Finally, there she was headed toward us.

"Where were you?" I asked Linda.

"I was with Rodney Bailey," she reported. She looked like she had slept in her clothes which she probably had.

"Oh, really," I replied.

"I suppose you had sex," Brenda accused.

"I did not," she insisted.

"You liar," Brenda responded.

"Knock it off," I insisted. "We have to get back to the car."

Brenda continued to mumble as all three of us made our way back to Ed's car. Linda had been drinking because I could smell it on her. She didn't appear to be drunk, however. Several days later, she would confess to me that she had sex with Rodney that night. That wasn't the worse part, though. She also confessed that she had oral sex with him, too. Now she was having anxiety attacks about returning to school and facing him.

I couldn't imagine doing what she had done. I was still a virgin. It seemed very wrong to me, but Linda was still my friend. I wondered why she behaved like she did. I wasn't happy with Rodney, either. He got her to drink and used her. I wondered if he felt any shame. I doubted it.

The first week of June, the Burnham Jamboree began. It was a small fireman's carnival that was held in Burnham. Each year Brenda and I would attend with some of our friends. That event always signaled that the end of school was close. This in itself caused me to celebrate.

We generally would purchase our ride tickets from a member of the Burnham Lion's Club because we would get a discount. My Uncle Bill, Mom's sister Martha's husband, was a member. There would only be a few rides, which were generally a Ferris wheel, merry mixer, dive bomber, and several small children's rides. A number of food stands surrounded the grounds, including a barbecue chicken pit, and the Burnham Lions' French fry truck. Of course they had pizza, ice cream, candy apples, cotton candy, hot dogs, and hamburgers, too. Numerous game stands were also a part of the scene.

Cathy and Betsy accompanied me and Brenda that year. We went on Friday evening. When we arrived, we initially just walked the circle around the grounds. In our travels, we saw many of our friends. We eventually waited in line at each of the adult rides for several turns until we ran out of tickets. The entertainment that night was the "Four Spots," a local rock band. We spent the remainder of the evening standing with the other kids watching the group perform.

As we stood there, I noticed Tracy in the crowd. I hoped she had not seen me; however, I was much more confident with my friends. Cathy knew Tracy harassed me, and she didn't like her. Tracy definitely could not intimidate Cathy. She had too much self-confidence. I wished I did, too. However, the truth of the matter was that I had very little.

Later, when Tracy walked by with her boyfriend, Gary, she snickered. She was such a bitch. It angered me that she was capable of semi-messing up my evening. I was glad school would be over in two days. Then I would have only one more year to survive Tracy's harassment.

When we were leaving the Jamboree, we stopped at Guz's Pizza Shop and each got a cut of pizza as we waited for Cathy's mother to pick us up. Over all, I had a good time. I think everyone did.

The next day was Saturday, and it was very warm. Dad had decided that he would remove the upstairs windows so that we could repaint them. He had Brenda and me spread newspapers on the back porch so we could do the painting there without getting any on the porch. He told us that he also wanted us to repaint the white fence around our front yard that summer. Dad always had some project for us to work on.

Brenda decided to paint some of the fence that day, and I was to paint the windows. I didn't mind painting. It was much better, in my opinion, than helping with other things, like cleaning greasy tools. I did my best with the windows, and when I was finished, I cleaned the paint brushes in the garage. Dad was working on sharpening our lawn mower blade. He asked, "How do the windows look?"

"Okay," I answered. I finished and went into the house to get a drink. As I finished drinking my water, I heard Dad calling me. His voice didn't sound happy, and I felt pangs of anxiety.

As I went onto the back porch, I saw Dad hunched down beside the windows I had painted. "Come over here," he commanded.

Oh no, I thought. "What?" I asked as I approached him.

"What's this?" he asked as he pointed at the frames.

"What do you mean?" I asked.

"Well, bend down and look at this," he ordered. I did as he told me. "Now what is that?" he again asked.

I saw what he was referring to. There was some fuzz on the paint. "I don't know how that got there," I said, for I really didn't.

"I'll tell you how it got there," he bellowed. "You stirred up all the dust and ruined the paint." His voice was now roaring.

I was dumbfounded and attempted to think of an appropriate response, when he brutally back handed me across the mouth. I felt my front teeth cut into my lip from the force of the blow, and I could taste the saltiness of my blood as my tongue instinctively licked my lip.

Dad continued to blast me with all sorts of insults, but I could no longer absorb what he was saying. I did, however, catch his command to get out of there. So I left the back porch, cut through the woods, and found myself sitting in my grieving spot on the first step at the edge of the bridge.

I stared at the water as my tears gushed from my eyes and the sound of the rushing water covered my sobs. Again, I wondered how he could be so cruel to me. I had honestly done my best. I wasn't sure how that fuzz had gotten onto the paint. Surely he must have known I wouldn't do anything like that on purpose. No matter what I did, I could never satisfy him. He made no secret of the fact that he was never happy with me. I never received any praise in any form. All children need some praise. All I ever received was criticism. I wouldn't have known how to respond if he ever would have given me a compliment.

For the most part, my major depression was gone. I no longer was taken to the doctor, and I was able then to at least function without medication. Episodes like that, however, still depressed me. I so wanted compassion and visible signs of love. I often wondered why I angered my father so much. He frequently seemed pleased with Brenda's behavior, but never mine. I could see no difference between her behavior and my behavior. It was hard not to be depressed under those circumstances.

I continued to watch the water as I sat at the bridge until my sobs had subsided and my tears had stopped. I stayed there ten or fifteen minutes longer and allowed the soothing sound of the water to calm my soul. Again, I wished I could reach out to God, but I still could not. I knew He was there, though, and I wondered why He allowed my father to hurt me.

PART VI
JULY 1969 – JUNE 1970
Time Line

July 20, 1969 – Apollo 11; Armstrong and Aldrin first walk on the moon.
September 1969 – Linda starts 12th grade.
October 30, 1969 – Supreme Court orders immediate desegregation throughout the US.
November 19, 1969 – Congress passes random selection of draftees through lottery.
November 24, 1969 - Apollo 12: second landing on moon.
December 12, 1969 – Linda's 17th Birthday.
December 1969 – Over 100,000 Americans have died in Viet Nam; 65,000 troops brought home to US.
January 5, 1970 – Mississippi integrates first three districts of its public schools.
April 10, 1970 – McCartney announces dissolution of the Beatles.
April 1970 – Apollo 13 (third trip to the moon).
May 1970 – 30 ROTC buildings burned; National Guard on 21 campuses in 16 states.
May 4, 1970 – Kent State University, Ohio: National Guard fires into crowd at anti-war demonstration, 4 students killed and 8 wounded.
May 9 – 11, 1970 – 50-60,000 anti-war demonstrators gather in Washington.
June 22, 1970 – Voting age lowered to 18.

Popular Songs

"In The Year 2525," Exordium & Terminus; "Baby, I Love You," Andy Kim; "Honky Tonk Women," The Rolling Stones; "Sugar, Sugar," The Archies; "Abbey Road," The Beatles; "Na Na Hey Hey Kiss Him Goodbye," Steam; "I Want You Back," The Jackson Five; "Raindrops Keep Fallin' On My Head," B. J. Thomas; "Bridge Over Troubled Water," Simon & Garfunkel; "Let It Be, The Beatles," "Turn Back The Hands of Time," Tyrone Davis; "Which Way You Goin' Billy?," The Poppy Family

Chapter 31

On July 16, 1969, the Apollo 11 lifted off from the Kennedy Space Center to begin the first manned journey to the moon. The crew of Apollo 11 consisted of Neil Armstrong, Michael Collins, and Edwin Aldrin, Jr. I was extremely proud, as most Americans were, that in a small way I seemed to be a part of the mission since I, too, was an American. We all stayed glued to our TVs as we continued to watch as the Apollo astronauts arrived on the moon four days later, and then the Lunar Module "Eagle" carrying Neil Armstrong and Edwin Aldrin landed on the lunar surface. At 10:56 EST on July 20, 1969, Neil Armstrong exited the "Eagle" and took his first step on the moon and made the now famous statement, "One small step for man; one giant leap for mankind." Those words were heard around the world and would be repeated for centuries. I knew I would never forget them.

In the middle of that history-making event I recall that on July 18th, 1969, Senator Ted Kennedy was in an automobile accident at Chappaquiddick, and his passenger, Mary Jo Kopechne, 28 years old, was killed. There was much controversy over what had actually happened. My parents, along with many others, were wrapped up in all the news reports covering that incident. At sixteen, I had little interest in that; the Apollo 11 moon mission seemed much more important to me.

I remember thinking I was living during a very important time in history, but it also was a very important time in my life. That was my last summer before I would graduate from high school and join the "real world." I was looking forward to getting out of school, but I had no idea what I would do for the remainder of my life. Many of my classmates were preparing to go to business schools and colleges both inside and outside of our state. Still others planned to join the Armed Forces. A few even planned to marry after graduation.

The previous school year, when my guidance counselor, Mr. Middlesworth, had called me to his office to discuss my future plans, I told him I planned to join the Air Force. Later that evening, I told my parents about my meeting with Mr. Middlesworth. Dad immediately informed me that was not going to happen. To begin with, since I would be under eighteen when I graduated, I would need parental consent. He told me he would not give his consent. Of course, Mom couldn't either since he had forbidden it. His reasoning was that "good girls" didn't join the service. It was his opinion that only women with questionable morals entered the military. His response made me sad because I saw the service as a way of getting away and seeing the world. Dad was never in the service, but his three brothers were, so I was confused about why he objected so adamantly.

My friends and I continued to go to the Youth Park dances every Tuesday night that summer of 1969. I dated several boys occasionally, but I had no serious romances. Cathy was dating Steve Jones regularly. He lived in Reedsville, the next village toward Lewistown, after passing Milroy. He ran around with several boys, one of whom I was interested in, Dan Dahl. I thought he was cute, and I had seen him at Charlene's house and at the Burnham drive-in. It turned out that I was more interested in him than he was in me, so that romance just sort of fizzled out.

Cathy's mother had bought her a horse that summer which they boarded in Reedsville at a small stable. I often went to the stable with Cathy while she groomed and fed her horse, Chester. Generally, when we were done, she would allow me to ride him around the corral. I didn't mind helping clean the stall if I could get a horseback ride when we finished.

One August evening that summer, Faye was transporting Cathy and me to the stable for one of our riding sessions. I was riding in the back seat as I always did, and Cathy was up front in the passenger seat beside her mother. Faye had a newer model Corvair than Dad's; it was more rounded than boxy. She had turned left at the only red light in Reedsville onto East Logan Street and continued toward the bridge that led to Honey Creek where the stable was located. Just as she reached the bridge, a speeding vehicle rounded the corner on our side of the road, and hit us head-on. I heard Faye scream and the screeching tires and breaking glass.

Some minutes later, I sat up in the back seat, and I recall the eerie silence that surrounded me. It took me a while to recall what had happened. As it all came back to me, I realized that we had been in an accident. Out of nowhere, suddenly it seemed that people were everywhere. They were opening the doors, asking questions, and helping Faye get out of the car. I was shocked when I looked into the front seat, and saw a shattered windshield on Cathy's side. Her head was on the dashboard, and she wasn't moving. I felt fear engulf me.

As people helped Faye out of the car, I heard her cry: "Help my daughter; please help my daughter! Oh God, please let her be okay!" Cathy began moaning and stirring while that was going on. Someone helped me out of the back seat after Faye got out. It was a two-door car, so I couldn't exit until she was out. Cathy's head was bleeding. The blood frightened me. Faye was telling someone that her front teeth were missing. A middle-aged man asked me if I had any pain. I told him that just my leg hurt, but I was not bleeding anywhere. There seemed to be mass confusion as the ambulance and tow trucks arrived. It was then I realized that Cathy's boyfriend, Steve, had crashed into us. How ironic! Someone insisted that we all go to the hospital, so Cathy, Faye, and I got into the ambulance. Steve said he wasn't hurt and refused to go.

At the hospital, they took Cathy and Faye into a separate cubicle. They made me call my parents, and before they got there, the emergency room doctor bandaged by left leg. When Mom and Dad arrived, he told them that a piece of my leg tissue was torn on the inside and I would probably be very stiff for several days, but other than that, I was fine. The doctor assured me that Faye and Cathy would be all right, too. Cathy needed to get several stitches above her right ear where the windshield had cut her. The worst part was that part of her head had to be shaved. Faye needed dental work because her mouth had hit the steering wheel. None of us had seat belts on. All in all, we were very fortunate.

I returned home with Mom and Dad. Brenda had remained at home with her school friend, Kathy, who was visiting. When I got home, I told her and Kathy all about the accident. They couldn't believe Steve had crashed into us. We discussed all the possible scenarios that might develop.

The next day when Cathy and I got together, we talked about our accident in detail. Faye's insurance company told her they would have to file suit against Steve's insurance company. That really upset Cathy, and she didn't want her mother to do that. She was afraid Steve would get angry with her. In the end, Faye had no choice if she wanted to get another car, for her car was totaled.

Several weeks later, Cathy learned that Steve was dating two other girls and leading her to believe he was only dating her. She was glad then that her mother's insurance company took action against his insurance company. Maybe there was some sort of justice after all.

That last summer before my senior year passed quickly. Soon the rose-of-sharon bushes were blooming, which always signified that the end of summer was near. A week before school started, the *Lewistown Sentinel* listed all the homerooms. My homeroom my senior year would be Room 103, and Mr. Aumiller, the biology teacher, would be my homeroom teacher.

School again started on the day after Labor Day, and as I entered the building, I became aware of the elevated status of being a senior. I had a sense of pleasure knowing that finally our class was at the top of the class hierarchy. The seventh graders seemed so small. I wondered if we had looked that small when we were in their places. I remember thinking that seventh grade was such a long time ago; Grandma was alive then. I felt pangs of anxiety as I thought about the past five years. I would never want to relive those painful years!

In our homeroom class, Mr. Aumiller passed out our class schedules. The classes I was enrolled in were Health, Business-English, Office Practice, Phys. Ed., Problems of Democracy, and Bookkeeping II. In my sophomore year, I had decided I would not be going to college. My parents didn't have the money to send me, and I knew nothing about how to apply for grants or scholarships. My grades were not even close to being good enough to warrant any scholarships anyway. I believed the school just wrote me off as graduating and joining the labor force. Years later, that would annoy me, but back then, I, too, thought that was my only option. After all, I had no one encouraging me to do otherwise: not my parents and no one at school. It never occurred to my teachers and guidance counselor to even consider college for me even though my I.Q. was above average.

I had taken the minimum amount of classes permitted, so I had eleven periods of study hall my senior year. What a waste of opportunity! Why didn't the teachers encourage me to do more? Wasn't that their job? My second period during my senior year was a study hall.

During that study hall, I learned about the latest school scandal. Dale Carsteter and Carl Dixon were seated at the table with me, and Dale asked: "Did you two hear about what happened to Miss. Foster over the summer?"

"No," Carl and I answered.

Dale was more than happy to update us on all the current gossip. "Miss Foster was dating Mark Jones, and she is pregnant! Can you believe it? She was suspended for dating a student."

Mark Jones was "Amazon Annie's" brother. He was two years older than we were, but he had started school later than we did, and he was held back one year. Miss Foster had been one of the Business teachers. I had her the year before for shorthand. She was a good teacher, and she always treated me with respect. Miss Foster wasn't real attractive, but she wasn't ugly either. I wondered how she ever got involved with Mark. He was kind of cute, but he didn't seem to me to be the kind of person a teacher would be attracted to.

"No kidding," was my response.

Carl said, "Way to go Jones," as he chuckled.

Dale continued, "Miss Foster moved out of town. No one seems to know where. She'll probably end up getting fired and never be able to teach again."

"What's Mark doing?" I asked.

Dale answered, "He's here today. I saw him. I don't know what he's doing about the baby."

I said, "I wonder if she'll keep the baby."

Carl answered, "I don't know. Surely Mark won't marry her. She's a good bit older than he is, and he's not the type to settle down."

"That's for sure," Dale added. "You know he just wanted to get laid."

"Definitely," Carl agreed chuckling again.

"I like Miss Foster," I said.

"She's okay," Dale responded.

It was then that Mr. Seigler, the study hall monitor, walked over to our table and told us to find something to do. It wasn't like we had any homework yet, so for the remainder of the study hall, I just sat there and stared. I was thinking, however, about Miss Foster. I felt sorry for her. *She must love him*, I thought. She didn't look like the type who would jump into bed with just anyone. The romantic in me thought that maybe Mark loved her, too. It seemed unfair to me that she would be fired for loving someone. I didn't consider the inappropriate behavior of an authority figure at that time. I was troubled about what would happen to their baby. Secretly, I hoped they would get married and keep the baby.

For the next few weeks, there was much talk about the incident. After that, however, life went on and the subject was rarely brought up again. There would always be a new scandal that would come along with lots of gossip for people to move onto. I never did hear what happened to Miss Foster and the baby. Mark stayed in school and continued living in Reedsville with his parents.

Chapter 32

The last week of September, I entered the cafeteria, and went over to the row of tables to my left along the wall. I sat near Charlene and a group of eleventh graders she ran around with.

"Hey, Linda," she called, as I was settling into my seat, positioning my lunch tray before me.

"What?" I responded as I opened my milk container.

"Come down here a minute; I need to talk to you," she called.

I got out of my chair and squeezed down the aisle until I was standing directly across the table from Charlene. "What do you want?" I asked.

"I talked to my boss about you wanting a job, and she told me to have you come in this afternoon to talk to her about working at the hospital. You need to go right after school. I'm pretty sure she will hire you."

"Really?" I exclaimed. Charlene worked in the kitchen at the Lewistown Hospital, and I had told her I would like to work there.

"Yeah, just make sure you're there. Okay?"

"Sure, I'll be there. Thanks," I said.

"Ask for Mrs. Boova, and tell her I told you that you should come in," Charlene added, as I turned and went back to my seat and lunch.

Of course, I would be there. I couldn't believe it. I really wanted a job so I would have spending money. Mom and Dad just couldn't afford to give Brenda and me much. Often I would skip lunch and save my lunch money so I would have money when I went out with my friends. That day, though, they were serving hot pork sandwiches, and I couldn't resist them.

The remainder of the day all I could think of was getting that job. Time dragged on very slowly, but finally, I was on the bus and on my way home. When I got home, I looked for Dad's Corvair keys. I knew he wouldn't be home for about another half hour, and I needed to go to the Lewistown Hospital before then to meet with Mrs. Boova. Hopefully, Dad wouldn't be angry with me for taking the car without asking because there were extenuating circumstances. I found the keys on top of the television set, and said to Brenda, "Tell Dad I have an interview at the hospital. Charlene's trying to get me a job. I have to be there before he'll get home, so tell him I had to take the car and I'll be back as soon as my interview is over."

"You're going to get into big trouble," she informed me.

"I have to," I insisted. "If I don't go, I probably won't get the job, and I need this job."

"Well, you're going to get in trouble," she again informed me.

"Just make sure you tell him when he gets home why I took the car," I instructed her. I quickly exited the front door and walked across the alley into the woods where Dad parked the Corvair. He kept his Desota in the garage. I got into the Corvair, turned the key in the ignition, and pulled out between the two pine trees where it was parked, then onto the alley in front of our house. I was on my way; I was nervous and excited.

Shortly after I got onto the 322 bypass, Dad passed me going in the other direction in his Chevy. I saw him do a double take, and I was certain he was surprised to see me. I sure hoped he wouldn't be angry with me. He was a fanatic when it came to cars, and I was afraid I might mess something up. If I did, there was no telling what the consequences might be. It was too late to worry about that then, so I continued driving on the bypass until I got to the Electric Avenue exit that would take me into Lewistown; then I exited. Instead of going toward Lewistown, however, I went in the opposite direction toward the Lewistown Hospital. At the red light on Electric Avenue, I turned left, went up the hill, and pulled into the employee parking lot. I had been there before when we met Charlene after work. I parked the Corvair near the back steps that led to the kitchen, and entered the back door.

I had never been inside the Lewistown Hospital through that entrance, so I didn't know where to go after entering. While walking down the corridor, I saw a woman dressed in pink coming toward me, so I stopped her and asked, "Could you tell me how to get to the kitchen?"

"Sure. Just continue down this hall and take the next right, then go straight. You'll come right to the kitchen entrance. It's on your right."

"Thanks," I said as I quickly moved in the direction of the kitchen.

When I got to the entrance, there were two large wooden swinging doors. I pushed the one on my right inward and went into the kitchen. I stood there for a moment until someone noticed me. A large woman in a yellow uniform and white hat came up to me and asked, "May I help you?"

"I am supposed to speak to Mrs. Boova," I told her.

"Oh, follow me," she said. She led me across the kitchen toward an office with two windows that looked into the kitchen. When she got to the office door, she knocked. Through the glass on the door, I could see a gray-haired woman dressed in a white uniform sitting behind a desk.

"Come in," the woman instructed.

"Go on in," said the woman in yellow.

I opened the door, entered, and said, "I'm Linda Bishop. Charlene Osborne told me you requested that I come in to see you."

"Yes, I did," Mrs. Boova responded. "I've been told that you're interested in working here in the kitchen. Is that correct?"

"Yes, it is. I would like to have a part-time job."

"Have you worked anywhere else?" she asked. "Yes, I worked at Semple's Kennels cleaning, and I had babysitting jobs," I answered.

"Do you know what kind of work we do here?" Mrs. Boova asked.

"Yes, Charlene has told me about it."

"The hours after school are four-thirty until seven for dinner. Then on weekends, the hours will vary depending on what shift you work. The breakfast and lunch shift starts at six-fifteen and ends at two-fifteen. Sometimes you will be required to work a split-shift which means you will work from six-fifteen until two-fifteen; then you will have a break until four-thirty. Then you will again work from four-thirty until seven in the evening. Do you think you can handle those hours?"

"Yes, I'm sure I can," I replied.

"The work consists of a variety of tasks. You will work in one of the tray line positions while the food is being served, and then move to a position in the dish room in the back where the trays are sent down and cleaned and the dishes are washed. Are you still interested?" Mrs. Boova asked.

"Yes," I answered enthusiastically.

"Well then, you may start work this coming Monday. Be here a little early so we can complete the paperwork. Take this application with you, complete it, and bring it with you when you return," she instructed, handing me an application.

"I will," I said, taking it, and standing up. "Thank you," I said, then turned and left, retracing my steps until I was again at the top of the stairs by the Corvair. Now I felt as if I could breathe again. I was extremely nervous, but all in all, I thought it had gone quite well. Now I had to go home and face Dad. I sure hoped he wouldn't be mad about me taking the car.

When I reached the top of Lingle Valley Road, my heart rate increased in anticipation of explaining to Dad why I took the car without his permission. *Please let him be in a good mood!* I thought.

After parking the car, I went into the house and found Dad in the living room. He was watching TV, and when I entered, he just stared at me, waiting for an explanation. "I hope you're not mad about me taking the car," I started. "Charlene told me that Mrs. Boova, her boss at the hospital, wanted me to come in for an interview right after school. I wasn't able to ask you if I could take the car, but I got the job! I start next Monday after school," I ended, almost breathless.

Dad hesitated for a moment, letting what I had just said register; then he said, "I'm not happy about you just taking the car without permission, but I can understand why you did. I guess you had a good reason."

Wow, what a relief! I thought. Then I began excitedly explaining what I would be doing. Dad was okay with everything, but I still had to sell the idea to Mom. She would be home shortly.

Mom arrived home from work about fifteen minutes later. When she came into the house, the rest of us were in the kitchen preparing supper. We were having goulash and green beans. Mom deposited her coat and hat on the couch and entered the kitchen. Dad turned around from the stove and said, "Linda has something to tell you."

I again explained with enthusiasm what had transpired that evening. When I ended, Mom said, "I don't know if you should work while you're still in school."

"Why not?" I asked defensively. "Charlene works and she has a car and money to buy clothes and lots of other things."

"How does she have time to do her homework?" Mom asked me.

"We get out at seven-fifteen, and there's lots of time to do homework. I have a bunch of study halls, so I don't have to do much homework anyways."

She asked, "How are you going to get back and forth to work?"

"Charlene said I could ride with her when we work the same schedule and when we don't, I thought Dad could let me use his car" I explained.

Mom just looked at Dad and didn't say anything. Finally, Dad said, "Maybe I could sell the car to you. I suppose you'll be needing a car of your own now since you'll be working."

"Yeah, that would be great!" I exclaimed. This was wonderful!

Mom didn't say anything else, but she didn't seemed pleased. I, on the other hand, was ecstatic! I had a job, and I was getting a car of my own!

Things were looking fantastic; I was happy.

The following Monday, I started working in the kitchen at the Lewistown Hospital. I reported to Mrs. Boova's office when I entered the kitchen that night. I gave her my completed application, and she had me complete a few other papers for payroll. She then had Anna Mary, the dietitian on duty that night, show me around. Anna Mary gave me three yellow uniforms and told me to go to the locker room and change. I knew where the locker room was located because I passed it on my way in. She had given me size fourteen uniforms; the smallest size they had in stock. She said I was allowed to have them hemmed, but not to cut the bottom off in case someone else would get them later. She also gave me a white paper hat and hairnet.

I went to the locker room and changed. I wore size seven, so the uniforms looked like sacks on me. I tied the cloth belt as tight as I could get it, then rolled up the uniform until it reached my knee and tucked it in my belt. I stuffed all my hair into the hairnet and pinned on the paper hat. I felt ridiculous. Nothing looked right, but I returned to the kitchen in my new outfit. Anna Mary saw me and instructed me to go with Wanda to train for the "bread and butter" position on the tray line.

Prior to the start of the tray line, we had to prepare all the specialty orders. There was salt-free bread and butter pats. We also had to place all the regular and salt-free bread slices in separate baggies. In addition, we prepared the skim milk orders.

I learned that the remainder of the evening-shift people had other specific jobs prior to the start of the tray line. An employee named Flo was in charge of preparing the dietetic food. Jane prepared the coffee and tea, and Jean prepared the desserts for the full-diet menus. Maude and Helen had to wash the pots, pans, and steam kettles. I quickly learned that no one envied their positions.

When the foods were ready, the tray line began. Anna Mary controlled the line from her position at the end of the tray line. She instructed the porter, who also ran the tray line, when to start and stop the line. Each tray was checked by her prior to going up to the patient's room.

Jane began the trays on the tray line. She placed the silverware, napkin, metal plate container, and diet card on each tray and sent it down the line. Flo and Sarah were on the same side of the line as Laurel, and Jean was directly across from Flo. Flo would read the special diet cards and place the foods for those individuals on their trays. Sarah stood beside Flo and would fill the full-diet plates. Jean placed the desserts on the trays. Next the tray came to

Wanda. She placed the bread and butter, milk, and any other special diet drinks on the trays. The tray was then stopped in front of the dietitian where she would check to make sure the proper foods were on the tray. She then would instruct the porter to place coffee or tea on the tray, and it would go up to the room. The porter that evening was Bill Baughman. He constantly teased Anna Mary as she checked the trays. He pulled his hat over his eyes and pretended he couldn't see, he started and stopped the tray line in short jerks, and he made many jokes as we all worked. He certainly kept work interesting.

The conveyor took the trays up to the different floors, and someone would be on each floor to pull the trays out as they reached them. The trays set on metal slides on each side. When they were going up, there usually were no problems, but sometimes when they were being sent down to the dish room, one would not be placed properly on the metal slides and there would be a crash.

The dish room was my least favorite part of the job. There were four positions in the dish room. Jean was on silverware. She had to soak all the silverware in a special solution, scratch off the dried food, and stand them in containers to go through the dishwasher. Jane got the trays off of the conveyor, separated the dishes and silverware, and threw away the uneaten food and garbage. Sarah sprayed the dishes and placed them in racks to go through the dishwasher. Wanda was on takeout. She had to wear rubber gloves to pick up the racks as they came out of the dishwasher. The glasses were stacked and stored in the racks, but the other dishes had to be removed and stacked along the tray line in their appropriate spots.

Since Wanda was training me, I helped with takeout. It was a very hot job. Each time we picked up one of the trays, we would be sprayed with hot water and steam. By the time I got out of the dish room, I felt sweaty and grimy. I still was glad that I had a job, though. I joyfully returned to the locker room, gathered my purse, jacket, and other uniforms, since we were not permitted to keep our belongings in the lockers overnight; then I rushed down the corridor, up the stairs, and out the door to my Corvair. I had survived my first day of "real" work, and I felt great.

Chapter 33

It was Saturday night, and that evening Cathy, Brenda, and I were going to the Burnham Hop. The previous night, I had received my first paycheck from the hospital, and I felt I was rich. The dances at the YMCA in Burnham every Saturday night were held from eight to eleven when school was in session. In the past, Cathy's mother and my dad had taken turns providing us with transportation, but that night I would be driving. When I got my job at the hospital, Dad sold me the Corvair for one hundred dollars. I made my first twenty-five dollar payment on my car as I had agreed to do. I liked my new semi-independent days

They always played the latest rock-n-roll records at the hop. The dances were held in the gym, and we paid at the door prior to entering. It cost one dollar. There was a table near the door where all the girls deposited their purses. Theft wasn't common during that time in Burnham. During all the times we attended the dances during the sixties, I recall only one girl having her purse stolen.

Mini-skirts were popular. I wore a dark green, pleated mini-skirt, a two-inch wide black belt and a white pullover sweater that I tucked in. My shoes were black slip-ons with a two and a half inch wide heel. I thought I looked good, and I was ready to dance.

As we walked into the gym, the song that was playing had just ended, and they started playing "Baby, It's You." Cathy said, "Come on guys," as Brenda and I followed her onto the dance floor, and we all started dancing in a circle. That was the customary procedure. Boys would then cut in and dance with us. As we were dancing, I noticed the boy I worked with, Bill, standing on the other side of the gym talking to a girl I recognized from Chief Logan High School. Soon they, too, started dancing. When the song ended, the band immediately started playing, "Sugar, Sugar." We danced for several more songs, then I announced, "I need a bathroom break," and started for the door.

As I passed Bill, he said, "Hi, Linda," and he winked as I walked past. He was very forward, and I don't believe there was a shy bone in his body.

"Hi," I answered as I continued out the door. I kind of liked him. He was going with Cindy, though, the girl he was with. He had told me about their relationship at work.

In the lobby, we went to the purse table, located our purses, and waited in line outside the door to the bathroom that was located on the left of the corridor. When it was our turn, all three of us entered even though we knew there was only one toilet. There was nothing unusual about that. Girls always travel to the restroom in packs. We fixed our hair and makeup, then exited. Our purses went back on the table, and we returned to the gym.

When I entered the gym, I again noticed Bill. He was on the dance floor, dancing to "Na-Na Hey Hey Kiss Him Good-bye." Cathy, Brenda, and I found our way closer to the center of the dance floor and started dancing. Tab Shaeffer came up, cut in, and started dancing with Cathy. A few minutes later, Doug Bitner and Gary Earnest started dancing with Brenda and me. The three of us had a good time dancing the remainder of the evening with numerous partners.

Gary Earnest sure seemed to be taking an interest in Brenda. They danced together almost every dance. He really thought he was a Casanova, and he was really cute. Cathy and I had numerous partners.

I made sure that I watched what Bill was doing as I danced throughout the evening. When eleven o'clock arrived, no one wanted to leave. We gathered our purses, paraded down the steep steps leading from the YMCA, and crossed the street to Heller's funeral home parking lot. Almost everyone parked there since it was closer than parking at the back of the YMCA and walking the whole way around the building.

I had a junior license, so I had to have the car home by midnight. We chattered continuously as we traveled home. Cathy said to Brenda, "Boy, that Gary Earnest must really like you! I don't think he danced with anyone else all evening."

"Do you really think so?" Brenda asked.

"Yeah, I do. Don't you Linda?"

"It sure seems like it," I answered.

"That guy you work with kept watching you," Cathy informed me.

"He was with his girlfriend," I reminded her. "I think he's kind of cute, but like I said, he has a girlfriend."

"Yeah, well he still kept watching you," she insisted.

We dropped Cathy off at her house and drove down the alley to our house. I parked the Corvair in the woods, and we walked across the alley and went into the house. Mom had waited up. She always did that because she said she couldn't sleep until we were in the house.

"It's late," she said. "You two better get to bed."

Brenda was already starting up the stairs, and I said "okay," as I, too, went through the living room, into Grandma's old room, and started up the stairs. Things were nice on the weekends. I wasn't thinking about Grandma very often anymore, but I still missed her. I never wanted to forget about her.

As I lay down that night, I thought about Bill Baughman. I wondered what he thought of me. I wondered if he even thought about me. I fell asleep thinking pleasant thoughts.

The next morning, Sunday, I thought of the previous night and felt happy. But, that feeling was soon replaced with feelings of anxiety as I realized it was back to school the next day. I sure wished I didn't have to go to school. Even though I was a senior and had elevated status, I still didn't like school.

When I went downstairs in the morning, I couldn't help looking at the clock on top of the TV. It was almost a compulsion. It was eight-ten; I had slightly over twenty four hours before it would again be time to go back to school. I would be so much happier if I could avoid Tracy and her flunkies for the remainder of my life. That was just not meant to be. I drove Brenda and myself to church. We met Cathy there, and we all sat together.

When church was over, Brenda and I decided we would skip Sunday School, and go running around. Cathy really wanted to go with us, but her mother made her stay at church for Sunday School.

I drove up to Burk's Drug Store, and we went in. There was a bar with stools inside. We each took a seat on a stool and ordered cherry cokes, and bought a ten-cent bag of Hartley's potato chips from the rack. Hartley's were made in Lewiston in a small, family-owned factory. They were the best chips ever. We sat there chatting while we drank our drinks and ate our chips. After we finished our snack, we returned to the Corvair and decided to go to Lewistown.

Many of the kids from the area hung out in town on weekend nights. We really didn't expect to see anyone on a Sunday morning, but it was something to do. After taking several laps around Lewistown, we decided it was time to go home so Mom and Dad wouldn't become suspicious. I had a portable cassette player I had gotten for Christmas lying on the seat, and Brenda put one of my Bee Gee tapes in for us to listen to as we drove.

When we got home, Mom was placing lunch on the table. We always had a big Sunday lunch. In the evening then, we would eat leftovers. That day Mom had made roast beef and potatoes. She also had prepared brussel sprouts. I truly enjoyed Mom's cooking.

Throughout the day, periodically I would mentally calculate the remaining time left in the weekend. I despaired more each time as I realized that my weekend was diminishing. Thank God, at least I was a senior. There was a time when I thought it would never happen. June's graduation date got closer each day, but at times it seemed to be going very slowly.

December finally arrived. I was still working at the Lewistown Hospital kitchen. Now I was trained on all the tray line jobs. I liked Flo's and Laurel's jobs the best. When you were scheduled for those jobs, you didn't have to go to the dish room because you prepared foods for the meals after the tray line. You also got to work independently. I liked that.

The second Saturday of that December, I was scheduled to work a split-shift, so I had to be there at six-fifteen. Charlene was riding to work with me that morning. It had snowed during the night, and Dad was outside plowing the driveway and the little patch of woods where I parked the Corvair so I could get out of the alley to get to work. It was a dead-end alley, so the township never took over the responsibility of the upkeep of the road. Dad would plow from Mrs. Lyter's house to Lingle Valley Road. The Fultzes, the family on the other side of Mrs. Lyter, plowed the remainder of the alley. Mom was also outside, removing the snow from the sidewalk.

I bundled up in my blue winter coat, put on my gloves, hat, and boots, and went outside to brave the snowstorm to go to work. As I got into my car, Dad gave me last minute instructions on how to drive in the snow. I didn't listen very closely because I thought I knew how to drive in the snow. Dad had started my car so the engine would warm up. Mom shouted over the noise of the tractor and my car to be careful as I got into the driver's seat and closed the door. I eased onto the alley and then Lingle Valley Road.

The Corvair was fairly good in the snow. Dad said it didn't slide as much as other small cars because its engine was in the back, and that weight allowed the vehicle to have better traction. The State had Route 322 cleared and salted. I had no trouble getting to Charlene's house. I stopped outside of her house, and she came down the stairs and got into my car. I noticed that the snow had stopped as we went up over Siegler Street, took a right onto Hill Street, and headed back to Route 322. It was then that we ran into trouble.

Snow had drifted across the road, for that little stretch of road had no snow fence along it. I remembered Dad telling me that my car was good in the snow, so I told Charlene to hold on as I speeded up to make a run through the drift. The Corvair chugged along quite nicely through the first part of the drift, then stopped dead in its tracks. I hadn't realized how deep the drift was. When I got out of the car, I saw that we were in a three-foot snow drift. I considered my options. The car was still running, so I told Charlene to stay there and I would walk to the nearest house to call Dad.

I had to walk approximately 100 yards to get to the house at the crossroad where I turned onto Hill Street. It was cold and still dark. The blowing snow stung my face as I walked against the wind. My coat was short, and I only had on my thin uniform underneath. Fortunately, I had my boots. The snow crunched beneath my feet as I walked. When I finally reached the house, I knocked at the door. There was a light on, so I hoped I hadn't gotten someone out of bed.

A middle-aged man answered the door, and I explained what had happened and requested to use his phone. To my dismay, the phone line was dead. The man offered to drive me home. He probably would have taken Charlene, too, but in my despair, I forgot to tell him about her.

He dropped me off at the top of Lingle Valley Road because he was afraid he would get stuck if he drove down through the valley. I rushed down the road as much as I could under the circumstances. When I arrived at our house, I noticed that Mom and Dad were no longer outside. When I went inside, Dad woke up at the sound of the door opening. He had fallen asleep on the couch. I explained what had happened, and he instructed me to get the shovel while he put his coat and boots back on. I met him in the driveway, and we got into his 1959 blue Chevy and headed to Milroy.

The entire time driving there, he lectured me about how stupid I was to leave Charlene there in the car. I explained that I didn't want to leave my car stranded in the middle of the road, and I thought I would just be calling him. When we turned left off Route 322, Dad's Chevy began to slide and it went into a snowbank along the road. Dad got out of the car and began shoveling the snowbank. It didn't take him long to get us out, and we continued to Hill Street where my car remained.

When we arrived, we discovered that Charlene had turned the car off because she feared it would run out of gas. The windows all had frozen steam covering the inside, and Charlene was shivering so badly, she had difficulty speaking. Dad told me to get into the car and start the engine so Charlene could get warm. I did as he told me to do and then sat there while he shoveled a path in the snow behind the car.

When Dad had finished shoveling the path, he yelled for me to back up the Corvair. I put the car into gear and began backing. I had very little practice backing, however, so it didn't take me long to have the car back in the snowdrift. That really infuriated Dad as he again shoveled a path. When he was done shoveling, he ordered me to get out of the car, and he backed it out of the snowdrift.

After that, he kept telling me how stupid I was for trying to drive through a three-foot snowdrift. He asked if we were still going to work. I decided I was definitely going even though we were late, because it would be much better to be at work than to listen to Dad lecture me all day. Charlene still wanted to go with me. We arrived at work late, but they were glad we braved the snow and made it in. We were fortunate that everyone eventually made it in that day. After going through the tray line and the dish room, it was ten o'clock and time for a break.

Working on the breakfast and lunch schedule, entitled us to two fifteen minute breaks. A break room was provided in the back of the hospital on the first floor. In the break room, I discovered the way the hospital was color differentiated.. The housekeeping staff wore blue uniforms, the kitchen staff wore yellow uniforms, the emergency room staff and operating room staff wore green uniforms, and the other nurses wore white uniforms. To further differentiate the nurses, the registered nurses wore larger hats than the practical nurses. The candy-striped volunteers wore red and white striped uniforms. It was strange how the colors affected one's status. The green seemed to have the greatest status, and the remaining order of the status from highest to lowest was as follows: white, registered; white, practical; yellow; blue; and red and white striped. I learned a lot about what was going on within the hospital during my breaks by listening to the full-time employees. Some of them had worked at the hospital for a long time, and they were aware of all the gossip.

Often Charlene and I worked together. Even though I had a car of my own, and she did, too, we would still ride together to cut down on the cost of gas. During our rides to work, many times we would discuss our boyfriend problems. At that time Bill and I were dating sometimes. Charlene was going with Benny Morris, who had been at our tent a few summers before. He was a year older than I and two years older than Charlene. Benny had graduated the previous year.

Charlene dated much more than I did. She lived with her mother and two sisters in Milroy. Her parents were divorced. When I first met Charlene, her family lived at the lower end of Milroy. Since then, her mother had bought The Valley Tavern at the upper end of Milroy. Charlene, her mother, and sisters moved in, on the second floor over the bar. Her mother was not nearly as strict as my parents. Charlene had gone with Phillip Henry when she was in ninth grade. Phillip was already out of school and in the service. Phillip lived at the top of Lingle Valley Road prior to leaving for the service. When I was younger, I saw him on the school bus. Since then, Phillip and Charlene had broken up.

Charlene dated some between Phillip and Benny. She was crazy about Benny and saw him as much as possible. He worked at the Esso Station in Milroy. Benny had black curly hair and was very cute. I had a feeling, though, that Charlene cared for him much more than he cared for her. I saw him on occasions when stopping for gas, and whenever he was around other girls, he sure was a big flirt.

Charlene had admitted to the gang once at Linda Jones' sleepover that she and Benny were having sex. The girls always discussed things like that. Sonja Himes, who was at the same sleepover, was known to be one of the town sluts. She told all kinds of sexual secrets. Many of the girls admitted they were sexually active. It was embarrassing when they started questioning me since I was not. Virginity should have been something to be proud of, but in 1970, those teenagers experimenting with sexual freedom were held in high esteem. I had mixed feelings. Part of me craved to be sexually free, but my religious background and family's years of lectures kept me moral physically, if not mentally.

On our drive to work the day after the snow problem, Charlene said, "If I tell you something very important, do you promise not to tell anyone else?"

Of course, I wanted to know the secret, so I responded, "What is it? I promise I won't tell."

Charlene sighed, hesitated a moment, then with concern said, "I think I might be pregnant. My period is late, and I don't know what I'm going to do." I was speechless. What could I say? If I was in her shoes, I would be terrified. My dad would probably kill me. Knowing Charlene's mother, though, I didn't think Charlene would get in nearly as much trouble. She continued, "Benny doesn't even know; I don't know what he'll say. Mom doesn't know, either." Her voice cracked on the last sentence, and I was afraid she was going to cry.

How could I advise her what to do? I didn't know what I would do. We drove in silence for a few miles, then I said as reassuringly as possible, "Maybe you're just late. I read somewhere that nerves can affect the timing of your period."

"Really?" she asked, grasping for hope.

"How late are you?" I asked.

"Three weeks. I feel strange, too…sort of bloated and my ankles are swollen."

"You probably should see a doctor." They didn't have the home pregnancy tests back then.

"I guess I better," Charlene said absently as I pulled into the parking lot and parked in my usual spot.

We deposited our coats and purses in the locker room, then went into the cafeteria where we sat until it was time to start our shift. The large cafeteria was open to all hospital staff and the public, and there was a smaller cafeteria for the kitchen staff. We went into the small cafeteria. Charlene and I took a seat at a table where Bill was sitting. He was smoking a Tarreyton cigarette. I was surprised that his parents allowed him to smoke. In 1969 you were allowed to smoke in the hospital.

Once I had asked him what his parents said about his smoking. He said his stepfather, Phil, had told him years ago that he wasn't allowed to smoke until he was old enough to earn the money to buy his own cigarettes. Since he was working, he started smoking.

"Hi, what's up with you two?" he asked as he flicked his ashes into the blue ceramic ashtray on the table..

"Nothing much," I answered

Charlene added, "nothing exciting." Charlene had a piece of Juicy Fruit gum in her mouth and as usual, she was chewing like a cow chewing its cud. When she chewed like that, it was more noticeable that her front teeth were crooked.

"Are you going to the Burnham hop this weekend?" Bill asked me. Charlene never went to the hop because she was usually with Benny, and Benny didn't like going to hops.

"Probably," I replied.

Charlene was now carrying on a conversation with Peg Franklin, a large-framed woman who worked as one of the porters. Peg was one of a kind, very wild and often vulgar; she was seated at the table next to ours. She had all of her hair scrapped back and pulled into a ponytail. She too was smoking a cigarette.

"I'm going, too. Maybe we could dance together some," Bill continued.

"Maybe," was my answer. I liked Bill, but he sure was a showoff. There was no doubt about him being an extrovert. On the dance floor, he got carried away. His outgoing personality probably contributed to him being chosen the Chief Logan High School mascot, which was an Indian. In addition, Bill's flexibility was amazing. He could do headstands and flips with no apparent effort. It would be mild to say that we were opposites. Sometimes while dancing with him, I would become embarrassed because he would drop to the floor, hold his arms, and dance like a Russian. People would stand around us and watch; I didn't like the attention. I valued my privacy. It was safer to blend into the woodwork; that way, you had no demands to meet, and people wouldn't make fun of you.

By then it was four-thirty, and we had to start our shift. Flo was the first one to stand up and leave the kitchen. The rest of us wandered out behind her and took our work stations along the tray line. Bill was the porter that night, and I was again in the bread and butter position. That put me close to Bill since Verna, the dietitian that night, was the only person between us. Verna was an older woman who acted like she wouldn't tolerate any nonsense. Bill goofed off, though, and Verna couldn't help but smile even though she continually reprimanded him. He also flirted with me throughout the evening.

Later, I had the takeout position. As I recovered the dish racks as they came out of the dishwasher, I would carry them out of the dish room into the kitchen. That gave me numerous opportunities to see Bill as he was completing his duties. He was such a ham. I couldn't help but like him.

Takeout was one of the better positions in the dish room. At least you handled clean dishes instead of dirty dishes. Sometimes, though, you would burn your hands through the rubber gloves. Whenever I was in a position where I was required to clean the dishes or silverware, my nylons would stick to my legs because of the food that fell on me. It was disgusting.

As Charlene and I rode home after work that night, out of nowhere she asked, "Do you like Bill?"

"He's okay," I answered.

"Well, he told me that he wants to go steady with you, but he's afraid to ask you."

"He's afraid? I can't believe that. He's never afraid to do anything." I was shocked. He wanted to go with me! I really wasn't sure how I felt about that.

"That's what he told me. He may ask you on Saturday at the dance."

"No kidding! Why did he tell you?"

"Probably because he knew I would tell you, and then later he'll ask me what I think you will say. What will you say?"

"I don't know. I have to think about it." *What would I say?* I asked myself.

Changing the subject, I asked, "Are you going to tell Benny that you might be pregnant?"

"Not until I know if I am."

"What do you think he'll say?"

"I don't know."

"If you are pregnant, would you want to marry him?"

"I don't know. I just can't be pregnant. It would mess up everything."

We talked on until I pulled up at the back of Charlene's house and she got out. She said, "see ya," and disappeared up the back stairs.

I continued my drive home. The idea of Bill wanting to go with me was on my mind. I had only steadily dated one other person, Bill Griffith, when I was fifteen. He didn't have a car, so we had only gone out on an actual date alone when he had borrowed a friend's car. We had double-dated on numerous occasions with my friend Cathy and his friend Steve in Steve's old green Plymouth. Cathy and Steve had dated for several months, also.

Steve worked at the Sinclair Service Station near the YMCA. Bill Griffith hung out there, and on Saturday nights, Cathy and I would leave the YMCA and walk down to visit them. I never really had any serious attachment to Bill. He was actually suffocating. He tried to control everything I did. I certainly wasn't ready for a relationship like that. When I got my driver's license, Bill was history.

The next day after school, I again took Charlene to work. She said, "Well, I have an appointment with Dr. Walters on Thursday, after school." Dr. Walters was the only doctor in the village of Milroy.

"You do?" I responded.

"Uh huh…I'm really scared," she admitted.

"I would be, too. Does Benny know that you're going to the doctor?"

"No. I didn't want to tell him yet. This morning, I threw up. Not much, but I think it must be morning sickness. I'm always very tired, too."

"Did anyone hear you throw up?" I asked.

"I think Teresa did, but she didn't say anything," Charlene looked pale and stressed. I was getting worried about her.

"You know, Betsy's sister Francine is Dr. Walters' nurse," I informed her. "Do you think she'll say anything to anyone?"

"She better not. That should be confidential."

"Yes, I guess it should be," I said as I pulled into the hospital parking lot and parked near the steps that led into the basement level.

A few minutes later, we were both entering the employee cafeteria. Charlene and I took a seat at our usual table with Bill. He attended school at Chief Logan High School near the hospital, so he always got to work before we did. "Hi," I said as I sat down across the table from him.

"Hi," he answered.

As I looked at him, I really started studying him. He was about five-feet ten inches tall. He had very short, very curly light brown hair and blue eyes. Bill wasn't what you'd call handsome, but he wasn't ugly either. His personality was unique. No one intimidated him, and I liked that about him. Yes, I decided, all in all he wasn't bad.

Bill flirted with me throughout the evening on the tray line and again in the kitchen as I carried the dishes from the dish room. Our romance was beginning to blossom. I was glad he was planning to go to the YMCA dance on Saturday. I couldn't believe he would like me even when I was wearing that ugly yellow uniform that was much too big and a hairnet and paper hat. At the end of the evening, Bill followed me from the kitchen to the girls' locker room, and said good night. Charlene came in a few minutes later; we gathered our belongings, and went out to my car. Bill was standing beside his light brown Dodge Dart as we exited the hospital. He got into his car, waved to us, and drove away. Charlene said, "He's got it bad!"

"What?" I asked.

"You know what. He's got it bad for you, and you know it."

"I don't think so," I shyly responded.

"Of course not!" she exclaimed.

I said nothing more. I didn't want to argue about it. Secretly, I hoped she was right, but I was afraid to believe it. I thought time would tell.

On Saturday, I worked the breakfast and lunch schedule. I was glad because it would give me more time to get ready for the dance. Cathy wasn't going with Brenda and me that night. She had a date with Mark Nelson. Robin Powell and Linda Jones were going with us. Robin lived in Naginey. She was only in tenth grade, but she had run around with us on numerous occasions. Linda lived in Reedsville. I would pick Robin up, and then take the shortcut over to Reedsville to pick up Linda. Then we would drive on to the Burnham YMCA.

Later that night, Brenda and I picked up Robin and Linda and headed for

Burnham. When we reached the YMCA, we parked in Heller's Funeral Home parking lot, crossed the street, and walked up the steep stairs to the YMCA. There were several pool tables right inside the door. Bill was standing there with several other guys playing pool. He spotted me as soon as I entered the door and came over to talk to me. "I was watching for you," he informed me.

"Oh, really," I responded.

"Make sure you save some dances for me," he instructed.

"I'll be sure to do that," I answered.

As we continued to the gym where the records were already playing, Linda said, "Who's that?"

"A guy I work with," I answered.

"He's kind of cute. Maybe you could introduce us," she said.

I didn't answer because I didn't want her showing any interest in Bill. Linda liked any guy she saw, and even though I liked her, her reputation was far from lily-white. Her interest in Bill only made *me* more interested. I never could understand how girls could just go out with a guy and have sex even if they hardly new them. That seemed wrong to me. I had even heard that Linda had sex with her older brother Ed. In fact, she, herself, had told a group of us about that one night. I still wasn't sure I believed it. She didn't think anything was wrong with that, but the rest of us thought it was sick. Still, I hated to judge her, and I did like her.

Before long, Bill wandered into the gym, and we were dancing almost every dance. I particularly liked the slow dances. I could smell his Brut, and I liked it. As the evening progressed, we danced closer and closer. Then as they played, "Easy to Be Hard" by Three Dog Night, Bill and I were dancing, and he whispered in my ear, "Do you want to go steady?" I was intoxicated by the evening; it almost seemed magical.

"Yes," I whispered back into his ear. As the dance ended, he slipped his class ring from his finger and pressed it into my right hand, then squeezed my fingers closed, enclosing it in the palm of my hand. I felt that I loved him. I wanted love. It was nice to have someone care for me. Many times I felt all alone; I didn't want to be alone anymore.

When the last song ended, Bill said, "I'll walk you to your car."

"Okay," I responded.

Linda was walking out with Pee Wee Forrester, and she said, "Linda, Pee Wee is taking me home. I'll talk to you tomorrow."

"All right. See you later," I said.

Robin and Brenda were trailing behind. Brenda had danced a lot with Gary again. He was leaving with a bunch of guys and yelled to Brenda, "I'll give you a call."

"Okay," Brenda replied happily.

Bill kissed me on the cheek as he said, "I'll see you tomorrow at work."

"Good night," I said, looking deep into his blue eyes as we stood beneath the street light by my car.

As I drove home, I was ecstatic. I was going with Bill. I had his class ring on the middle finger of my right hand. I would need to wrap it with yarn like the other girls did with their boyfriends' rings. Bill had placed my class ring on his little finger. It only went to his first knuckle. My ring was a woman's size five; his was a man's size ten.

After getting into bed that night, I had trouble falling asleep for I kept replaying every minute of the night in my mind. The feeling I was experiencing was great; I hoped I would never lose it. As I finally drifted off to sleep, I thought it was too bad that I wouldn't see Bill until four-thirty the next day since we both worked the evening shift.

The next morning, I awoke and dreamily remembered the evening before. I pulled my hand out from under the sheet and looked at Bill's class ring. It was still there; last night had not been a dream. I was happy; I hardly thought about having to return to school the next day. Bill was good for me.

As I was doing the dishes after eating lunch, the phone rang. Mom answered it. "Linda, it's for you," she informed me.

I picked up the phone and said, "Hello."

"Hello, Linda."

"Oh...hi," I said, somewhat surprised. It was Bill.

"Would you like to go for a ride?" he asked.

"Sure. Where to?"

"Well, since we work tonight, why don't you just meet me at the hospital parking lot, and then we'll have more time since we'll only have to go back there."

"All right; that sounds good," I said, feeling the blood rush to my neck and ears. I always got red blotches on my neck and upper arms when I felt any deep emotion.

"Could you be there in about an hour--say one-thirty?" he asked.

"Sure, I think I can make that," I purred into the phone.

"Okay, see you then."

"See you."

"Bye."

"Bye."

I hurriedly finished washing the dishes, changed my clothes, gathered my work clothes, told Mom and Dad my plans, and said good-bye as I left the house and loaded everything into my Corvair. As I drove to the hospital, I put the Bee Gee's cassette into my portable tape player that I still had in my car. Since it wasn't installed, I just laid it on the passenger seat. I couldn't wait to see Bill.

He was already in the parking lot when I arrived. I pulled my Corvair next to his Dart, got out, and walked over to his car. He got out of his car, also, and walked me to the passenger side, opened the door, and stood waiting until I got in. Then he got in and drove us out of the parking lot. "Where are we going?" I asked.

"I thought maybe we would drive down to my house, and you could meet my parents," Bill said.

"Oh" I responded.

"Is that okay?" he inquired.

"Sure," I answered, not too convincingly.

Bill looked over at me as he drove on. He said, "You'll like them. They're really not that bad."

My anxiety level increased the longer we drove for I realized we were getting closer to his parent's house. Bill lived on the other side of Vira, which was a few miles outside of Burnham. You just continued east on Freedom Avenue out of Burnham for about two or three miles, and ended up in the middle of Vira. There were only twenty to thirty houses in Vira. They were on both sides of the road. The road name changed to Old Stage Road as it left Burnham. You continued on Old Stage Road for another few miles; then you would encounter a row of houses on the right-hand side of the road. Bill's house was the last house in that row.

He pulled into his driveway, got out, came around his car, and opened my door. I walked with him onto the side porch; he opened the door for me, and I entered his kitchen with him right behind me. His mother was standing at the sink washing dishes. When she heard us enter, she turned around and said, "Hello."

"Hello," I answered in reply.

Bill said, "Mom, this is Linda, the girl I've told you about. Linda this is my mom, Maxine."

"Hi," I said. She was about my height with short dark hair, and she wore dark-framed glasses.

"So what are you two up to today?" she asked.

"I just brought Linda down to meet you and Phil, and we both have to work at four- thirty today," Bill explained. He then asked, "Is Phil here?"

"Yes, he's in the basement. Go on down. I think he's watching a football game," said Maxine.

Bill said to me, "Come on," and he led me down their basement stairs.

As we descended the stairs, I saw that they had made their basement into a family room. There was a bar in the center of the room, and on the other side of it, a pool table. A TV stand against the far wall, a couch along the stair wall, and numerous chairs were scattered throughout the remainder of the room. A man with black hair was sitting on the couch with his feet propped up on the coffee table. I assumed that was Phil.

"Phil I'd like you to meet Linda. I work with her, and she's the girl I told you about. Linda this is my stepfather, Phil," Bill stated in his introduction.

"Hi," I said.

"Well, hi. I finally get to meet you. I've heard quite a lot about you," Phil said as he removed his feet from the coffee table and leaned forward.

"Really," I said with embarrassment. I could feel my ears begin to heat up.

"Yes, I think Bill tells us everything you do at work in detail," Phil teased.

"He does!" I exclaimed in disbelief.

"You can calm down, though. It's all good," Phil said, and I noticed the twinkle in his eye.

Bill laughed and responded, "Phil, you're unbelievable."

We sat on the couch beside Phil and chatted for a while before Bill said, "We have to get going so we're not late for work." He stood up, and I stood beside him.

Phil rose, too, and said to me, "It was nice meeting you, Linda." It was then that I noticed his left hand was deformed. Actually, his left arm was smaller that his right, and his left hand had never completely formed. There were only three partially formed fingers on his hand. I noticed, too, that his arms were very hairy, and there was a tuft of thick, black hair sticking out the top of his buttoned shirt. I recall thinking that his chest must be extremely hairy.

"It was nice meeting you, too," I responded.

Bill led me back up the stairs and into the kitchen. His mother was finishing the dishes. She turned around and said, "You're not leaving already, are you?"

"We have to, Mom," said Bill. "We're going to the snack bar to get a sandwich before work starts, so we have to get moving."

"I could fix you something here ," Maxine offered.

"No thanks, Mom. We're going to meet Mike and some other people at the snack bar. See you later," he called as we exited the house and headed toward his car.

"Good-bye," I called.

"Good-bye," I heard her reply.

I breathed a sigh of relief as I settled into the front seat of Bill's Dodge Dart.

"Well, what do you think of them?" Bill asked as he drove out of their driveway and back onto Old Stage Road.

"I think your parents are very nice," I said. "Phil's a real teaser, though, isn't he?"

"Yes, he sure is. Did you notice his hand?" Bill asked.

"Yes I did. Is it a birth defect?" I asked.

"Yeah. I hardly ever notice it anymore since it has always been like that. It doesn't stop him from doing anything, either. He has a lot of strength in that arm," Bill informed me.

"Do you get along well with Phil?" I inquired.

"Yes, I like him. He's been very good to me and my brother. My mother really needed him after Dad left her and remarried."

"Does your brother like him, too?" I continued the conversation. Bill's brother's name was George. George was four years older than Bill. He had been drafted into the Army and was fighting in Viet Nam.

"Pretty much so. They did have some arguments, though, but I think Phil respects George since he was drafted into the service, especially now since he's in Viet Nam."

"Does he write much to you and your family?" I asked.

"Not a lot, but he does write. He is engaged, so he writes to his girlfriend a lot, but his girlfriend is running around on him. My parents are really upset about that. We don't think he knows about it yet. They don't want to tell him until he comes home."

"How do they know she's running around on him?" I inquired.

"Friends of my parents told them. Rumor has it that she is pregnant. It couldn't be George's child. They are afraid she will try to convince him that he's the child's father. So when he comes home for Christmas, this will all come out. I'm sure not looking forward to that."

"I guess not! I wouldn't either."

By that time, we were driving up the hill to the hospital parking lot. It was three thirty, so we still had an hour to eat and get changed before our shift started. We had a fun day. I liked Bill, I liked his parents, and I wanted to be a part of their lives.

Bill and I went to the snack shop and met Mike, Bill's friend who was also a porter at the hospital, and Charlene. We all had a sandwich and a cherry coke. When we finished, Charlene and I went to the girls' locker room to change into our uniforms and then to the kitchen to start our shift. I was on bread and butter again, which meant I had to go to the dish room when the tray line was finished. Time passed quickly while I was on the tray line, but it was hot and disgusting in the dish room and seemed like it would never end. Charlene got out of it that night because she was filling in for Flo. After tray line, she was able to stay in the kitchen to prepare meals for the next shift.

When I was finished taking the last tray of glasses out of the dishwasher, I carried them out into the kitchen to stack them with the other clean glasses. As I was removing my rubber gloves, Charlene walked over from the other side of the kitchen and asked, "Are you finished?"

"Yeah, " I responded, and we both headed for the locker room.

This was the first time I had been alone with Charlene since she had her appointment with Dr. Walters. When we entered the locker room, and I was certain that we were alone, I asked, "How did your appointment with Dr. Walters turn out?"

"Not good…I'm pregnant…He gave me some vitamins with iron, and suggested that I tell my mother and the baby's father…I still haven't told either," Charlene sadly reported.

"Did you tell anyone?" I asked.

"My sister, Tina. She won't tell anyone. I wouldn't dare tell Teresa; she'd tell Mom. I went out with Benny last night, but I just couldn't bring myself to tell him. I don't know how I'll tell Mom either."

"Charlene, you can't keep this a secret. People are going to find out. Why don't you just tell them and be done with it?" I suggested. It was easy to give that advise, but I probably would not have told anyone either if it had been me.

"I'm afraid," Charlene sobbed as her tears flooded her confession.

"I know you are," I said with true compassion. "But, you have to make plans for you and the baby," I added. It was strange, but abortion had never occurred to either of us. It was just out of the question. Besides it was 1970, not 1973, when abortion was legalized.

"What if he hates me and never wants to see me again?" Charlene sobbed as she expressed her hidden fears.

"Well, if he feels that way, then you're too good for him," I declared. "He's just as much to blame for this pregnancy as you are. You know that, don't you?"

"I don't know anything anymore. I'm just so mixed up. I can't have a baby. I'm still in school. Benny never even mentioned marriage. He just likes sex. I just wanted to make him happy and make him love me. He'll never love me now," she continued to sob.

In my heart, I knew that what she was saying was true. All Benny wanted was sex. I didn't think he loved Charlene, and I certainly didn't think he wanted to marry her, but this was not the time to express those feelings. To Charlene I said, "You can't be certain of that until you confront him with the facts. Only then will you know the truth. Charlene, you don't want to live a lie, do you? It would be better to discuss this with Benny, so you know where to go from here. You must protect yourself and your child. Your mother may be upset, but I really think she would help you. I'll do whatever I can to help you," I offered.

Charlene continued to cry as we got changed and headed for our cars. We drove separately that night. "Are you okay to drive?" I asked as we reached our cars. "You could leave your car here and go home with me."

"No, I'll drive home," Charlene insisted.

"Okay, but please talk to your mother and Benny," I urged. I wanted to help her so much, but I didn't know how. After all, I had no idea what it was like to be pregnant. I had never even had sex But, instinct told me she needed to reveal the truth and take it from there. "Drive carefully," I instructed as we went our separate ways in the parking lot.

"I will," she promised.

On the way home, I thought about Charlene's dilemma. I hoped I never had to face a similar problem. That made me more certain that sex outside of marriage was wrong. It only caused heartache. I wondered what Charlene would do. She was only sixteen, but she was going to be a mother. I also wondered about the child. What would the child think in later years? What would she think of her mother's morality? What would she think of her father's lust and desertion? These were issues much too deep for a sixteen year old; I wished Charlene could escape the consequences of her actions. The lesson I had learned from that would stay with me forever: what you do today can affect the remainder of your life and the lives of others.

Chapter 34

My senior year progressed slowly through the winter months and then spring eventually arrived. Prom plans were begun. It was decided by the prom committee that the prom theme would be Roman Holiday. I would not attend my high school prom for Bill had asked me to his prom to be held at Chief Logan High School. My sister was attending the Kishacoquillas prom with her date, Scott Schultz.

Charlene, Brenda, and I agreed we were going shopping in Harrisburg for our prom gowns. Charlene was only four months pregnant and still not showing, so she planned on going to the prom with Benny. She had told Benny about her pregnancy, and he informed her that he had no intentions of getting married. I think Charlene was hoping he would change his mind. She had told her mother, also. She wasn't happy about Charlene's pregnancy, but she was supporting her emotionally.

We decided to skip school on Tuesday, April 4th, to go shopping for our gowns. Prior to my senior year, I had never skipped school. In fact, after I had passed through the usual childhood diseases, I had missed only one day of school for seven years straight. That was the day I had called Mom home due to my depression. After I got my driver's license and my own car, that all changed. I missed many days of school my senior year. It was just too easy to skip.

The day we were going for our prom gowns, I said I would drive. There was a portion of the old road near Naginey that had never been removed after they opened the new road. Charlene hid her car on that old road. It ran parallel with the new road, but it was hidden behind spruce trees and bushes that grew between the two. After her car was adequately hidden, we were all off to Harrisburg in my car.

We went to the Colonial Mall. It was the only indoor mall in Harrisburg at that time. There were numerous stores in the mall that sold formal dresses.

Brenda found a dress first at Clare's Boutique. It had a princess style sheath of pink, ribbed twill fabric with a velvet bodice dotted with flower clusters of glass beads. Since it was sleeveless, she planned to wear long white gloves with it.

Charlene found her dress in the same store. She decided on a red nylon strapless gown. It had hundreds of rows of red nylon ruffles attached to a net that made up the gown and covered a full taffeta underskirt. White lace adorned the bodice. She said the gown looked so great that maybe Benny would change his mind and marry her. She planned to accent her gown with her mother's white pearl necklace.

I found my gown in a different store. It was a long-sleeved yellow and white gown. The inside lining was a silky yellow acrylic material, and the entire gown was covered in a layer of delicate white lace. The sleeves were made entirely of lace. There was a bow attached separately at the waistline made of a fabulous chiffon type material as was the waistline décor. I was not particularly fond of yellow; however, I loved that gown.

We all were extremely happy with our purchases. As we ate lunch in the mall at a small pizza stand, we discussed our gowns and upcoming prom plans. After lunch, we looked for purses and shoes. Everyone ended up with white heels and small white clutch bags. By then it was late afternoon, and we decided it was time to return home.

The next day at school, to our dismay, we discovered that Mrs. Riden, a teacher's aide at our school, had seen us head out on our journey the previous day. We all got called into the office by the assistant principal, Mr. Schnell. When we realized we were had, we confessed. Mr. Schnell threatened that we would not be permitted to go to the prom. I wasn't going to that prom anyway, but Charlene and Brenda were very upset. In the end, however, he permitted them to attend. I believe he wasn't real hard on us since we had never been caught skipping school before.

A week later, Mom bought Brenda and me each a fake white rabbit fur stole to wear with our gowns. I was excited and nervous about the upcoming dance, but Brenda acted as though she could take it or leave it.

When prom night arrived, Bill and Scott arrived at our house together. Scott didn't have his license, so Bill and I were dropping him and Brenda off at the Kishacoquillas prom before we went on to the Chief Logan prom. They had another way home since we would be attending different after-prom parties. Brenda and I had both had our hair done at the beauty salon at the local strip mall in Burnham. She just had hers washed and styled, but I had mine done in French curls. After it was done, I wished I had not gotten the curls, but it was too late to undo it. Dad took pictures of us and our dates.

When the photo session was finished, we were off to the prom. After dropping Brenda and Scott off at my school, we went to Bill's. He parked in the parking lot in front of the gymnasium, and we made our grand entrance along with all the other dressed-up kids. I was very self-conscious and felt everyone else looked better than me. All in all, though, we had a good time. After the prom, we went to Bill's house and his parents took numerous pictures of us. When they were finished, we changed clothes and headed to the after-prom party, which was held at the Burnham YMCA. There was a live band playing all night. I had purchased a new outfit for the after-prom party. I wore blue and orange plaid pants with a matching blue shirt. Bill had a new outfit, too. He wore navy blue and white striped pants and a navy shirt.

Once you signed in at the YMCA, you were not permitted back in if you left. We stayed for several hours before we left to go to another party near Poe Valley State Park with some of Bill's friends. That party was outside at a camp, and there was some alcohol. I had one mixed drink, and Bill had a couple of beers.

I was still a virgin at the time, and I had decided this would be the night I would change that status. Someone must have been watching over me, though, because it just didn't happen. I was certain I would be the only girl in my graduation class who was still a virgin. That should have made me happy, but I felt like a loser.

When we arrived back at my house, it was after four a.m. Bill and I sat in his car in the woods across from my house making out for a little while before Mom started flashing the front porch light on and off. How embarrassing! I gathered all my belongings, Bill kissed me good night, and I went inside. Mom was waiting. Dad had gone to bed long before that. I gave Mom a quick summary of my evening, omitting the second party and went to bed.

The next day, Dad never asked me anything about the prom. Some parents had even gone to the high school to take pictures. I knew my parents would never do that. Again, I felt like I was different from everyone else. Dad didn't seem to care how I felt.

I was glad I was able to go to Bill's prom; I probably would have been harassed if I went to mine. I was certain that Tracy and her flunkies had attended. I was happy that school would soon be over, and she would never be able to harass me again, because if I had my way, I would never see her again. Maybe life wasn't that bad after all, and maybe there was a God. I still believed there was even though I couldn't communicate with Him, and I felt He must be good. I wished I could feel close to Him.

June was almost upon us, and my classmates and I were preparing for our approaching graduation. We had received our graduation announcements, pendants, class hats, and rented our maroon and white caps and gowns. I had sent graduation announcements to all my aunts and uncles. Baccalaureate was scheduled for Sunday evening, May 31st, at eight o'clock in our high school auditorium. Graduation commencement exercises were scheduled for Monday evening, June 1st, at eight p.m.

Dad had already informed Mom and me that he would not be attending my baccalaureate or commencement ceremonies. He had never attended any of our school functions. Dad hadn't graduated, and I believed he was afraid people would discover that. Years later, I learned that he was practically illiterate, and then I realized that was what he had feared would be revealed. I have come to believe he was dyslexic, too, but it had never been diagnosed.

Dad had attended a one-room country school. He had memorized what kids ahead of him read, and that was how he covered his learning disability. My grandfather made him quit school at the end of sixth grade to help work at the sawmill he owned. As I reflect on my years of growing up, I now understand why Dad didn't read us bedtime stories, why we didn't go into restaurants to eat, and why my mother read the map when we traveled. He had covered his "secret" well, so I did not understand, then.

Mom was not happy about Dad's refusal to attend my graduation, even though she knew his "secret." She had invited two of my aunts, Mabel and Marie, to accompany Brenda and her. I had asked Bill to go. I thought everyone would really think I was weird if they knew my father wasn't attending my graduation ceremonies. After all, graduation was a milestone. Under the circumstances, I thought most parents would be very proud of a child who had surpassed their accomplishments. As usual, though, I said nothing about my feelings and Dad's refusal to attend; it would have made no difference.

May 31st came and went. My baccalaureate had been, for the most part, uneventful Then it was June 1st, 1970, my graduation day. It had finally arrived. There were times when I thought it would never happen. My high school years were not happy times. I believe the combination of puberty, the death of my grandma and resulting grieving period, and switching school environments all contributed to my depression during those formative high school years. I had been so incapacitated by my grief caused by Grandma's death, and depression about my life situation, in general, that my social skills were frozen at a time they were needed to adapt to the new circumstances in my life. Due to all of these factors, I lived a sad, lonely existence during much of my high school years. I was afraid to reach out to other students. To be a friend, I had to make myself vulnerable. My self-esteem was so damaged, it was just easier and safer just to hide.

The need to belong to a group, however, was very much a part of me. I longed to belong and be accepted. Because I cried a lot during the beginning of my high school years, and I didn't participate in many activities due to my depression, I had earned myself the reputation of being somewhat of an oddball. I believe this is why some students gave me such a hard time. I had learned that whenever one's behavior varied from the norm, she became the victim of harassment. It was during those years that I learned to root for the underdog because I *was* the underdog.

I had felt firsthand the pain created by cruel words and gestures. Young people could crucify anyone who didn't conform to their rules and expectations. If they attacked someone else, it was less likely that they would be attacked themselves. The lessons I learned during my high school years would be remembered throughout my life.

The many social issues occurring during the sixties also contributed to the overall "me" that emerged. The first half of 1970 was no different. I witnessed through television, bombings on the college campuses, thousands of American soldiers fighting in Viet Nam, student demonstrations against the Viet Nam War, draft card burnings, and the integration of southern schools. It was a turbulent time in history as well as a turbulent time in my life.

We had a rehearsal the morning of graduation. I planned to wear a white dress I had gotten at Easter time under my graduation gown. Also, I was going to wear white shoes with a small heel. I hoped that I would not trip going onto the stage. Things like that always worried me. After practice, we were dismissed and were to return at seven p.m.

Later that evening, as a member of the graduating class of Kishacoquillas High School in Gardenview, Pennsylvania, I sat in my seat on the stage of the auditorium as our commencement program began with an organ prelude, "Prayer for Peace." How appropriate that seemed since we were in the midst of the Viet Nam War. It was followed by the processional, "Trumpet Voluntary in D Major." Reverend Thomas Kramm from Saint John's Lutheran

Church in Belleville gave the invocation. The audience remained standing during the processional and invocation; they were then permitted to be seated. Next Richard Metz, our senior class president, gave the welcome address.

The student orations followed with the theme: "America's future." I sat there wondering what my future would be. Connie Romig's speech was entitled: *Discrimination Terminates in Extinction.* It was a nice thought, but would it ever happen? I only semi-listened to Marcene Farrell's *Today's High Schools – Room For Improvement* and Cynthia Downing's *The Fight to Save America.* Barry Heading's *Moon Landing: Inspiration Or Hollow Triumph* caught my attention somewhat, but Cathy Madden's *Why?* almost moved me to tears. It was not the speech itself, but what memories it stirred that moved me so deeply.

I too asked: Why? Why did my high school years have to be so sad and lonely? Why did a small group of students have to be so cruel? Why didn't the teachers notice? Why did the world in general have to be so brutal with so many killings as a result of the Viet Nam War and racial bigotry, especially in the South? Why couldn't my parents be different? Why wouldn't my father attend my graduation? Why did Charlene have to get pregnant? Why did Grandma, Joyce, and Mrs. Semple have to die? Why, why, and why?

I continued asking myself the "why" questions as Dr. Edward Shore, President of the Mifflin County School District Board of Education gave us greetings from the Board, and then Mr. Murphy, our principal, presented to the audience our class of 1970. The handing out of the diplomas followed, with Mr. Frank Walk, Jr., Superintendent of the Mifflin County School District, making the presentations. When it was my turn to receive my diploma, I gladly accepted it from Mr. Walk and quietly breathed a sigh of relief as I realized it was finally over. I considered myself very fortunate to be getting out of the red brick building that had often seemed like a prison to me.

The entire senior class and audience again stood as we began singing our Alma Mater:

"To the school that we love may we ever be true.
We pledge love and honor Kishacoquillas to you.
We'll remember your name as our lives bring you fame.
May the Lord up above bless the school that we love
And in peace may you lie Kishacoquillas High.
Mid the mountains of blue – neath the pale azure sky
Stands our Alma Mater – sweet memories there lie.

And may nothing impair the friendships we share.
May the Lord up above bless the school that we love
And in peace may you lie Kishacoquillas High."

Some students had begun to cry before the song ended. I was not one of them. Reverend Dale Sultzbaugh from the Saint Paul's Lutheran Church in Milroy gave the benediction, and more students began crying. I still was not one of them.

I had no clue what the future would hold for me, but I knew it had to be better than the last six years of my life. It seemed as though freedom was just on the other side of our graduation ceremony, and when I walked my last steps as a senior, down the aisle of the auditorium to the recessional, "Pomp and Circumstance," for once there were *no more tears for me*. Everyone around me, though, seemed to be crying: the students, the parents, and even some of the teachers. When I passed my family members and Bill, I noticed Bill even had tears in his eyes. I suppose the students were sad that that period of their lives was over; I was happy. In white cap and gown I exited the door at the back of the auditorium, crossed the hall, accepted the red rose they handed me on my way out of the front door, and anxiously entered the freedom that awaited me on the other side of the door as I joyously faced the rest of my life.

Epilogue

Jamie and Jessie, my two daughters, entered Mom's living room and saw me staring at Grandma's picture. Mom was still in the kitchen. "What are you doing?" Jamie asked.

I blinked as I returned to reality. "Hi. When did you two get here?" I asked, ignoring Jamie's question and slipping Grandma's photo back into the box.

"We just got back from Indiana," she answered. Jamie was attending Indiana University of Pennsylvania. Jessie was still a senior in high school. She had been visiting Jamie for the weekend. "So what are you doing?" Jamie asked again. John spoke up and said, "I'm working on a time-line project for school, and I need some family pictures to go with it."

Jessie walked over to the couch where John was accumulating the pictures he had chosen from the cardboard box, and asked, "What do you have so far?"

Jamie joined Jessie and John on the couch, and all three of them looked through the photos. They laughed and joked with each other as they reminisced about what had been happening when the photos were taken.

It was then that I experienced one of those rare moments when you get a glimpse of the meaning of life. I realized how everything has a purpose, and there really is a time for everything. It may not, and generally does not, correspond to how we believe it should be, but in the end, it may just all work out. No matter how hard you try to hold onto those moments, though, they slip away as quickly as they come to you, and you just have to wait for the next one to come along.

As I sat looking at my three beautiful children, I realized that my life had turned out okay. My journey had been far from smooth, for I had many rocky spots along the way as most people do. The death of Grandma Bishop was the first tragic event in my life, and there were many more that followed. It was all a part of growing up and maturing. All of our life circumstances are different, and we all grow up at a different pace. Along my way, I even found God again. He had been there all along, but I had distanced myself for I had felt betrayed. Also, it took me much time to realize that God really was a loving, caring, and compassionate God. Often God is referred to as our father, and maybe I just had trouble equating Him with *my* father.

Time had even allowed me to come to peace with my relationship with my father. Before he passed away, he told me he loved me. It was the only time in my life that I had heard those words come from his lips. It is strange what a healing effect a few words can have on your soul. I still grieve for all that has been lost, yet rejoice for what I have had and have. I came to realize that my parents were not perfect and they had problems of their own to deal with, but they did the best they could. Age often tends to mellow people. This happened with my father. My children had been close to him; they remain close to my mother.

Charlene dropped out of school and had a baby girl who looked just like Benny. She and Benny never married each other; however, they did marry and have their separate families. Bill and I continued to date, and in July, 1971, we eloped and moved to North Carolina where his father lived. Five years later, our marriage became a teenage marriage statistic when we divorced. I have no ill feelings toward Bill; I believe we just married too young and, perhaps, for the wrong reasons. I returned to Pennsylvania, and a few years after our divorce, I married my husband Larry. We have three children.

Through the years, I lost contact with Cathy, Charlene, Betsy, and the others. But, I heard Cathy moved to Delaware and Betsy to Florida. Charlene still lives near her previous home in Pennsylvania. I never again saw my "special" Steve who helped me through a very difficult time during the summer of 1965.

Throughout all of these years that have passed since my grandma's sickness and death, there has always been that little twelve-year-old girl deep within me. We become what our pasts have made us. I like to believe that through my tears for Grandma and all the tears that followed, I have learned to be compassionate and in turn have strived to improve the quality of life for those around me.

I currently work at the Pennsylvania Department of Public Welfare as a caseworker, and my sister, Brenda, works there, too. We are in the middle of "welfare reform" as our state and nation attempt to resolve the poverty issues that have been with us throughout the ages. Whenever an elderly client sits across from me in one of the interviewing booths, I remember when Grandma was on that side of the desk. My memory of her continues to inspire me to reach out to others in need.

Printed in the United States
24192LVS00003B/154